The Art AND SCIENCE OF Success

VOLUME 2

D1616102

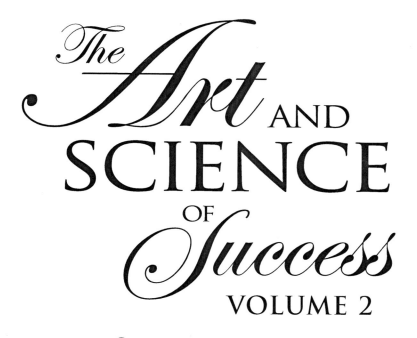

The Art AND SCIENCE OF Success

VOLUME 2

PROVEN STRATEGIES FROM TODAY'S LEADING EXPERTS

SUCCESS YOU PUBLISHING
CARROLLTON, TX

© 2011 Matt Morris

Success You Publishing, Inc.
2810 Trinity Mills Road #209-142
Carrollton, TX 75006

SUCCESS YOU PUBLISHING   questions@mattmorris.com

ISBN: 978-0-9830770-1-5

Printed in United States of America

Cover Design: Chris Collins
Interior Design & Layout: Ghislain Viau

Contents

Chapter 1: 5 Proven Principles to Million Dollar Results
by Matt Morris   1

Chapter 2: Fail. Fail. Fail. Fail. Succeed!
by Austin Walsh   9

Chapter 3: Wrong Turn. Success Is This Way
by Traci Williams   17

Chapter 4: Creating Your New Wealth and Freedom Lifestyle
by Daven Michaels   25

Chapter 5: Your Passion, Your Power!
by Darlene C. O'Keeffe, CHC, PTF   33

Chapter 6: Opportunity Is Calling
by Adam Spiel   41

Chapter 7: Transforming a Vision into a Dream
by Clay Johnson   49

Chapter 8: Success Is Where the Heart Is
by Mark Call   57

Chapter 9: The Conversation
by Tim Zimmerman   67

Chapter 10: OUT! Outrageously Unlimited Thinking
by Thell G. Prueitt   75

Chapter 11: The One Thing All Successful People
Have in Common
by Mike R. Phillips   83

Chapter 12: Focus on What You *Really* Want and
Follow Your Passion
   by Christian Schnubel   93

Chapter 13: Dare to Dream . . . *Act* on your Vision!
   by Gerri Krienke   101

Chapter 14: The View from the Top
   by David Sapp   111

Chapter 15: The Most Resilient Parasite—An Idea
   by Jérome Vaultier   119

Chapter 16: The Biggest Myth About Career Success
   by Bud Bilanich   127

Chapter 17: It's Never Too Late to Reinvent Yourself
to Live Your Dream Life
   by Dr. Joe Rubino   137

Chapter 18: Live the Uncommon Life
   by Justin Tillman   145

Chapter 19: You Too Can Succeed!
   by Godfrey E. McAllister, Ph.D., DTM   153

Chapter 20: Success Comes Before Work
Only in the Dictionary
   by Betty Wong   161

Chapter 21: A Sense of Balance
   by Anand Ferco   169

Chapter 22: You Can Do Anything You Want . . .
   by Ayn Ulm   177

Chapter 23: Birthing Success
   by Tanya MarCia   185

Chapter 24: A Child of Africa—Yes, We Can, Too!
   by Colette Bowers   193

Chapter 25: My Vertical Success
   by Cecilia Matthews   201

Chapter 26: In Times of Struggle, We Often Become
the Most Resourceful
   by Mikkel Pitzner   207

Chapter 27: Change Starts in the Mind
   by Rev. Dean Decastro   217

Chapter 28: Success through Mental Martial Arts
   by Roger J. Aston   225

Chapter 29: Extraordinary Ordinary Women
   by Victoria Rei Ristow   233

Chapter 30: Success—Work Hard, Follow the Leaders,
Have Fun!
   by David S. Velasquez   241

Chapter 31: Briarley's Story
   by Briarley Nicholson   249

Chapter 32: It All Starts with This . . .
   W. David Medina   257

Chapter 33: Grateful Farm Boy
   by Mike Pawlowski   265

Chapter 34: The Breakthrough Mantra
   by Joe Rodrigues   277

Chapter 35: What You *Do*
   by Margie Stacey   285

Chapter 36: Letting Your Spirit Guide
   by Christine Kasik   293

Chapter 37: What Everybody Ought to Know
for Success in the 21st Century
   by Evelyn Cole   301

Chapter 38: Possibility
           by Joanne Haslam   309

Chapter 39: A Success Bigger than Self
           by Sabrina Williams   317

Chapter 40: The Power of Thought
           by Melanie Greenough   325

Chapter 41: From a Poor Farm Boy to a College Professor
  and an Entrepreneur
           by Robert Boyd   333

Chapter 42: Success Turned Upside Down
           by Wayne Sharer   341

Chapter 1

5 Proven Principles to Million Dollar Results

by Matt Morris

Formal education will make you a living, but
self-education will make you a fortune.
— Jim Rohn

Nine years ago, I was $30,000 in debt. I was living out of my beat-up little Honda Civic, bathing in gas station bathrooms, and selling above-ground swimming pools door-to-door in the hottest two months of the summer. I had hit absolute rock bottom and had absolutely no idea how to pull myself out.

Then, as many of you will have from reading this book, I had an awakening late one night. By that, I mean that I was exposed to a set of principles and strategies that allowed me to completely reinvent my life. From the ages of 21 to 24, I went from being homeless and living out of my car to earning a six-figure income, working for myself, taking exotic vacations around the world, and living what, at the time, was my dream lifestyle. From the ages of 24 to 29 I became a millionaire, and I have helped countless other people earn six- and seven-figure incomes.

I've compiled my overall philosophy on creating success into seven specific strategies that I've used to create seven figures in revenue, not once, not twice, but SIX SEPARATE TIMES in my life, all before the age of 30. To date, the same strategies I'm about to share with you have allowed me to generate over eight figures!

1. Dream Big!

You will never live life beyond your wildest expectations until you first have some wild expectations.
—Anonymous

When we're children, we have an amazing ability to dream big dreams. Unfortunately, as we grow older, people begin to tell us we're being unrealistic, that we should aspire to be something we can accomplish more easily. For many children, society steals their dream, and just as a child lowers her level of thinking because of practicality, most people lower their level of thinking because they've given up. They've made goals like getting out of debt instead of having goals like owning their own multimillion-dollar home. Puny goals—like having enough money to pay all their bills—instead of having enough money to live on the interest created from their investments.

It's no wonder that children stop looking up to their parents at a certain point in their lives. When a child is 6 years old, his parents are his heroes, but when he's about 16, he wonders what happened to them! He sees his parents have gone from grown-ups to given-ups.

It's also no surprise that most young adults end up giving up on their dreams. They're simply following in the footsteps of their parents.

As I look back at myself and at so many others I've been able to assist in accomplishing success, a character trait that's common among us all is our ability to dream big dreams.

As the great Art Williams once said, the key to winning is desire. A burning desire is what you *must* have in your gut to do what's necessary to succeed. If you want to harness your passion, your drive, your discipline, your determination, you have to have a desire level that borders on obsession.

The surest way to bring out that burning desire from within yourself is through having a massive dream, for "Dreams are the fuel that fire desire!"

2. Become an Expert.

My definition of an expert is someone who is in the top 1% knowledge level compared to everyone else in the world.

What's the quickest way to get yourself to that 1% quickly? Simple. When you read five books on one single subject, that's more than what 99% of all other people in the world will ever learn on that particular topic. So to become an expert, you're only five books away.

Here's a way to advance your mastery even further: With every book, read it as if you have to give a training course on the information as soon as you're finished with it. Take notes on these books and create your own "book report" just like you did in school. Create a "success journal" with your studies and you can use this as a reference guide for the rest of your life through your journey to success.

3. Create a Game Plan.

What this strategy is really talking about is goal setting. I grew up playing sports, so for me the words "game plan" get me excited and motivated, so you can call this strategy whatever you like, but the important part is using a specific strategy for setting and achieving your goals.

1. Your goal must be *specific and measurable.*
2. Your goal must have a *deadline.*
3. Your goals must be *written down.*
4. You must have a *why* for your goal. (Figure out why your goal is not just an option, but a *must.*)
5. You must develop a specific *action plan* to achieve your goal. (What are you going to *do* to achieve your goal?)
6. You must *review* your goal weekly if not daily.

Let me share another powerful tip: Your goal should always be written as an affirmation as if it's already happened. This way, every time you see it and read it aloud, it makes an imprint in your subconscious mind as if it's already true. And every imprint made in your subconscious mind creates your ultimate reality.

4. Take Massive action.

This point goes right along with the formula for success:

$$\text{Your Success} = \text{Effort} \times \text{Skill} \times \text{Financial Vehicle}$$

You may be incredibly talented and have a great financial vehicle, but if the "effort" variable is not put into play, none of that matters. Every self-made millionaire I know got there by not being scared to work hard—really hard. A mentor of mine once told me that if you want to experience the exact same success in any endeavor as someone who has ten times your level of ability, all you have to do is work ten times harder.

I took this as a challenge when I heard it. At the time, I was working a full-time job and was also involved in a network marketing company. The top leader in this network marketing company was a full-time networker who had earned over a million dollars in the industry and previously built an organization of over 70,000 people. The best thing I had ever done was to build an organization of about 150, so I was a long way away from the top leader's ability level.

But I had a massive dream to change my life, so I decided that I would just flat-out outwork every other person in that company, including this seven-figure earner. I knew this seven-figure earner was really only working the business about 20 or so hours a week.

So here's what I did, whether you consider this wise or not: I quit my full-time job, and I made a commitment that I would do whatever it took to become the top earner in that company. I essentially gave myself no other option. I would either go absolutely broke, or I would achieve the success that I had dreamed of my entire life. I backed myself into a corner, I burnt the bridges behind me, and so I had absolutely no way to retreat. I created an action plan for working like a madman to achieve my dreams.

I worked 80-100 hours per week for a solid 90 days before taking a break. I personally enrolled about 30 people my first month and after six weeks was earning about $1,000 a week. Within 90 days, I was earning just over $2,000 a week (a six-figure income!), and within six months I was earning $40,000 a month.

Not only did I achieve my financial goals, something interesting happened. My level of skill went through the roof, and I became the #1 money earner in that company with *no* prior success—all through the power of *massive action*.

5. Follow the Laws of Leadership.

My core belief is that everything rises and falls on leadership. Whether you're a leader in network marketing, of a nation, of a company, of a military unit, or in your family, everything rises and falls on your ability to lead and influence others.

Here's a rule of leadership: People will only follow others they perceive as a higher-level leader than themselves. So if you're a 5 on a scale of 1 to 10, you're going to have a bunch of 4s and 3s following you. To get 8s, 9s, and 10s, you'll need to develop yourself into a 10.

Here are a few Laws of Leadership for you to follow in order to become a powerful leader:

- *A leader must have a dream larger than those they lead.*
  Big dreamers inspire others to dream big. People are not moved and influenced by the depth of your logic. They are propelled to action by the height of your passion and inspiration. Sharing your dreams for the organization is the quickest and most straightforward way to motivate your team to act.

- *A leader must have an attitude superior to those they lead.*
  Leaders fill themselves with positive thoughts; they act in an upbeat manner at all times when they're in front of those they lead. Positive attitudes are contagious, just like negative ones. But negative attitudes have an even greater impact on your people.

- *Leaders must always display a commitment to integrity and character.*
  People before profits—enough said. Make a goal of being transparent with your intentions for the organizations and be the first to admit it when you've made a mistake. You'll never be followed unless you are trusted, and the more open you are, the more trusted you become.

- *Leaders have a commitment to personal growth.*
  Personal stagnation is the cause of decay and failure in most people's lives. People want to be around someone who's moving forward in all areas of life. "When you're green you're growing; when you're ripe you're rotten."

- *Leaders have pig-headed determination.*

  Realize it takes time to achieve greatness. I spent five years as an entrepreneur before I earned a full-time income. A true leader will always find a way over, around, or through any challenge that arises and will do whatever it takes to be a winner.

- *Leaders convey an inspiring vision.*

  Not only are great leaders comfortable sharing their vision, their passion overflows and spills out so that others can't wait to be a part of it. People want to be inspired to do something remarkable with their life, so figure out how your vision can help them make that a reality.

These were several of the guiding principles, along with my faith in God, that have allowed me to create my dream lifestyle. They've proven to create seven- and eight-figure results over and over again in my entrepreneurial career.

Here's my disclaimer: It may not be easy. Achieving your dreams may be a fight. It may be a struggle. You may lose sleep. It may require you to experience rejection. In fact, it will probably hurt. But fighting for your destiny, fighting for your dreams, is the one fight you will never regret.

Far better is to dare mighty things, to win glorious triumphs, even though checkered by failure, than to take ranks with those poor spirits who neither enjoy much nor suffer much, because they live in the gray twilight of mediocrity that knows neither victory nor defeat.
—Theodore Roosevelt

Biography

Matt Morris

MATT MORRIS is the international best-selling author of *The Unemployed Millionaire*. A serial entrepreneur since the age of 18, Matt has generated tens of millions of dollars through his companies while generating over 100,000 customers in 180 countries around the world. As a dynamic speaker, best-selling  author, and young success story, Matt has been featured on international radio and television and has addressed audiences in over 20 countries worldwide. Matt is widely known as one of the top Internet marketing experts and is the founder of Success You Publishing, Inc.

Contact Information

www.MattMorris.com

Chapter 2

Fail. Fail. Fail.
Fail. Succeed!

by Austin Walsh

*A*t the tender age of 10 years, I decided that I needed to become financially independent. Or, more accurately, I wanted to make a boatload of money. Therefore, I opened up a lemonade stand at the end of my street. Each day that I made a slight increase in profit, I became more excited by the possibilities of what I was capable of earning for myself. Eventually it dawned on me that on the best sales day, I would make only 80 dollars. This didn't work out for me when I calculated how long I would work and how much of that money would go back into buying supplies. So it was time for a new plan.

What did you think was the coolest way to make money in middle school? Well, I decided that becoming a DJ would be the most awesome way to make money while also having fun. (After all, what good is it for you to make money if you don't enjoy what you're doing while making it?) Little did I know that I would be creating a cool theory for kids around the world—start by being a DJ and work your way to becoming a speaker. It was pretty awesome at 12 years old to be DJing with a nice sound system, basically going everywhere and anywhere that was willing to pay my going rate of 400 dollars. That's a *ton* of money for a 12 year old, and considering I was just playing music for a couple of hours every night, I figured that I had made it big.

The wheels in my head started turning again. . . . Being a DJ was cool, but throwing parties was even cooler! I knew I would be good at throwing the coolest and biggest parties, so I dove right in. Just as I predicted, I could get 100 people to a party location like clockwork. Unfortunately, as my popularity increased, my mother's lenience in using our family basement decreased—my parties were just getting too big. Using my own bash to experiment, I was set on finding the perfect place to throw a *huge* party. I was about to turn 16, and I searched everywhere for the perfect location. That's when I found Eclipse Night Club, and over 500 kids showed up after a month of advertising through my favorite social network, Facebook.

With how successful the party was, I figured, why not throw a New Year's Eve bash a month later? As I started to plan the party, the venue owner and I did some quick numbers and figured that $20 a head would be a great split for door entry. Everything was *perfect!* We had a Facebook promotions page rocking and rolling with about 1,700 people confirmed that they were coming to my big party. *It was going to be insane!* That is, until I got a call three days before the party that went a little something like this:

"Well, Austin, since there's going to be so many people, instead of doing a door split, we can only pay you like 500 bucks."

What the heck! It didn't take a math genius to see that I was supposed to make *$10,000*, and instead the venue owner was only going to offer me $500. I was young, but I wasn't stupid—I was going to get ripped off if I stayed with that venue. So, I quickly made the decision that my team had 72 hours to find another venue, and I went to work at the speed of lightning.

Now this brings up a great point. *Don't cry to give up. Cry to keep going.*

I started driving everywhere and talking to anyone that had adequate space for me to throw my party. Rejected... Rejected... Rejected... Rejected... That's all I got.

Finally I walk into a little place called Mojoes, and after much conversation and a little help from my dad, the perfect venue was rebooked. Now the only thing I had to worry about was making sure that my attendees would cross over to the new venue with me. So I sent out *one* Facebook message, and everyone showed up to the new venue, Mojoes! That's right—not a single person showed up to Eclipse. *The party was insane,* and the cash flow was even crazier!

The party business was going good, so I began working with my dad, Bill Walsh. Now, if you don't know him, he is one hell of a seminar speaker with a huge worldwide following. Funny enough, *I didn't really know,* because I was 16. I just thought that my dad was in real estate!

This brings up good point #2. *Tell your kids what you do.* Please, people! Do it! They want to know.

My father greatly influenced the way I wanted to live my life, run my business, and develop my personal relationships. Learning what he did, why he did it, and how it reflected in the relationships he had not only taught me how to be a successful business developer, but also how to be a successful human being. Happiness is key in this life, and there shouldn't be a day you waste not being happy about what you do, who you're with, and where you're going. Life is as tough as you make it, and when you share your principles of success with those you love, you help them learn how to make life a little bit easier for themselves. So parents, listen up! Share your work with your kids!

Because I swear to you, this world is getting crazier by the day.

I have heard countless people constantly complaining about failure, and how they just cannot seem to get this game of "success" figured out. I have a lot of friends who constantly tell me how much they would like to switch places with me and live my "dream" life.

Let's clear something up about this "success" thing right now! You have to fail over and over again before you get it right. Now, there are a few steps you can follow to minimize your failure rate (which I want to share with you), but failing is still essential. Don't be surprised when I share that even with the amount of success I have had in my 19 years of life, I have failed much more!

- I quit my dream of playing basketball.
- I have about an idea (or 10) a week that is a total flop. (I have another 10 ideas that are awesome and succeed!)
- I have let a few friends down, because of the lifestyle I have chosen, rather than the normal college life.
- I choose to stay out of relationships so that I can focus on working successfully and moving forward.
- I am still so young that I couldn't get a credit card at Best Buy, among other stores.
- One of the parties I spent a *ton* of "traditional" marketing money on had fewer than 100 people show up.
- I moved out of my house at 17. That was an accomplishment and a failure!
- I have spoken on multiple stages where I haven't made a dime.
- I couldn't even get hired as a gas station clerk.

Trust me, there are a ton more than that, but most important, I *accept* and *embrace* all the failures I've had in my life. Life can, and will, move forward if you allow yourself to get back up and try something new. The key is to take the lesson from the failure and don't get stuck!

I mentioned earlier some ways to stop some of these failures. Here they are:

- Get a *great* mentor. Who cares what it costs? No cost should get in the way of your success

- Get a system. The reasons small businesses fail and franchises succeed is because franchises use a system!

- Create an amazing team with people you trust and can do business with for years.

- Learn to learn. If you can't learn in this new economy, your company will not skyrocket to what you desire—in fact, you'll be lucky if it takes off at all.

- *Marketing!* I cannot stress enough that you *have* to have a solid marketing plan that you can implement with your business's system. This is *huge* for success.

Apply these to your business and watch your biz start getting small victories. Do not go for huge wins. It's like setting up a domino pattern—trip the wrong domino, and the tiles will turn over the wrong way without revealing the pretty work you've done. If you set things up methodically, and let things grow *with* you, your business will flourish.

Read back through the progression of how I began as an entrepreneur. I guarantee you that every single one of the principles I just listed were used along the way—and I still use them today! Running a top-5,000 business website that I *love* and obsess over wouldn't be possible if I hadn't learned along the way from my personal choices and my wonderful mentors.

Remember: Continue working hard, playing hard, and always being you. All the success in the world doesn't mean a thing if you're not having a good time!

Biography

Austin Walsh

AUSTIN is a quickly rising tech entrepreneur and Internet marketer committed to uniquely driven sales and business education grounded in firm values. At the age of 19, he has already been featured on stages alongside some of the world's most renowned speakers and business coaches. His  long-term clients include Mark Victor Hansen, Mark Accetta, Bishop Jordan, and Gary Goldstein, among others. Austin is the cofounder and marketing face of the highly profitable membership site www.isocialacademy.com.

Contact Information

www.isocialacademy.com

Chapter 3

Wrong Turn–
Success Is This Way

by Traci Williams

W hen I studied health and kinesiology in college, I assumed I was going to become a physician. As I got further into the curriculum, I realized I was drawn to the courses that challenged my core beliefs. It was neurobiology and behavioral psychology studies that really woke me up to what it means to be well. As I dug further, it became apparent that our attitude toward life is equally as, if not more important than, our eating habits and exercise routines.

You've heard the phrase, "Have an attitude of gratitude." When I heard it, I brushed it off as just being thankful for what I have. I think most people do that pretty well. But the challenge I share with you is to dissect that phrase a little further for its deeper meaning. Therein lies your true key to success, as was the case for me and many others throughout history. According to Cicero, "Gratitude is not only the greatest of virtues, but the parent of all others."

The benefits of living a grateful life have been studied extensively. According to a research project from the University of Miami, people who practiced conscious gratitude:

- made greater progress towards personal goals.

- exercised more regularly, had better overall health, slept better, and felt more optimistic.

- were more alert, enthusiastic, and could cope with stress more effectively.

I want more. I want to be better, have better, look better, feel better. Life is all about constant improvement for many of us. Maybe you picked up this book so you could become "more" or better yourself. If you're like me, you want to continue to improve in the areas of your life that aren't quite complete or those that aren't where you thought they would be right now. In my case, I'm a 37-year-old divorced mother who hasn't found that real true love of my life yet. For you, maybe it's where you are in your career. If you're saying in your head right now, "What career?", then I'm likely talking to you. Or maybe you haven't reached that financial goal. Maybe you're just struggling in general.

Our tendency to focus on those things we have yet to master or obtain can be our downfall. I know, I know. What about Constant Improvement, Traci? What about personal development? Isn't that what this book is about, achieving success? Yes. However, we could be approaching it all wrong. I've had and am having success in my life in many ways, and for those, I'm very grateful. However you define success, I believe there is one sure-fire way to get there—and most of us are going the wrong way.

Related studies have found other benefits to gratitude, such as better resilience, higher immune response, longer lives, closer family ties, and even a greater sense of religion. These results hold even when researchers factor out such things as age, health, and income, equalizing for the fact that the young, the well-to-do, or the wealthy might have "more to be grateful for."

Now that you fully understand the benefits of having an attitude of gratitude, let's explore what it really means in your daily life. Let's break down the meaning behind it.

at·ti·tude/'atiˌt(y)ood/

Noun: A settled way of thinking or feeling, typically reflected in a person's behavior.

grat·i·tude/'gratˌt(y)ood/

Noun: The quality of being thankful; readiness to show appreciation for and to return kindness.

So if you put the two together, you come up with *a settled way of being ready to show thanks and kindness through your behavior.* That's a pretty powerful statement, implying that we need to be ready to behave in a way that doesn't always come naturally to us. Let me give you a personal example.

My mom was and still is my greatest inspiration. She was the oldest of four girls. She basically raised and protected them from abusive parents, men, and situations. She was the toughest person I knew. She married my dad at the ripe old age of 18, when she was pregnant with my sister Kristi. Within a few years, I was born, and then my little sister, Amy. The stress of farm life and marriage on two kids who had three kids was just too much, so they ended up divorced. Since there aren't a lot of jobs in White Deer, Texas, my mom moved us to the big city of Amarillo, Texas! Mom really struggled to make ends meet. In fact, she had three jobs, and one of those was in a beef-packing plant. We were dirt poor, but Mom somehow made it pretty fun with games like, "How big can we make this garage sale?" and "food stamp-licking races," and I have very fond memories of "camping out" on the living room floor on mattresses.

Eventually, Mom married again and we moved "uptown." It was a true rags to riches kind of deal. We had a Delorean, a pool, and went to a great school. That lasted a few years until my stepdad's business went under due to a crooked business deal. He went into a major depression, and life got tough again. We moved to Oklahoma, where Mom went back to school for nursing. Keep in mind she's only about 37 with two kids in high school and one in middle school. We were totally starting over. Throughout all of this, she kept the best attitude and continued to bring in people worse off than us. We had a family of four move in for several months. We all learned how to care for a quadriplegic child so her mother could get out of an abusive situation. We're stretching dollars, but Mom knew we had to help. It was our responsibility.

She continued to work as a nurse for a few years while Kristi and I went to college on scholarships and grants. She taught us to dream big, picture it, and go for it. We knew how quickly life could change on us and that how we respond to that is what builds character. She was a shining example of manifestation, gratitude, and resilience.

While I was still in college, she moved to Austin, Texas, where she managed an assisted living facility. I joined them while in graduate school. She continued her good deeds while in Austin and shared her love for life. Growing up, she'd always had horrible migraines and had to take lots of different medications to manage the pain. As she got older, the medication had taken a toll on her digestive system. She continued to change her diet to help the situation, but it didn't get any better. Then, when Mom was only 49 years old, she went into a catatonic state. My stepdad called 911, then called me. I knew she was dying before he could even tell me what was happening. My sisters, her sisters, and our friends gathered in the emergency room and near her bed. The doctors had given her only hours to live. She lived for three days waiting for everyone to arrive and say their goodbyes. Only when we told her it was time to let go did she look up at us with a peace in her eyes focused on Heaven. She took her last breath on November 1, All Saints Day.

I was 28 years old when this happened. I could have been angry with God, the world, or even her, but I was thankful to have been blessed with such an amazing mother. Her light burned so bright during her time here and affected so many people in ways I believe will be seen through generations.

I realize now that I was so fortunate to be raised by a woman who valued gratitude and lived it daily. I learned by example and practice it every day. That's what it takes to get to *a settled way of being ready to show thanks and kindness through your behavior.* It doesn't matter that you're new to this. I can share with you tactics that have worked for many people, but you do need to practice. Success comes only from consistent application of this concept.

Dale Carnegie recommends the following to cultivate a mental attitude that will bring you peace, happiness, and success:

1. Fill your mind with thoughts of peace, courage, health, and hope.
2. Never try to get even with your enemies.
3. Expect ingratitude.
4. Count your blessings not your troubles.
5. Do not imitate others.
6. Try to profit from your losses.
7. Create happiness for others.

Reflect on your present blessings—of which every man has many—
not on your past misfortunes, of which all men have some.
—Charles Dickens

As with all things, success requires consistent persistence. A little bit of gratitude every day can, over time, *make a big difference to your level of happiness and overall well-being.*

Your Call to Action: Spend a few minutes at the start of your day listing three things that happened the previous day for which you are thankful as well as the three things you plan to achieve that day for which you are thankful in advance. This allows you to be both thankful and hopeful—the most powerful way to start your day.

Keep in mind that it is good to be grateful even for those things that do not seem positive at first glance, like the death of my mother. I'm thankful for the life we shared. Maybe you were in a toxic relationship and need to find a way to be grateful for it. Maybe you are thankful that you're able to love again; even though it's not going to be that person, you realize you're open to it. You've heard entrepreneurs say they've learned more from their "failures" than their success; without them, they wouldn't be the business people they are today. Do you see the difference?

On a neurobiological level, gratitude resides within the social emotions, along with awe, wonder, transcendence, and pride. It can be both practiced and experienced.

An example of practicing gratitude is helping others in return for having been helped. As an experience, it is felt in the same frontal regions of the brain that are activated by awe, wonder, and transcendence. Dopamine and serotonin, the "feel good" chemicals, reside here. In short, feeling gratitude and appreciation regularly helps heal us at every level of our being.

I don't think anyone can question that gratitude makes us feel happier.

How we think about happiness and success has profound implications on the way we choose to run our lives. For instance, if we believe that success mainly leads to happiness, then we are more motivated to focus on success while foregoing any happiness right now, assuming that happiness will naturally come from success once we obtain it.

If the psychological research is right, though, the strategy would still be to pursue success, but not to the exclusion of happiness. Feeling better in the moment not only is more pleasant but is also likely to open our minds to opportunities in business, play, spirituality, and our relationships. Seeing, recognizing, and jumping on these opportunities will lead us to success.

We can only be said to be alive in those moments
when our hearts are conscious of our treasures.
—Thornton Wilder

Biography

Traci Williams

As a sought-after speaker, consultant, and entrepreneur, TRACI WILLIAMS is the president
and CEO of Success You Publishing, Inc. After
receiving her masters of education from the University of Texas at Austin, Traci worked with the top
executives of a multibillion-dollar corporation to
streamline operations and increase revenues, significantly adding to
the company's bottom-line profits. After leaving the corporate world,
Traci reinvented the learning systems for the #1 most-visited personal
development website on the Internet, which led to several hundred
thousand dollars a month in added revenues to the company. Today,
she runs Success You Publishing while maintaining her own global
enterprise helping entrepreneurs create a thriving business in the $8
trillion-a-year travel industry.

Contact Information

www.PartnerWithTraci.com
wayoflifeinfo@gmail.com

Chapter 4

Creating Your New Wealth and Freedom Lifestyle

by Daven Michaels

My entrepreneurial career that started at the age of 15 with a dream to have a designer clothing retail store on Melrose Street in Los Angeles. Being so young, I was turned down by everyone I knew for the start-up capital, so I turned to my supportive father for the money I needed.

My grand opening was a traditional Hollywood-style fanfare, with champagne flowing, cheers, and slaps on the back. The days that followed were the most nervous days of my life. For the next few days I had no customers, not one. I recall feeling extremely anxious and worried. What if I had failed before I even started? I remember thinking about the money I had borrowed and how long it would take me to pay back my dad. Even in those nervous moments, in my heart I still knew I could make this work. I had to make this work, and as fate

would have it, by the end of first week, Jack Nicholson bought out half my shop, and I was in business! From that moment, I knew I would always be an entrepreneur, and I have never looked back.

I have truly lived the American dream. I have turned multiple passions into prosperous businesses: I have been a best-selling music and television producer, author, speaker, and successful entrepreneur. I have worked hard, played hard, traveled the world, and been involved with incredible people, amazing projects, and exciting ventures. Some say I have been lucky, and maybe I have; however, early on in my entrepreneurial career, I became aware of a formula for success to which I attribute my ability to turn multiple diverse businesses into financial successes.

During my time as a record producer, I first became aware of a formula for creating hit records. This made me think there must be a success formula for running a business. I actively sought out mentors whom I knew were successful, and through their mentorship, I developed a system for success that I now teach to others.

In addition to running 123Employee, what I really enjoy doing is helping small business owners around the world create their new wealth and freedom lifestyle by showing them how to effectively leverage and delegate. Money alone does not translate into success. I know many rich people who are unhappy; they work long hours and are miserable. The definition of success, wealth, and freedom are relative—mine may be totally different from yours. My definition is simple—it's having the resources to live the lifestyle I desire and being happy.

While I achieved financial success in my businesses early on, I did not achieve freedom and expansion until I fully understood and embraced how to effectively *delegate* and *leverage*. No successful person has been able to establish a business without mastering these two core concepts. Learning how to delegate is the bridge between self-employed and being a business owner, and yet this is often easier said than done.

I think one of the reasons I am able to relate to solopreneurs and small business owners is that many of them tend to micromanagers, and I was one as well. Even today, my staff has to wrestle tasks from me, so I know how most people feel about hiring people to help them and then assigning tasks consistently to make an impact in the business.

Even though I manage a staff of 400 people, I still work from home. My management team and staff are all virtual, and I still consider myself a small business owner, working with the same challenges as the many entrepreneurs and small businesses who are my clients. Many key aspects of my business are delegated to employees all over the world, and this makes me uniquely positioned to share my experience with others.

Outsourcing is a form of delegation that is commonly understood as hiring people from countries like India, the Philippines, or Eastern Europe to do tasks for you. And while that is the common understanding, I believe we live in a global economy that is not limited by boundaries, nationalities, cultures. When I use the word "outsourcing" today, I think of assigning the task to anyone outside your company regardless of geographical location.

I have created a simple methodology for effectively creating a delegation plan that I call the 7 Steps to Successful Delegation.

Step 1: Deciding What to Delegate

The first step in creating a delegation plan is making a delegation table for *each* project/income stream as follows:

1. Take a sheet of paper (landscape). Create four columns and label as follows:

    • Column 1: List the tasks *you have to do.*

- Column 2: List the tasks you *have to* outsource to others (you don't have the skill).
- Column 3: List the tasks you are doing that could be done by others.
- Column 4: List the tasks you would be doing if you had more time or money.

2. Divide the columns into two rows and label as "Marketing-Related Tasks" and "All Other Tasks."

3. Enter all the tasks related to a project/income stream into the table.

Step 2: Prioritizing What Tasks to Delegate First

In an ideal world, it would be great to outsource *everything* you don't have to do or want to do. The reality is that we are all limited by resources, and we have to prioritize what tasks to outsource first.

1. Must Outsource Next

   These are task or projects you *must* outsource next for your business to proceed. They could be the creation of a website, lead capture page, sales page, copywriting. In most cases, the *must* do list are things you are not able to do, or that you don't have time for and have to hire someone to do them for you. In many cases, these tasks are project based.

2. Marketing to Increase Revenue

   The next set of tasks I would outsource should lead to the generation of more sales. This would mean either hiring someone to generate more leads for you or delegating the bust task you are doing so that *you* can generate more sales.

We often advise our clients to implement an outsourcing strategy to hire someone to generate more leads via Internet marketing, social media, or telemarketing. Although this might apply for many businesses, in some instances, our client is a great salesperson and simply needs more time to make calls, attend networking events, talk at events, and so forth. Identify tasks you are doing that can be outsourced so that you have more time to do what you are *best* at.

3. Outsource Your Dislike List, Not Good At List, and Boring List

    Once you have outsourced "must delegate" and "marketing tasks," you can outsource the tasks you really do not want to do, if you have the resources.

Step 3: Selecting Whom to Delegate To

Often new prospects will want to hire a six-dollar-per hour virtual agent (VA) when what they are really looking for is a consultant, specialist, or business/project manager. Knowing whom to hire for the right job is crucial for your success. Once you have completed the table assign the tasks to one of the following:

- Consultant: Someone who will advise you, create a strategy or plan of action; they typically do not do the work themselves

- Specialist: Someone with specialized skills (graphics, web, technology, accountant, etc.)

- Business/Project Manager: Someone who manages key aspects of your business

- In-house Employee: Someone who comes into your place of business, full or part time

- Remote Employee: Someone who works remotely

Step 4: Instructing How You Want the Task Done

Once you have identified the tasks to delegate, prioritized the tasks, decided whom to assign the tasks to, the next step is to create Basic Operational Sequential Steps.

The instructions should be simple, step by step, easy to follow. If you do not know how to do certain tasks, ask your agent to research or review any applicable training material.

Instructions can be as simple as writing the steps in a word document, recording phone calls, creating scripts trees, creating training videos, or using screen capture software.

Step 5: Allocating When You Want the Task Done

In addition to providing instructions, create a schedule and allocate time for different tasks throughout the week in Google Calendar or a similar program. This is often overlooked, often because you are too busy and don't have time to create the calendar for your employees. However, when the time is scheduled up front, you get better results.

Step 6: Understanding Why Outsourcing Might Now Work

Many people complain that outsourcing did not work for them, and they often blame their virtual employee or service provider. The reality is that there are six pillars of successful outsourcing. The following examples show when these pillars are not met.

1. The business is not well defined or structured. The funnel, websites, copy, and so forth are not great.

2. The employers do not know how to communicate or manage, or they overwhelm the VA.

3. The tasks are not appropriate for that level employee.

4. The instructions are not clear.

5. The employee/agent is not up to the task.

6. The employer has unrealistic expectations from their agent.

When these reasons are adequately addressed, the outsourcing relationship will be better.

Step 7: Know Your Role

Once you have made the decision to outsource, used the delegation process to decide what to outsource first to get through the first 30–90 days. We do our best to assist our clients with this process. The reality is that they are *your* employee, even if they are working in another facility. They will look to you for advice and guidance. Provide information and resources to allow their tasks to be done.

Remember: not seeking help, whether locally or somewhere in the world, is a recipe for disaster. Your business will not grow because you can only do so much. And you will never be free to do the things you want to do, when you want to do them. Make a plan and then get some help. You deserve to have a business that makes you a lot of money and affords you the free time to enjoy it.

Biography

Daven Michaels

Super entrepreneur and COO of 123Employee, DAVEN MICHAELS has made a career of living the American dream. Best-selling music and television producer, author, speaker, and entrepreneur, Daven shows the little guy how to play ball with the big corporations and beat them at their  own game. Daven Michaels has become an advocate for the small business owner and has appeared on numerous radio and TV shows and stages across North America.

Contact Information

www.DavenMichaels.com

info@123Employee.com

Chapter 5

Your Passion, Your Power!

by Darlene C. O'Keeffe, CHC, PTF

No to Death and Yes to Life

My story of triumph begins in 1992, when I was 32 years old. Until that point I had been living a life without direction or purpose. I had worked hard, treated people well, and always tried to do the right thing. But I wasn't passionate about much, and I had little personal conviction or power of my own. I was still drifting along, trying to find my way.

Everything changed when I awoke one morning knowing in every fiber of my being that I was dying. I got up and glanced back at my bed, where I saw a fistful of hair left behind on the pillow. Going bald at the age of 32 was the least of my problems. My calves were swelling to the size of my waist. I couldn't walk up two steps without stopping to rest. There were open sores on my skin that wouldn't heal, I was losing my eyesight, and there was nearly no food I could eat anymore—my digestive system was barely functioning.

So I went to a couple of doctors for help. One told me, "You're just getting to the age that when you get home from work, you need to put your legs up." Well, that advice wasn't good enough for me—I was only 32. The second told me that the last system to shut down before the body dies is the digestive system, and my digestive system was in the process of shutting down. I was told I had about two weeks to live.

At that moment, I knew that if I wanted to live, I had to save my own life. I didn't have much time to turn things around, and I still had no idea what was causing my problems. So there I was, in the doctor's office, standing at Death's door with a decision to make. Do I accept the advice I was given and die, or do I take matters into my own hands?

If I wanted to *live*, I had no choice.

I fully believe the body is an amazing thing—that if you give it what it needs, and remove those things that are hurting it, it will heal itself. This belief was the guiding light that helped me through the darkness, but it was my passion for survival that gave me the strength to live through this hell and make it back to health and happiness.

After I had been working with a chiropractor/nutritionist for six months, he turned to me and said with exasperation, "Darlene, you should be well by now. Your body is acting like it's been poisoned!" That's when my life changed—that was the moment I understood what had happened. Unrecognized by me or the medical professionals, I had experienced a gradual massive pesticide poisoning over that past year.

I had actually poisoned *myself* using flea foggers to kill the fleas in my home! My cat had become a flea magnet after moving to Miami, and my apartment had become infested. To kill the fleas, I had used flea bombs, setting off three in my home in succession. Over the next year, I had absorbed those pesticides from every soft surface that I couldn't clean. My research told me these pesticides work by exploding the cells from the inside. Can you imagine how much damage was done to my body over that year? It was massive!

Now that I knew the cause, I could do something about it. Realizing it was pesticide poisoning, I took more focused steps toward health that began to pay off. With no health insurance covering this and no one to guide me, armed only with my passion to live, I mustered enough energy to take those first steps toward my goal.

The first three years were a life-and-death struggle. I barely had enough energy to lift a brush to my hair or a glass of water to my lips. But my passion to survive wouldn't let me give up. I researched and experimented, as I could afford, and I learned firsthand what worked for me. I knew there were no magic bullets, and I didn't expect any. I listened to others' advice, but took action based on my own counsel, following only the actions that felt right and were true for me. Taking responsibility for the condition I was in, I did whatever it took to achieve my goal.

Knowing that the body constantly rebuilds itself and replaces old dying cells with new ones, I realized there was an opportunity here to reverse the damage. So, I ensured that each new generation of cells was less damaged than the ones before, and I was gradually able to reverse the damage and become healthy again. After those first three desperate years, I turned a corner. No longer in hand-to-hand combat with Death, I was rewarded with many great leaps in my physical condition over the next 10 years. And the payoff was enormous—I succeeded in achieving my goal to be vibrantly healthy again, and I also discovered how to rebuild a body.

Armed with this knowledge and a new passion to help others become vibrantly healthy and happy, my personal power emerged.

Thoughts on Success

My greatest tips for success in any area of life are simply this:

Don't give up, and Don't go it alone!

Know that you *will* succeed in overcoming your challenges and reaching your goals. Find others who have been where you are now and have succeeded. They can help you achieve your goals faster and with less expense than learning by trial and error as I did. Then simply don't let anyone or anything get in your way, including you!

In my viewpoint, success is not defined by how much you have, but by what you do, and how you live your life. It is expressed every day that you attempt to be the best you can be. Successful people have conviction and passion. They have purpose and a strong level of integrity. They don't blame others or circumstances for their failures—they are not victims. Instead, they learn from their failures, pack that lesson into their toolkit, and move on to the next failure until they ultimately achieve their goals. Successful people take the journey one step at a time, accepting who they are, frailties and all, and strive to make their life and their loved ones' lives a little better every day.

To build and have a successful life, discover what inspires you, what you're good at. What lights your fire? These things will feed you mentally, spiritually, and yes, even physically. When you're living your passions, your body can't help but respond. Take steps for self-improvement—do the inner work to become clear of your baggage and the voices in your head that tell you that you "can't" or "shouldn't" do something, or that you're "not good enough." Gain the knowledge and skills needed to live your passions. Focus. Set goals and take action toward those goals and dreams every day. Take one baby step at a time until you can take longer strides. Don't accept mediocrity in yourself or others and strive to be the best person you can be. But most important, share your love, your joy, and your passions with others.

Always remember, there's a reason, a cause, for everything that happens in life. To overcome challenges and be successful, we need to understand the cause of our challenges. Where and how did they start? What actions did *you* take that helped create the chain of events that led to where you are today? What could *you* have been done differently to create a different, better outcome? When you spot those answers, ask yourself what tools are available to help you solve that issue or problem. If you don't know, keep searching.

When you come across possible answers, pick the ones that feel true for you. Implement the solutions—try them out. Discover firsthand what works for you, no matter what others may think. If it doesn't get you closer to your goal, obviously it's not *your* answer, so get rid of it. Keep looking. Don't accept the opinions or advice of so-called authorities who have never overcome a similar experience themselves. Surround yourself with and seek out others who have experience with your type of challenges and who have overcome them. Surround yourself with positive people, not people who would stop you and pull you down.

If you continue to react and respond to challenges in your life the same as you've always done, how can you expect different results? Deepak Chopra once said, "If you change the way you look at things, the things you look at change." So to heck with what others say you should or shouldn't do, or what they tell you is right or wrong. To heck with what "authority" says can and can't be done. If what they're saying isn't helping you get well, thank them for their advice and then do what works for you. Don't let anyone stop you from achieving what you want or need to live the life you were meant to live. Life should be an adventure. Find out what it is you're passionate about, figure out what it is you want to achieve, don't be afraid of hard work, and most importantly, go for it!

Say no to the ordinary, and your life will become extraordinary!

Among many inspirational quotes about success, my all-time favorite is by Marianne Williamson. It speaks to what many of us do that prevents us from living with passion and inviting success into our lives.

Our deepest fear is not that we are inadequate. Our deepest fear is that we are powerful beyond measure. It is our light, not our darkness that most frightens us. We ask ourselves, Who am I to be brilliant, gorgeous, talented, fabulous? Actually, who are you not to be? You are a child of God. Your playing small does not serve the world. There is nothing enlightened about shrinking so that other people won't feel insecure around you. We are all meant to shine, as children do. We were born to make manifest the glory of God that is within us. It's not just in some of us; it's in everyone. And as we let our own light shine, we unconsciously give other people permission to do the same. As we are liberated from our own fear, our presence automatically liberates others.

Thoughts on Leadership

I believe leadership is having the ability to inspire passion and action in others. It's the ability to help others realize their goals. Through their actions, leaders show us what we are all capable of achieving. Being focused and dedicated, leaders must be willing to roll their sleeves up and do whatever is necessary to achieve their goals. A leader must also have creativity, vision, a high level of integrity, and above all, they must have a spirit of play. Leaders help spark the fires of passion within us and have the strength and conviction to blaze their own trail.

Are you letting others lead you or interfere with the creation of your life, or are you blazing your own trail? One path leads toward failure and pain, the other toward passion and success. We're all faced with this choice at many points throughout our lives. If you believe you've made the wrong choices, don't fret. It's never too late. You can always change your mind. The choice is yours!

Biography

Darlene C. O'Keeffe

Certified Health Counselor and Passion Test Facilitator

In 1992, DARLENE O'KEEFFE started on a path that led her from Death's door to vibrant health. During her journey, she realized that vibrant health and passion are tightly bound; most important, she discovered her passion for helping others reach their health and life goals.

As a result of her personal experimentation and her ongoing formal education, she has amassed a tremendous toolkit—a toolkit that contains the knowledge and steps she used to rebuild her body and health, and completely change her life. Nothing makes her happier now than sharing that toolkit to help others achieve their health and life goals. To find out more about Darlene and how she can help you create a more passion-driven, healthy, and successful life, visit her websites.

Contact Information

Passion website: www.YourPassionYourPower.com
Darlene@YourPassionYourPower.com

Health counseling website: www.DarleneO.com
Health@DarleneO.com
914-484-8200

Chapter 6

Opportunity Is Calling

by Adam Spiel

I remember sitting and watching Tony Hseih, CEO of Zappos, speaking at the SANG (Speakers and Authors Networking Group) conference in LA about the core foundation of why his company was so successful. He said, "Our goal at Zappos is for our employees to think of their work not as a *job* or *career*, but as a *calling*."

As he said that, I couldn't help but think to myself about the "job" I had, and the "money" I had made—but what was my calling? And how could I live that calling every day?

Sure, I had made a lot of money selling products and building businesses—and I had lost a lot of money too. Growing up, I had watched my dad spinning his wheels, working for corporation after corporation. He would fix all the problems in his department and perfect it to the point where he had worked himself out of a job. Every two years the cycle would begin again: He would find a new job, make his department absolutely excellent, and suddenly the corporation would assume they no longer needed him.

Not only did I see the pain and worry in his face every time this cycle ended, but I experienced that pain with him, at a very young age. Of course, we all know where my dad was coming from. He wanted to find a "job" or a "career" where there was security, fulfillment, and no frustration. Instead, he was hopping from job and career, attempting to "work the system" and finding that the system was actually working him.

Well, that's what I grew up observing—and I made a promise to myself that I would never be in that same position. I would always control my future by owning my own business.

I was a very bad employee because I would always challenge the status quo in any company and tell them that they could be more productive if they did things differently. Established companies don't like hearing that from a 19- or 22-year-old kid.

Have you ever done something that drains every ounce of your energy? While in college I spent some time working with the fund-raising department. Just a mere two to three hours a day speaking with alumni about donations to their alma mater felt more like a torturous and drawn-out 20 hours! I couldn't wait to get out of there, because it was a *huge* energy drain. Why?

Simply because I wasn't expressing my core talents and purpose through those activities.

On the other hand, when I started coaching, teaching, and working with entrepreneurs, I could go on and on for hours and it felt like minutes. Time just flew by, and I gained incredible energy, standing in a place of power aligned with my core purpose and talents.

Desperately wanting to blaze my own path, I began to try things on my own. I found myself living on credit cards with over $100,000 in debt as I invested in myself to lift my business off the ground. This investing came in the form of courses, mentoring, and overall learning of the strategies and mechanics of running my own business.

Don't think for a second that this was glamorous, either. Owning my own business had its own set of risks and stresses. There were days when I would talk to my wife to ask whether she should get another job or if I should simply give up and go get a "real job." But I knew that simply wasn't me!

That investment in myself has ultimately paid off. Today I work when I want and where I want. I take weeks off at a time, traveling and spending time with my wife and three kids. In fact, we just returned from 10 days in Maui, and we're planning a 12-month sabbatical in New Zealand and Australia.

After years of dedication, I have finally built a team and business that grows and makes money even when I'm not around. And I *love* the work that I do—working with young entrepreneurs to grow their online businesses, so they don't have to get a "real job" or play the infinite game of "the system."

Because the system is broken! You know that and I know that. During the numerous years when my dad should have started his own business, he spent working a couple years for one corporation and then another. He was good at what he did and he *loved* what he did. So what was he doing wrong? My dad needed to do it in a market where he could work for himself, or even better, create a business that worked for him.

Yet he never took that step because he was preoccupied with the fear of providing for his family, just like many of you are today. We all want security. And we're all taught that the corporate world offers that system of security. Funny enough, my dad is proof of how broken that system is. Starting over and over again at a new corporate position doesn't sound very secure, does it?

Today I can happily say that my dad has developed his own company over the last 10 years—*finally!* It was an honor when he called me the other day and thanked me for encouraging him to take that first, scary step. He has never been happier, truly doing the work that he loves and making a big difference with the companies he works with. My dad is truly living his calling and core purpose. The same opportunity and possibility exists for you right now, today.

We're taught at a young age to look outward for knowledge, in books, in the Internet, even in other, smarter, people. We're taught that the answers are always outside us.

Think about this dynamic paradigm shift, just for a moment: you have value within you, right now. When you share your talents, you create value for other people. And in case you're in doubt, you should know that there are people all over the world who desperately *need* what you have to share.

All of us have a core purpose—a unique set of talents, strengths, passions, and experiences to share and create value in the world.

How do you discover and find out what your core purpose is? What is the value that you have to share with the world?

As I coach people through this process, I have found that that the core purpose within them lies where their passions, talents, and experiences intersect. It's the sweet spot, where we experience the ultimate success, purpose, and fulfillment. It's where we can wake up every day, excited to create value and share our personal truth with the world.

These are just a few questions I ask my coaching students as the starting line to find their core purpose. I want you to begin this journey today.

What are your top three strengths?

Are you a dedicated leader? Good at teaching others? A fantastic writer? The best networker you know? Love to promote a party, idea, service to your friends? Good at closing a sale?

What are your talents?

Are you an expert at wiring your home? A great basketball player? Uncanny with numbers? The master at word-smithing? The creator of unforgettable events that bring people together?

What are your passions?

What is something you can completely lose track of time and space doing? Does it feel productive, natural, and uplifting? Why do you like it so much? Do others have a passion for the same thing? What would you do all day long even if you weren't getting paid to do it?

What do you do better than anyone else in the world?

Can you motivate anyone, no matter what the circumstances? Design the coolest websites in the fastest amount of time? Are you an expert at creating awesome videos or teaching and speaking in front of groups? What is so easy to you that you could do it in your sleep and still be the best at it?

What are your experiences?

What life experiences have you had that you could use to teach, inspire, or assist someone else going through the same situation? Are there problems that you have been able to solve that you could share the answer with someone else? Take some of your answers from above and write down the most poignant discoveries you have made in experiencing any of these strengths or talents.

What is your personal "Why"?

There's a reason *why* you like to do what you do, and *why* you just *know* that you're supposed to be sharing it with others through your business efforts. Ponder it for a moment, and write it down.

Knowing your core purpose and strengths also requires acknowledging that there are some things in this life that you are *not* good at and things that you do *not* enjoy doing—and this is as equally important for you to know. Because when you are doing activities that are not in alignment with your core purpose and strengths, you are standing and operating outside your certainty. Standing outside your certainty can, and will, drain you of your power.

Remember, it's not about "What do you want to be when you grow up?"—that's the wrong question.

The right question to ask is, "What is your calling? What unique gifts and talents do you have to share and bless the world with? What is the contribution you can make by living, expressing, and sharing your core purpose with the world?"

And more important than knowing your calling, it's about living, sharing, and expressing your core purpose and inner truth every day. When you do this, you can stand in that place of certainty and power.

I knew that my calling was to end the pattern of 9-to-5 game playing in everyone's lives. Working through my personal observations and experiences, today I not only end that pattern in other people's lives, but I'm living proof of beating the system.

So ask yourself, "How can I express my talents and core purpose starting *right now* and start *living* the life I was meant to live and making the contribution I was meant to make?"

Biography

Adam Spiel

ADAM SPIEL is a serial entrepreneur and Internet marketer committed to profitable and predictable results centered on value and purpose. He is the cofounder of Inspiration Generation™—a revolutionary movement introducing a new conversation of core purpose to awaken and inspire the next generation to live in their truth and power every day.

Contact Information

www.InspirationGeneration.org

Chapter 7

Transforming a Vision into a Dream

by Clay Johnson

It is Monday morning, and I am still trying to recover from the weekend of too much fun. I really just want to sleep in and take care of my own business today, but I have to go to work. Most people start their Mondays on Sunday afternoon. That feeling of anxiety begins usually around the late afternoon hours and weighs heavily as the evening progresses. This was my weekly ritual when I was working as a technology designer for Motorola. I loved my job, but Monday always came too often.

Weekends were never long enough, so my wife and I would have friends over on Sunday just to extend the fun a little longer. We would usually have a BBQ or maybe some seafood out on the back patio. On occasion I would reminisce about past vacations and have a déjà vu moment. I would dream of getting up from the dinner table, leaving all the dishes right in their place, and catching a flight to the British Virgin Islands. Arriving on the small island, hoping to find a place to stay was the adventure. The reward would be a week of enchantment at my favorite place in the whole world, the North Sound of the BVI, just off the island of Virgin Gorda, with the Caribbean breeze blocking the thought of where I was supposed to be. The best part would be firing my boss from location. *If only I had won the lottery last night* was what my mind processed as I got ready for work every Monday morning.

I did love my job. Wanting to fire my boss did not mean I did not like my boss. I just did not like having to be somewhere other than where I wanted to be. So one day, I did fire my boss, but for opportunity. I created an opportunity to start my life as a serial entrepreneur, an opportunity to rid myself of the Sunday night jitters and the Monday morning blues. I had hit a wall at my beloved job and wanted more. I'd had seven new bosses in two and a half years. I was trying to establish a relationship with each as a technical contributor and found myself having to re-prove myself over and over.

The company was not doing well, so I was not doing well. This is what you would call a corporate roller coaster. Meetings were an excuse not to work. They were gatherings of anyone who wished to waste yet another afternoon and pass on that waste to the shareholders for the purpose of restating the obvious, which had been outlined just a few days before by the interim mid-level manager of the month. This was a middle management technique called "cover your ass."

I had reached my fill of this game when my current boss held yet another meeting for our small team, stating that we would all lose our jobs if we did not find employment in another department. During that meeting, I asked a simple question: "What about our deliverables?" His response was "screw the deliverables!" The level of incompetence had reached an all-time high, and I really needed to be in control of my future, so I fired my boss. It was one of the most difficult decisions I had ever made, because I truly loved my job and the people, but I did not feel like I was in control of my own advancement. You see, I am a results-oriented person. Hard work should be rewarded, and Laziness should be discouraged. Well, in corporate America, it sometimes just does not work that way.

Ready to start my new career as a general contractor, the world was my office and freedom was just around the corner. But the reality is that although you are free from a boss, you always take work home and even sleep with it at times. Still, being your own boss is cool, especially if you are passionate about what you do. I was good at it, and my motivation was to level the playing field and keep the competition honest. I was more mobile, made all the decisions, loved the progress that each job provided, and my profit requirement was much lower than that of my competition. This meant that I had options the other guy did not have.

The reality of entrepreneurship sets in at some point after a few missed vacations and being stuck on a job site until well after normal business hours over and over. After about 12 years, I grew tired of getting paid at the end of each job and sometimes not at all. I had the constant fear that my trades wouldn't show up to finish their job. Did I calculate enough loan carry to get me to the sale and then to the closing? Most of all, I got sick of getting home late, after dinner, when my babies were already tucked into bed. How would this work long term?

You see, I loved my job again, and this time I was my own boss, but my responsibility was much greater and much more thankless. The payday was larger, but the loss of revenue and investment was far more risky than rewarding, especially during the difficult housing market. Even when contracts to construct new homes were abundant, it was at a cost of more time for less pay. This made my business model of keeping the other guy honest even more difficult.

I was a very good homebuilder; honesty was my motivation, and my client relationships were lasting. So I call this a stalemate in success. I knew that if I continued down this path, I would be just like every other builder out there, building homes until I ran out of money. The competition was not going to change, and neither was I. For the second time, I was faced with a career crossroad decision, but this time not as an employee but as the employer, so I fired myself.

As an employer of my homebuilding company and as an employee at Motorola, I was only able to give so much of my time to make money. The income was limited, and my time was limited. Time and money will always compete with each other, so the efficient use of them is the key to having more of both. Residual income taught me that time was really the most valuable resource we all have.

How do we get more time? Work fewer hours, be efficient, build multiple income streams, and buy time. How do we do that? Build those residual income streams either by saving money or by leveraging the time we have available to us. This allows us to spend less time working for others. Get more done early in the day by eliminating procrastination. Get to the places you need or want to go faster. Use resources that are available to you and weigh their cost to the value they bring to you.

Is your time best spent cutting your own grass, or can you pay someone to do it while you earn more dollars with the time you save? Paying your bills online and utilizing autopay can save time. Any way you can create extra time gives you more time to build a side business. My favorite way to increase the amount of time that I have is to fly instead of driving. This costs money, but it saves on time. There is a balance where the economics are in a state of equilibrium with the time. I will always look for a way to save time at a cost as long as there is a profit involved. Time is finite, and we all have the same 24 hours each day. The best way to have more than 24 hours for personal use is to build multiple residual income streams.

How do you get started with this idea of buying more time and creating this dream of residual income? Well, the first thing to do is to identify where you are and where you want to go. Identify what it is that you have and what it is that you want. We are trained to accept our needs at the expense of our wants; this is where life overcomes our ability to dream big like we used to do when we were children. Having more time affords us to daydream about the better life that appears to always be on the other side of the fence.

This is all part of your personal vision for your life. The experiences you have had since you were born have shaped this vision. Your internal programming is set through those experiences. In essence, you are what you have been told, you are what you believe, and you are a product of your environment.

Many of us inherited a vision from our parents, our educators, our siblings, our peers, our mentors, and our employers. They each had their own idea of how to achieve goals and turn them into what we all know as a productive life. Where did they get their ideas and goal-setting methodology? From the same stamped-out plan that we all have come to know. The only thing that really separates our inherited plan is the depth and size of our dreams.

One thing for sure is that goals can be made and goals can be lost, but a dream is forever. When I was very young, I used to dream big—the dreams we all talked about with our friends: a nice new shiny sports car, a big house, a dream job, lots of friends, travel, plenty of financial security, a college degree, and a beautiful family. Don't forget about going to the moon. These dreams were the vision that I had for myself at a very young and impressionable age. The only problem was that the method of achieving these dreams was defined by a vision that I had inherited. So many of them would seem unattainable.

In many, many ways, the path of my life was already planned for me. Through my decisions, I was able to distinguish where my comfort zone wanted to keep me and where my heart and soul were guiding me. My dreams were met, but I needed to dream bigger.

I was 42 years old when I saw an opportunity to create a shift in this paradigm, and it was not disguised as a mid-life crisis. It was, however, distinguished through hindsight—you know, that thing we all know as 20/20 vision. The vehicle was opportunity knocking. It only happens every once in a while. This was the crossroad: no more time stealers, which are the same as dream stealers. I made the decision to break the pattern and change the vision from someone else's to my own.

This all happened by accident, because my life was just as I wanted it. My finances were great, my wife and children were and are amazing, my experiences were peak, but my work as a homebuilder held me as a captive audience. Pride, perfection, and a love of my work made the decisions for me.

I guess you could say my priorities changed. I could see the damage that I was doing to my family and myself by donating so much time to the spinning wheel of life. Going in circles was no longer my interest. I wanted my time, and I wanted it to take me places. I wanted the freedom and the opportunity to buy more time and compound that investment.

Nothing we do is free, and the cost of making a decision to change something we have become so comfortable with can literally change everything in our lives. Life can be simplified to a basic formula, Time plus Money equals Freedom. All we have to do is change the way we use our time, but first change our inherited internal programming. We can decide to work super hard for a little while, or we can work at our current pace for eternity. I personally like the idea of working double time now and having a chance of freedom later. The worst thing that can happen is that I just learn a great life lesson—or I might just hit that homerun. With time on my side today, I hit the homerun and am well on the road to total time and financial freedom.

Biography
Clay Johnson

CLAY JOHNSON is the owner and operator of Rienzi Custom Homes, Inc., Johnson Ranches LLC, CGJ Land LLC, Five J Marketing LLC, and Five J Holdings LLC. He has proven himself through excellence, dedication, and a commitment to keeping quality as the pinnacle of all business  endeavors. As a general contractor and multiple business owner for the last 14 years and a technical contributor with a major technology company for the 8 years prior, Clay has worked to exceed the expectations of peers and customers.

Despite this personal commitment to excellence, there are only so many hours to trade each day. Clay's focus is now to show the masses how to make a fortune and have more time. To fulfill his goals of helping others find the freedom they deserve, Clay coaches people on fiscal financial responsibility, future/forward planning, expertise in multiple skill sets, and dream building. Help someone show someone how to help someone and the reward will be a better world.

Contact Information

512-762-5659

Chapter 8

Success Is
Where the Heart Is

by Mark Call

Our definitions of success are as individual as paintings, and we each bring our own brush to the canvas of our lives. Even when we try to imitate another's successful artwork, our own work bears our hand, our signature. The art of success is the skill of bringing our own beauty and emotion to the canvas, to create a masterpiece that comes from the soul, that moves and inspires everyone around us.

Many people are afraid to take a chance on their own vision. Instead, they take the safe route, the paint-by-numbers approach guaranteed to make a profit. Sometimes this approach works, but often it doesn't. Either way, they're left unsatisfied. Why is this? They've followed the instructions and painted themselves a beautiful house and an expensive car, . . . but now what?

Lots of people have beautiful houses and expensive cars. Many of them probably painted from the same kit! But their own dreams are still unexpressed inside them. As long as this is true, they will never feel successful.

Now, you may be thinking, Hey, I *tried* to follow my own vision. I failed. Let's face it, I'm just not an artist.

Here's the thing: Although *what* you create is your vision and yours alone, *how* you create it requires skills—skills you can learn from those who have studied and applied the science of success.

That's why this book is about both. Each chapter is by an artist whose vision is unlike any other. Yet the science behind their success is proven. We all offer techniques and tools you can use to create your own masterpiece. In fact, you'll run into a few methods that most of us use—*because they work.*

But you'll notice we are all very different people, and although we used some tried-and-true techniques, we ended up with different yet equally amazing levels of success. We may have used some of the same brushes, or some of the same colors, but the art we have created is distinctly our own.

My success is based on 10 basic principles, rooted in art and science. I want to share them with you because your success is my success. Why? Read on to find out.

1. Live "As Is" not "As If"

The very first step, before you can do anything else, is to know who *you* are and *be* that person. Not the person everyone else thinks you should be, but the successful, happy person you have buried inside you. Decide who this person is and take small steps every day to embody that person.

I hate the saying "Fake it till you make it." Who are we supposed to be fooling? If we know we're faking it, then we know we're *not* who we want to be. If you live as is, you are not faking it. You are training yourself to be the best person you can be, and you are showing yourself and others who you truly are. "As is" means that you *are* a success where you are in this moment, and more importantly, where you will be in the next. This is a science that your subconscious will take hold of and eventually live by.

2. Know What You Want and Ask For It

Most people never ask for what they want and instead beat around the bush, hoping someone will get the hint. Usually people do this because they do not really know what they want. When you don't know what you want, you often get what you don't want.

Just as important as figuring out who you really are is figuring out *exactly* what you want. When you have a detailed vision in mind, you will see what you need to fulfill it. Then you can ask for it without any misunderstanding. Don't be afraid to ask people for help with your vision. You would be amazed at how many people appreciate your ability to articulate what you need and your courage in asking for help to get it.

And don't be afraid to throw your desires out to the universe. Be as specific as possible, and it will somehow provide. Don't ask me how because I really don't know, and I know it sounds flaky or weird, but it works.

3. Don't Let Anyone Stand in the Way of Your Dreams

You have heard this before, but I can't emphasize it enough. Don't share your aspirations with people you *know* will rip them apart, including (often well-meaning but patronizing) friends and family who think they know better than you. Remember: Your dreams are yours, not theirs. Instead, move forward, and as success comes, those who doubted you will be asking what your secret is.

You do, however, need to have at least one person you can trust with your vision. Open your heart to the person closest to you—your spouse, significant other, or best friend. Truly listen to each other's dreams and acquire them together. You'll find that as your success grows, so will your relationship, deepening your bond and giving you both the strength and courage to reach even higher.

4. Be Patient!

Delayed gratification can be hard, but even worse is trying to do too much at one time and ending up with nothing to show for it, which of course delays gratification even more! Take small, consistent steps toward your dreams every single day and they will add up quickly to success—much faster, in fact, than attempting to do it all overnight. I don't know anyone, including all the great coauthors of this book, who were overnight success stories. Be consistent in your business, but more importantly, be consistent with your loved ones. These daily actions will make you a better person and will become habit.

Assess your entire day every evening for a few minutes when you go to bed. Reflect on the day and what you accomplished toward your goals. If you got off track a little, think of your next day and what *small* steps you can take toward your focused goal. This is where the art of success comes in. Did you know that Leonardo da Vinci worked on the Mona Lisa for about *15 years* before completing it? He focused on one brush stroke at a time. And of course, he achieved many other successes during that time. The art of success, to me, means being an everyday artist, taking consistent small daily steps toward our greater cause.

5. Schedule Work Time and Schedule Family Time

Too often we schedule work time and get side-tracked. When you schedule work time, shut down everything else and truly work on the task at hand for the full time allotted. You will be surprised at how much you will get done.

On the same note, we often let work time interfere with family time. This may sound crude, but you need to schedule playtime with those you love: Shut down the computer, don't answer the phone, don't respond to e-mail—focus on the family. Not only will you recharge your batteries in this way, making your work time even more efficient and creative, your family will respect you more for your hard work and have a sincere appreciation for you. They will also get behind your dreams, knowing that one of your goals is to spend more focused time with them.

6. Go M.A.D. (Make a Difference)

Zig Ziglar said it best: "You can have everything in life you want, if you will just help other people get what they want." Make a difference in others' lives, and you will see the difference in your own. Success is not so much about who you know as it is who you care about. If you don't care about your customers, clients, and colleagues, why should they care about what you have to offer? Be honest with people: Don't sell a product or service that you have not used yourself and had success with, that you don't believe in with all your heart.

Always make a point of finding out what others want and show them that you are sincerely willing to help and support them in any way you can—then do it. When you interact with friends, family, and strangers alike, make it about them, not you. Ask questions and see if you can help that person and make a difference. Challenge yourself to make a difference every day in the lives of as many people as possible.

This is fun and you will become a success from this alone. Always be the first to ask about them in a conversation. The less you make it about you, the more successful you will be, and believe me, the more successful you will appear to everyone around you. You can make a difference by simply listening to others and grow the involvement from there.

7. There's no Such Thing as Problems, Only Solutions

If you look at problems, no matter what they may be (financial, relationship, etc.) as challenges and not problems, you will be ahead of the game. A challenge is an *opportunity* to be creative, to figure out a solution. If your brain is fried and you are frustrated, put it up for a while and come back and address the challenge in a new light. I personally find that if I sleep on a challenge, it solves itself. Your subconscious is an amazing solution machine—let it do its job! Every successful person is faced with challenges. You are no different from them unless you do nothing to create the solution.

8. Never Stop Learning

Always strive to learn new things about life, love, relationships, business, and most importantly, yourself. We always have room to learn. Again, *consistent* small steps to educate yourself are the key. Reading is an amazing way to learn and develop expertise, and becoming an expert in something is a surefire way to be successful. Think again about step 6. Where can you make a difference in the lives of others? That's what you need to become an expert on.

I actually hate reading; however, I read something every day. If the average book is 300 pages, and you read only 10–12 pages each day, you can usually get through a full book in under a month, which equates to 12 books a year. I don't know about you, but I don't think I read 12 books during my entire time in school, and now it has become a habit to educate myself through reading!

How long will it take you to read 10–12 pages of a good book per day? Not long, and think of the knowledge you will attain. In no time, this will become habit, and you will become more educated and knowledgeable than you ever dreamed. It's also fun to refer to what you read in conversation with others as it relates to their situation. Makes you look great, and helps you make a difference in their lives.

9. Surround Yourself With Success— You Are Who You Associate With

Okay, do this exercise. Take the five people you most commonly associate with, add up their total income as a group (c'mon, you know what they make), now divide it by 5—that is what you make. Worked, didn't it? Isn't that amazing?

Now, surrounding yourself with success does *not* mean dropping your best bud who is unemployed and down on his luck; it means *bringing others* into your life who will impact your success. At every point in my life, no matter where I have been, I could read my own success meter by looking at the people I most commonly associated with at that time. It's not all about the money they make but also the quality of their relationships and lifestyle—how they live their life. Associate with people who live successfully according to your definition. This is something that will repeatedly come up over time, and you will find your associations change and grow as you change.

10. Never Give Up!

This is one you have been taught since you were a little kid, because it's true! So many people just plain give up. It's heartbreaking how easily people give up on themselves and in turn their loved ones. Giving up should not be an option.

Success is not supposed to be easy. If it were, everyone would be the huge success that you read about, and in a way, no one would be successful because we'd have to redefine what success even means! Sure, you may have some challenges along the way, but finding solutions is all that matters. Maybe your masterpiece isn't turning out the way you thought it would, but you don't give up painting. Try a different brush, a different color, a new technique, or use the challenges as an opportunity to go in a new and better direction. Just whatever you do, don't stop painting.

You are already successful, exactly where you are. All you have to do is show the world that success by putting brush to canvas, using scientifically proven methods that have worked for thousands of successful people.

Success is where the heart is. Create a masterpiece that comes from your heart, and your art will make a difference in the lives of others, which in turn will lead to even more success and meaning in your life. *You* are the artist painting the life of your dreams. All you have to do is pick up that brush.

Biography

Mark Call

MARK CALL has been an Internet marketer and network marketer since 1991. He is now an online business and marketing coach, MLM Trainer, author, and motivational speaker. He does a minimum of two free live webcasts per week, teaching people the methods to be successful online  and in their home business. Why free, you ask? Well, it is just a small way for Mark to pay back to an industry that has been so good to him.

His latest comprehensive e-book, *The Book on Webcasting: Network Marketer's Edition,* will soon be available in print. Mark lives in Maine with his beautiful and supportive wife, Dina. They have four children with a wide range of talents: three sons, Marky, Brandon, and Hazen; and one daughter, Jensyn.

Contact Information

http://markcall.com
http://MarkCall.com/helpdesk

Chapter 9

The Conversation

by Tim Zimmerman

When it really comes down to it, why are we here? What is our true purpose? Is it to be a good father or mother, to give our children a better life than we had, or to be a good grandmother or grandfather, to be a good employer or employee, to create an empire? Why?

When we get down to our last breaths, and we know we are going to pass, what is going to be important? That we became a millionaire or billionaire, that we traveled the world, helped a lot of people, gave away a bunch of money, and have a lot of friends? That we overcame the Karma of the past or created as little Karma as possible? That we accomplished our bucket list?

According to Plato, the greatest achievement in life for any human Being is attaining the state of Divine Self-realization. This means to Know-Thy-Self as a eternal spirit, as a spiritual Being One with God. We are said to be of mind, body, and spirit—a body with a mind containing a spirit or soul, yet we truly are a Spirit with a body and mind to use in the world.

Is this noble goal of achieving divine self-realization something you want to achieve in this lifetime? I hope so, because that is what this chapter is about—how to understand your God Consciousness right now!

So, let's begin by asking a simple question. Do you believe in God, Infinite Intelligence, a Supreme Being? Most of you reading this probably do, yet there is more to understand.

In believing in God, then you would normally agree that the three attributes of God are Omnipotence (All Powerful), Omniscience (All Knowing), and Omnipresence (Everywhere Present at Once) . . . Do you agree with this?

So, being *Omnipresent* means that God is emanating throughout your body, my body, this computer I am typing on, the paper or computer screen that you are reading this on . . . emanating through the air we breathe, through what we see and what we do not see.

Yes? Do you agree?

So if God is emanating throughout your body, my body, everything we see and do not see, that means God is emanating through you, every atom and molecule of your body, through your brain, through every action, organ, and function of your body, though your mind, through your thoughts, through the words you say to yourself. God is closer to you than the air you breathe, closer than blood pumping through your heart, emanating through your entire Being, so

You are already One with God, for God is One with you.

Understand and realize this:

You are One with God, for God is One with You.

Now that is enlightening isn't it? Wow. Say this to yourself, "I am One with God because God is One with Me." Repeat it again and again; make it an affirmation. It is an incontrovertible truth.

So does this mean the you should go running around, saying "I am God, I am God"? Well, you could, yet until you bring this intellectual knowing into its physical equivalent, no one would believe you.

Paramahansa Yogananda said it this way: "You are as much one with God right now as you ever will be, you only have to increase your knowing." Remember Jesus' quote of the Bible, "Isn't it written 'Ye all are Gods'?" and in John 10:30, "I and the Father are One." Jesus said this because he knew and believed; he had the God Consciousness, or what some call the Christ Consciousness; he believed "I am One with God for God is One with me."

So, do you get it, do you see it, can you now realize this truth? When you realize fully that you are already One with God, this truth can truly set you free.

For in realizing and accepting this truth, at least three "ah ha moments" happen:

One realization is that everything that has happened to you, or because of you, happened to get you to this point in time, to the Here and Now, to your understanding your Oneness with God. Really, what would you have *not* done or not experienced to get to knowing you are one with God? Hasn't your Spirit continued to ask about God, asked where He was, what He was doing? Unknowingly, you were on The Path to finding God, right within your Self, within your Being.

A second realization is that you are already a *Perfect Manifestor*. You may not have known it, yet the things you thought about came about. You may not have "wished" for it, yet you thought about it, someone suggested it, or worried about it, or just *knew* it was going to happen. And remember, you had to go through it to get to the Here and Now, to get to this teaching.

The third realization is that since you were the cause of all the pain and pleasure in your life so far, and since you created all that you went through, *you can create what you really want from now on, from the perspective of your Oneness with God, from the Here and Now.*

It is said that God works in mysterious ways. Are His ways mysterious only because you have not sought the One that is dwelling right within your own Being, the One that animates you?

Since God is emanating through you, since you were born in His image and likeness, you must have all His attributes, His creation abilities, and much more than you understand and use right now. How could you understand and use them when you were raised to believe differently?

You are bound to create. You have created all of your life. You create through the words you speak (to yourself and to others); through the thoughts you think; through your actions and reactions to these thoughts and words; and through your thoughts, actions, and reactions to the thoughts, words, actions, and reactions of those in your world; and with previously sown thoughts, words, and deeds from all in your world. How cool is that? You are already a Perfect Manifestor!

Realize, though, that it is important to watch and control the words you speak to others, and especially the words you speak to yourself. For these words you speak to yourself create the habits of thought, patterns of thought, vibrations of thought that you continue and consistently project and sow, from moment to moment, and thus must reap consistently, continually, and consequently.

Understand that you are living your life as actions and reactions to the manifestations of your words and thoughts, your words and actions, your words spoken to yourself and to others. Also as a result of thoughts, words, actions, and reactions developed from your perceptions of this creation, your world. This perception is your consciousness, your belief system, that has been developing since the beginning of your time on this earth, and possibly before. Realize that this perception is uniquely yours, and others see from theirs, and now you all can do the work and exercises to change your thought to what you really desire to manifest from this new God Consciousness. SM3 Success Seminars was divinely inspired to conduct seminars to help you become more effective in the materialistic, mental, and spiritual aspects of your life.

One exercise you can do now to control your thoughts is to take time to consciously relax your body and take deep, rhythmic breaths to slow your mind, and just watch your thoughts, like clouds in the sky. Remember when you were a kid and you watched clouds? Do that with your thoughts. Write me after one week, and I will give you the second part of this exercise. It may seem silly, yet it is important. There is a celebrity you all know that did this with amazing results. Do it and see for yourself. To remind yourself, take 20 sticky notes, write "Watch Thoughts" on them and put them up in your home, in your car, and at the office. You will be amazed at the result, I promise. Once you control your thoughts, we can work on creating more Power in them.

Another thing you can start doing is to look back at your life and thank everyone and every situation that happened. Without any one of those "things" happening, no matter how hard or how bad, you would not be reading this right now and you would not Be coming into this God Consciousness. See them as a blessing and know that since God is Omnipresent, God is and was emanating within whoever helped you to get to the Here and Now. In thanking and loving them, you are loving God. That is why Jesus said, "Love thy enemies," "treat others as you would be treated," and "that which you do to the least of your brothers, you do until me"—unto God, for God is emanating though everyone and everything. And didn't you create it anyway?

There are specific ways to increase your "knowingness," specific ways to let go of your past beliefs and hurts, which block your empowerment, for good. There is specific training to develop not only your basic business skills, but also your latent, dormant God-conscious abilities. As humans, we are all bound by the Laws of Creation, and other Universal Laws, including the Laws of Success. So, let's work on the specific ways to gain control over all aspects of our lives—willful control over our thoughts, words, and deeds. Let's look at the law that trumps the Law of Attraction, and the Law of Karma. Let's look at everything you do on a day-to-day basis and see how to become 10%, 20%, 30% more effective in each of those areas, and come to know our Oneness with God even better. Let's look at the ways to use more and more of our brain and mind capacity, more than the 5-10% we currently use. Contact us and find the ways to achieve more success and work toward Conscious Deliberate Instantaneous Manifestation and more.

Biography

Tim Zimmerman

Over the last 30 years, TIM ZIMMERMAN has been on the Quest of a lifetime, a quest to seek and find *the Best of the Best* training and instruction in "Mastering Your Universe." He is now bringing these mental, spiritual, and business techniques and specific training programs to you and the world.
Being trained in his early 20s to teach the five world-renowned Dale Carnegie Courses, Tim is able to use this time-tested, proven successful material and training techniques as a base to build his training platform—to train all those who want success in all ventures. Over three decades, Tim has trained thousands of others in all subjects he mastered: human relations and leadership, effective communications, professional salesmanship and Fortune 500 management techniques; Silva Mind Control, mind development, alpha/theta thinking, NLP, EFT, and Body Talk; the teachings of Earl Nightengale, Napoleon Hill, Jim Rohn, Bob Proctor, Zig Ziglar, Tommy Hopkins, Todd Duncan, Brian Tracy, Mark Victor Hansen, Tony Robbins; and the more esoteric aspects of rebirthing, Raja Yoga, Kriya Yoga, quantum jumping, spiritual healing and meditation; and Ancient Egyptian, Yogic, Tibetan, and Taoist mysticism, initiation, and empowerments, including the techniques for physical and spiritual regeneration and healing. Tim is also considered a Reiki Master and has been through five Tibetan Empowerments, two with the Dalai Lama. All this leading

ultimately to being able to train others in all of these areas, for success in all ventures, God Consciousness and a better quality of life, now and beyond..

View SM3 Success SeminarsSM for the training that will empower you to become who and what you were meant to be in this life.

Contact Information

www.GreatPyramidProductions.com/sm3

Chapter 10

OUT!

OUTRAGEOUSLY UNLIMITED THINKING

by Thell G. Prueitt

I believe in you. All I need is for you to believe in you too!
—Amanda Marshall, from the song "I Believe in You"

*T*here are no wasted experiences in life; only how I choose to respond to them determines the value.

My youngest daughter, Amanda, at age 33, chose to experience death.

I turned around . . . and she was gone . . .

　　She left in the night

　　　　Her sleep took her away . . .

It's a Bright Day where she is

　　But my tears are not always Joyful

　　　　And my Dance not always light

I miss her and she knows

But our Hearts are as always One

Love is all there is

　　And when my spirit soars or drags a bit, we always meet again

Before she left, she gave birth to a most beautiful and bright-eyed son. He was not conceived in love, but her heart of love wrapped around him like the warmth of spring. There was never a doubt in her spirit that this child would be born and be given the best chance at *life*; she agonized over what that was to look like. I was privileged to walk with her through that adventure. Not as counselor, but as a sounding board, encouraging her to follow and trust her instinct.

She searched far and wide for Asa's parents. Amanda reached deep within her to find the courage and persistence needed to find them. They had been searching, and many disappointments created an openness to Amanda. The marriage of Asa, the son, with Mike and Kimberly as parents was certainly made in heaven; Amanda was the intuitive matchmaker.

Her troubled psyche was always brightened by being in her son's presence. The mental debilitation brought on by well-meaning doctors and medicines given her led her to another decision, the decision to end her life on this plane. I characterize in my soul of souls this decision as:

A Dad's heart-thoughts about our love-filled & courageous Amanda—

Life is eternal There is One Life

There is no separation Love is all there is

There is not a person in Amanda's Life

That did not give her every ounce of Life and Love that they knew how to give

Keep on giving—

There is not a person in Amanda's Life

That she did not give Every ounce of Life and Love that she knew how to give

Keep on receiving

It is important for me to remember that Amanda's decision to transition to her Home was made from her Center of Love.

I honor her decision by remembering her physical other—centered, giving Presence and the Spirit she is walking now. Several of those who loved her have seen her dancing and laughing with the angels, who are also enjoying her Presence. For me, when I dance, I am dancing with Amanda. There is one Spirit—I embrace that Love, and I embrace Amanda. Love is all there is—I love you, Amanda.

I have experienced life from the tops of the mountains, and from the depths of my soul mind. The above experience was pivotal in reaching out to attract what later became my Outrageously Unlimited Thinking Mastermind Group based on Napoleon Hills' *Think and Grow Rich*. Part of my vision is to help spawn other Mastermind Groups, to help entrepreneurs like yourself find and experience your voice.

I am going to use the responsible "I" in the following writings; *you* can take in the information and make it your own. I believe you are reading this to find your voice, but you get to decide if this will be embraced for your life.

When I was sent (some use the word "born"), deep within me was placed a passion and a mission; the world is yearning to accept and value my gifts and talents. The vision God has for this world is incomplete when I play small. I must find my Voice and roar!

I am recognizing daily that I am entitled to miracles. Miracles are simply shifts in my perceptions. The same God that parted the Red Sea and raised the dead is *in me*. In my Voice. Releasing my Voice, I can say to this mountain, Be moved! And it is moved.

I love the story of how Moses used a shepherd's staff to part the Red Sea—talk about Outrageously Unlimited Thinking! The angry children of Israel, and an even angrier Pharoah and his army on one side, mountains on either side, and the Red Sea on the other. As ridiculous as it appeared to all the Children of Israel, Moses followed his Voice, reached out with a stick, touched the water, and the Red Sea parted! Remember this when you get an Outrageously Unlimited Thought.

And I have the power to move *your* mountains. When Jesus raised Lazarus from the dead, Lazarus didn't have a thing to do with it—he was dead! My challenge is to remember the Truth of who I am. When I focus on my problems, or yours, and not the solutions that are all around, I forget my Voice. One of the common threads I see in all the chapters of this book, and in the many books I have read on busting loose from my assumed limitations, is to speak my Truth; use my Voice. Then I pay attention, and I take action within my Voice's direction. I cannot be limited even by your perceived limitations, which again is the power of the Mastermind Group. We help each other find and release our Voices, even when we can't find it within us to do so.

It is no accident you are reading this chapter; *you* have wanted a way to find your Voice and release it. This chapter will move you to action, and I will have accomplished part of why I was sent. Thank you for participating in not only releasing your Voice but empowering others to do the same.

You cannot find your Voice and give it full expression by yourself. Outrageously Unlimited Thinking requires a Mastermind Group of like-minded people, to hold you accountable to your Vision and your passion, and to allow *you* to mentor others in theirs. "Where 2 or 3 are gathered in HIS Spirit of Life, mountains are moved, the world is made a better place." My Mastermind Group is why I am part of this best-selling book; any success I have ever achieved has been because of the people around me. I know if just 1% of the people reading this chapter develop the Mastermind Mentality, Giants will walk the earth again, creating harmony and joy like has never been seen.

OUT!—Outrageously Unlimited Thinking

My definition of success is knowing who I am and fully expressing my Voice, which I was sent to express. I have been given an entire company (World Ventures) of people who see beyond limitations daily, creating fun, health, happiness, and fulfillment for the world. You can find your Mastermind Group now. Feel free to reach out to me, or to anyone Spirit guides you to, speaking your passion, writing down your dreams. Whatever limitations you have felt you had, let them go. Place your faith not on the challenges but on the solutions that abound around you. Your Mastermind Gang is waiting for you. They need you; you need them. By the power vested in me, I am calling you OUT!

At the end of the first evening of one of the many OUT trainings my company provides (this one was called "Millionaire Boot Camp"), our director of training Marc Accetta asked us to find a quiet place and ask for guidance, then just to be still and listen, writing down what we heard. I am coachable, and I did just that. I sat and wrote exactly what God was saying to me in the free flow of the moment; in less than 15 minutes I got what I needed. You will have a time, if you haven't already, when God's Voice speaks to your Voice; in the meantime, I will lend you mine.

God's Voice to your Voice:

My arms and heart are around you—I've got your back. Touch lives. Live full.

Serve the freedom my children deserve.

Open the valve to the flood of wealth and abundance. Make room. I believe in you. You have only tasted my bounty. Dig in. It's a feast!

Call on me at all times.

Look my children into their soul eyes and see Me. Call Me forth so they can see.

There are hundreds of thousands of my children coming your way.

79

Leaders who are yet to know my leadership. We will laugh and be strong together.

I am on your team. Feel my presence in every call, every handshake, every gathering, every event. Open your arms and heart to everyone I send.

The words I send you from my leaders are true. The world I show you is my world. All the thoughts in your Passion Statement are true. *You* are true.

Like the lions roar, you are safe. Nothing can harm you. All the health and wealth you ask for is yours! ASK BIG!

Dance as if there were no tomorrow. Invite others to the dance with you.

Your strength will come
From standing in the center of a place no one else can see
Knowing what no one can verify
And dancing to a tune no one else can hear

—Emmanuel

Biography

Thell G. Prueitt

Called by his peers "The Master of Fun," THELL plerks (plays/works) hard at living up to that title! He has been blessed with two awesome, loving, talented daughters who have gifted him three brilliant grandchildren. Thell's mom and dad surrounded him with loving mentoring that has helped him be successful at co-pastoring a church for several years, build many lucrative businesses, and endure the sadness of not-so-lucrative ones. His total joy is in seeing individuals, families, businesses, and organizations come alive when they see and feel their own Outrageously Unlimited Thinking.

Contact Information

www.themasteroffun.com
thell@themasteroffun.com
325-388-2813

Chapter 11

The One Thing All Successful People Have in Common

by Mike R. Phillips

When written in Chinese, the word "crisis" is composed of two characters. One represents danger and the other represents opportunity.
—John F. Kennedy

$\mathcal{M}$ost of us know how to dream big. Many (though not all) of us know that we have to set goals and work toward them to achieve those dreams. There really isn't much difference between people who are successful and people who aren't. Successful people breathe the same air, have blood running through their veins, and have human strengths and weaknesses, just like everyone else.

We don't all share the same definition of success. Some strive for wealth. Others strive for the top position in their company. Many dream of owning their own business. Most of us have multiple dreams. For me, success is having time. Time is the only resource that we cannot replace. The money I make is directly related to supporting and having more time to spend with family and friends and to do what I love to do most—travel.

No matter how we define success for ourselves, however, there's one thing all successful people have in common: They see obstacles as opportunities. Everything else flows from this one perspective.

By approaching obstacles as a chance to fine-tune their plan for success or to take a new, often exciting direction with their plans, successful people easily overcome any problem before them. Every time they do so, they build confidence in themselves, which only makes it easier and faster to achieve higher goals and one dream after another.

True success is not only obtainable, but it is also sustainable.

This confidence is key to success, and the beauty of it is that you don't need to be naturally confident (and certainly not arrogant). By approaching every problem as an opportunity, you will build confidence and make your dreams come true.

This is why you hear about so many successful people who had to overcome some kind of adversity in their lives. In a way, their lack of good fortune was fortunate because they learned early on how to survive by overcoming problems using perseverance and flexibility, skills they could then apply to achieving their dreams.

I was born multiracial at the height of the civil rights movement and raised by my grandmother, mother, and sister. Money was scarce, and the environment was often challenging, to say the least. I learned to be adaptable to adverse situations. While I was in elementary school, several of my friends and classmates lost loved ones, some both parents, when a plane crashed carrying Marshall University's entire football team and several of my friends' and classmates' parents. (A great movie was made about the crash and its aftermath: *We Are Marshall*.) This tragedy, and the strength of my friends who lost loved ones, inspired me throughout difficult personal times. These events in my early years prepared me to be a successful professional—hard working, goal oriented, flexible, determined, focused, and with the strength and faith to continue.

When you are not used to facing challenges, your confidence recedes and you lose your focus when an unplanned obstacle arises on your path to success. Many people get stuck. They make excuses or they give up, thinking this particular dream just wasn't meant to be. Some will move on to a different goal—until another challenge rears its head. It's easy to become a habitual goal setter instead of a habitual goal achiever.

If you are waiting for your moment in the sun, when you'll hit it big, when everything will fall into place, you will likely wait a long time, if not forever.

Success is not an event. It's a process.

I think of this process as having three intertwining steps:

1. Theorize
2. Visualize
3. Realize

Theorize

The most important first step in this process is to set attainable, realistic goals. This doesn't mean you don't dream big. In fact, if you dream of making a million dollars, you'll limit yourself to a million. Why not dream of more and just hit that million along the way? You just need to have a feasible plan, with small steps for achieving your big dreams.

When you set goals that you can achieve, and continually set new ones that take you a step further, you not only reach your biggest dreams much more quickly, but you gain confidence along the way, making each successive goal easier to accomplish.

For example, my 5-year-old son wanted to hit a home run, which was physically impossible. His big dream was to hit the ball far into the outfield. So when he was learning to bat, I would draw a line at the farthest point he had hit. His goal would be simply to hit the next ball farther than that line. When he did, I'd draw a new line at that spot (and we'd call it a home run). His next goal would be to hit farther than that line, and so on. Before he knew it, he was hitting that ball much farther than either of us ever expected. Make the impossible possible with creative ideas.

This is progressive learning, and if you apply it to your own goals, you will succeed much more quickly than if you have unreasonable expectations for yourself and your timeframe for achieving your dream. Then push yourself with each goal, as you gain confidence and ability. After all, no one is born walking.

Part of coming up with a realistic plan is to anticipate obstacles, understanding physical limitations. Be sure to plan for life to get in the way, including what you will do when it does. This doesn't mean you won't be surprised by the unexpected, but the more you prepare for the most likely challenges, the easier it will be to address them without losing momentum.

Having a strong support system in place is one way to ensure you stay motivated. Who these people are depends on the person. Decide early on who you will turn to when your motivation is low, and who can help you brainstorm and see new perspectives and opportunities when you're frustrated. Respect both your mentors and the people you lead and lean on with a humble and confident approach. This will ensure that they don't just hear you—they listen.

Finally, don't forget to continue to set new goals. There is life after you achieve your biggest dream. What will you do then? Keep growing and planning for the next step. From the beginning, build your blueprint assuming you will grow beyond it. Make it flexible, not static. You have to be just as prepared for success as you are for failure. Just ask one of the many lottery winners who went bankrupt because they had no plan for their success.

Visualize

The next step in the process of being successful is to not only visualize achieving your dream, but to visualize every step along the way, including obstacles and how you will handle them. Experience the entire process in your mind.

For example, if you will need to network with people, see yourself in a specific group and visualize the script. How do you want to present yourself? What questions will you ask? How will you adapt your interaction for different types of people and situations?

If you know that one of your challenges will be to stay motivated during the mundane tasks, visualize achieving these tasks and see yourself doing whatever you need to do to keep going even when you'd rather be doing something more interesting. Visualize finding happiness and fulfillment in what you are doing because you know that everything connects to a greater purpose.

Many people visualize only the end result. They know exactly what kind of car they will have, and they've mentally furnished their dream house. This is great because it can help you stay motivated, but if you aren't also visualizing taking the steps to get there, you might find yourself unprepared to deal with the sacrifices and persistence required every day to achieve your dreams. Imagining every step will prepare you, which will give you the confidence to make every day a success.

Remember, you aren't doing these things because you have to. You're doing them because you want to.

Realize

Ultimately, of course, you have to take action to realize your goals. Without acting on your plan, taking steps up that ladder, your dream will always be out of reach. Quoting my uncle Wesley: "Application is the key." Stay focused and let the reward of accomplishing each small step help keep you going, along with constant visualization. Because I have a long commute, driving is the perfect time to visualize and practice in my mind what I need to do to achieve my next dream. Make time in your daily life to do the same.

And remember that no plan is perfect. Realizing your dreams requires going back to your plan and making adjustments. Some obstacles require a creative approach to see the opportunity inherent in them, but doing so will always pay off. Some challenges may be rooted in factors outside your control, it's true, but too many people use that as an excuse to just give up instead of adapting their plans and controlling how they respond.

The economy, for example, has introduced many obstacles beyond our control. The challenge is to adapt to the changing circumstances. The dream you were pursuing in a healthy economy may need some realistic adjustments. You may even need to go in a completely new direction to reach the same endpoint.

I have worked in the financial services industry for more than 26 years. I have been able to achieve my definition of success over and over again, earning the money I need to support and spend time the way I want to spend it, and to travel while I'm still young and healthy enough to enjoy it. I didn't want to wait until I was retired to have the money I needed at a time when I might not be as fit to enjoy my travels. I've flown over a million miles, all over the world, the Mediterranean (Luxury Cruise), Monte Carlo, Paris, Asia, Rio de Janeiro, you name it. I have also had the free time to spend with the people I love.

But then the economy tanked. Suddenly people did not trust anyone in the financial services industry. The path I was on toward continued success suddenly hit what seemed like a clear dead end. I had to create a new path. My brother Kenny was both a solid supporter and a benefactor to pursuing this opportunity.

This was actually an opportunity for professional reinvention. I did not have to throw out my years of expertise in financial services. I could build on it and branch out into a field that did not have the stigma of my current field. Not only have I gone back to school to become a certified financial planner, but I am forming a new company, which will offer comprehensive financial planning, with several branches of expertise. This obstacle taught me the importance of having multiple opportunities available, so that if something happens to one, I'll have the others still going for me. Not only am I successfully adapting to the challenge, I am well on my way to achieving a bigger and better dream.

Sometimes the best things that happen to us
are the worst things that happen to us.

No matter who you are or what your situation is, there is no such thing as an insurmountable obstacle. If you have tried and failed to climb that wall in front of you, take a step back. The solution may be to go around it, to tunnel under it, to pole vault over it, or to get someone to help give you a leg up. In many cases, you can make that wall part of a new and innovative approach to your dreams.

As long as you don't give up in the face of obstacles, you *will* be successful. You may achieve that success in ways you don't foresee when you are first mapping out your dreams. But seeing success as a process, and making that process a part of your everyday life, will enable you to handle anything life throws your way. After you achieve one dream, that process will be in place for you to achieve the next, and the next, and the next. With the confidence you gain, it only gets easier.

Soon you will see that the only impossible dreams are the ones we give up on.

Biography

Mike R. Phillips

MIKE PHILLIPS is the president and CEO of Dan Ryan & Associates, Inc., an insurance investments firm. He is a licensed insurance and former securities agent with 26 years in the business as well as sales in the tens of millions. Mike is currently working toward becoming a certified financial planner as part of his new endeavor—starting his own financial planning firm, offering multiple layers of services and expertise.

Mike is a decorated soldier, serving in the USAF from 1978 to 1982. He was educated at Lamson Business College and Pima Community College, both in Tucson. He has two children, Michelle, 25, and Michael, 5, and lives in Morro Bay, California.

Contact Information

danryaninsuranceservices.com

mp2020@comcast.net

800-987-3300

Chapter 12

Focus on What You Really Want and Follow Your Passion

by Christian Schnubel

Ever since I can remember, I always wondered why people behave the way they do. What moves them? What is the driving force behind any human behavior?

I grew up in a small town in Germany. Having too much money was never really our biggest problem. I always used to look up to successful people and wondered how they became successful. In our town most businesses were family based, which made me believe that to become successful or rich, one must be born into a rich family! Well, our family was poor, so what did I say to myself? Right. "Christian, there is no chance for you in this life!"

But I never really accepted this. I knew from a very young age that I wanted more. So I was constantly looking for an opportunity. During my education as an electronics technician, I took any job possible. One day a friend of mine suggested that I become an insurance salesman. Well, I wasn't really into that, but I said I'd give it a try. This is now about 25 years ago, and I remember going to my first seminar like it was yesterday. I was blown away when the speaker talked about success and how to make money in this insurance company. This was what I was looking for.

I started selling insurance from a small room of my favorite pub, calling one friend after another into the room and presenting my program to them. In a short time I became a top salesman, making five times more money than from my main job. I was excited! I became even more excited when I received my first award on stage in front of hundreds of people. The Ferrari wasn't far away anymore. But as soon as the money came in, I'd spend it. I spent more than what I made, and of course my banker loved me. You can imagine what happened. A few months later, I was broke. I wasn't ready. I had made money, but my mind was still in the frame of a poor guy.

I didn't give up. I had tasted success for the first time in my life. I started reading books about success, and the first one was *Success Through a Positive Mental Attitude,* by Napoleon Hill. I was blown away and kept reading one book after another, studying any available material, and going from one seminar to the next for years. Then I started my own seminars, teaching people the success strategies I'd learned, but I wasn't successful at all. I remember doing a seminar tour, "How to Practice Positive Thinking," in ten different cities in Germany. Some friends and I put up hundreds of posters and gave away thousands of flyers in each city. We expected 150–200 people for each presentation, but only 20 to 30 showed up. I was frustrated and completely down. I tried so many things, nut nothing really changed. Until one day. . . .

It was 1996, and I had the opportunity to see Tony Robbins live. I called and made my reservation without even thinking about the cost. Now here was the challenge: I had no money at all. Not for the flight, the hotel, or the seminar ticket. But I knew that I had to see this guy, no matter what. I was committed. Sure enough, I found a way: A friend of mine who was working for a travel agency organized the flight, and at the hotel check-in, I told the clerk I'd forgotten my credit card (I did not even have a credit card at this time). At the seminar registration desk, I pretended that I had to speak urgently to Mr. X—the guy who had made my reservation—and that he was expecting me. I was in!

So here was this guy, no money, no credit card, flying to Belgium, checking into the hotel, and getting admission for the seminar. (I did pay everything back two months later.) But it gets even better: At the end of the seminar, Tony pitched his Mastery University: Hawaii, swimming with the dolphins, three weeks with the man. But the price was US $10,000, plus travel expenses to the States. No chance.

Tony's pitch was so attractive that I saw people throwing their credit cards toward the registration desk to get "one of the last available spots" (even today I have to laugh about this). And me? All I knew is that I wanted to be in Hawaii in three months, swimming with the dolphins. I put down the required deposit with a personal check, which of course bounced, and never thought that this was going to happen. However, a couple of weeks later I received a big envelope from the Robbins company. While opening the envelope, I expected some promotional stuff, but to my amazement, I read the magic words: "Welcome to Life Mastery!" Sure enough, I had found a way to get to Hawaii and did eventually make it.

> *People who say it cannot be done*
> *should not interrupt those who are doing it.*
> —Jack Canfield

If you really want something, if you are passionate about something, whatever it is, be assured that there is a way to make it happen.

Always! There is always a way if you are committed. Imagine someone you really love who needs an operation that costs $10,000, and neither of you has it. You need to raise this amount within 48 hours to save this person's life. Would you find a way to get the money? I bet you would! There is *always* a way!

After meeting Tony Robbins, my life changed completely. Because now, I knew *exactly* what I wanted and *why* I wanted it. I had found my passion. I started promoting Tony in Europe and became an internationally known public speaker. I moved from cold middle Europe to a sunny island. I had the privilege to travel the world and learn success tools and strategies from the best teachers on the planet. If you ask me about the most important key that I've learned in achieving success over the last 20 years, I would say focus and state management. If you do not consistently focus on your goals, you end up being distracted, and you will never succeed. If you do not learn how to manage your emotional state, you will miss out. We all go through times when we feel frustrated, depressed, or overwhelmed. The good news is that those feelings do not appear out of the blue—you create them. To "feel" a specific way, you have to focus on specific things.

Here is a small exercise for you to try: Take a deep breath, pull your shoulders back, then turn your head up and watch the ceiling, or the sky if you are sitting on the beach, like I am doing right now. Now, put the biggest smile that you can on your face. If you think you cannot smile right now, then fake it! Here comes my challenge for you: While doing that, try to be depressed. It's physically impossible to be depressed in this state. You can create any desirable emotion by using your body and focusing on something that makes you feel a specific way.

But what do I focus on? Focus on what you really want in life. Follow your passion. Most people are still running around doing a job they don't like, spending money they don't have, and buying things they don't need to impress people they don't like. Sounds funny, but that's reality. Why do people do that? Because they have no clue what they *really* want! They still think that happiness comes from making money and buying expensive things. They don't buy a specific car to get from A to B. Most people buy a new car because they associate a specific feeling with it.

I know people who spend half their life working like crazy, ruining their health and relationships just to get rich. And then they spend all their money in the second half of their life to get their health back! Does that make sense? I don't think so. Don't get me wrong. Making a lot of money is a great thing, and it does give you many options. The problem is that most people believe that making money is hard. Making tons of money has never been easier. Look at how many are making millions today by using the power of the Internet.

But many others try to make money on the Internet because it seems so easy hardly make anything. Why is this so? Because they are focusing on making money! They try every new so-called money-making system, bouncing from one opportunity to the next just to find out that this stuff doesn't really work for them. Would you like to know the secret of making money?

Stop focusing on making money!

Start focusing on what you really want and what you like, based on your God-given talents. Follow your passion and turn it into a business. Money will be a result sooner or later. The reason for this is simple: If you do what you love doing, you will be better than most people at it, and you will improve your skills regularly simply because you like it. And if you do something better than most, you'll get well rewarded! It's as simple as that. And the best part is, you are now enjoying what you're doing.

Every single *really* successful person on this planet knows exactly what he or she wants and why. It is not enough to know what you want; you need to know why you want it. If you do not have the minimum five compelling reasons for what you want, I would advise you to not even think about going for it. If you have enough reasons, compelling reasons, for what you want, you will always find a way to make it happen. Compelling reasons will give you the drive and will make you unstoppable. People who know exactly what they want and why they want it have charisma. You can see their focus and passion in their eyes. Whenever you make a list of goals and targets, always ask yourself: "Why do I want this?" If you cannot come up with enough reasons, stop wasting your precious time. If you do have enough strong and compelling reasons, I can actually guarantee you that you will find a way to make it happen.

The truth of the matter is that there is nothing you can't accomplish if: (1) you clearly decide what it is that you're absolutely committed to achieving, (2) you're willing to take massive action, (3) you notice what's working or not, and (4) you continue to change your approach until you achieve what you want, using whatever life gives you along the way.
—Anthony Robbins

So what do you want? What is your passion? What are you excited about? What makes you move? When I was a young boy, I used to dream about becoming a rock star. I still have a passion for music and singing, but I never became a rock star. But when I had my first keynote speech in front of 5,000 people, how do you think I felt? Yes, exactly. I felt like a rock star! If you want to become a rock star you do not even need to be on a stage in front of a raving audience to feel like one. All you want is the "feeling" of being a rock star! Raise your standards, give more than you would expect to receive, and you will experience this feeling. From your clients, your family, your friends, and anyone who is important to you.

Having feedback from the audience and receiving success stories from participants and coaching clients is, for me, the greatest gift. You cannot achieve this with money. And by the way, actually seeing results from what you are doing, and getting amazing feedback from your clients, is much more valuable than all the money in the world. And money will no longer be an issue anymore once you are there.

Find your passion, follow it, set your goals according to what you really want, keep focusing on it, and you will rock the world, your world! We all have a reason why we are walking on this planet. What is yours? What is your mission? Once you have found it, get ready for miracles and for all the amazing things and opportunities that life has in store for you.

Biography

Christian Schnubel

As a public speaker, author, and success coach, CHRISTIAN SCHNUBEL has inspired tens of thousands of people all over the world for more than 20 years. He is among the people who brought Anthony Robbins live to Europe and helped the company grow from $1 million to more than $20 million in annual sales as a sales manager and company trainer. Today, Christian is living in Dubai and Cyprus as a speaker, coach, and business consultant.

Contact Information

www.ChristianSchnubel.com
www.facebook.com/ChristianSchnubel
info@CMSseminars.com
CMS seminars & Consulting, Ltd.
PO Box 54351, CY-3723, Limassol, Cyprus
+357-25-693350

Chapter 13

Dare to Dream…
Act on your Vision!

by Gerri Krienke

I am the youngest of seven kids, and my mom raised most of us on her own after my dad passed away when I was four years old. Needless to say, I grew up poor and without the advantages and opportunities that my friends had. I struggled, particularly as a teenager, becoming more and more rebellious and unhappy. I had a deepening void inside of me and the person I really was, the person I knew I could be, was lost somewhere in that void.

After high school, I began to turn my life around and nurture my spiritual and intuitive side. I knew there was more to life, and I wanted to learn as much as I could to become the person I felt that I was inside. This process involved a lot of change from the inside out, which included deep personal growth and really getting to know who I was and who I wanted to become.

I began doing affirmations to increase my self-esteem and replace negative thoughts with positive ones. The idea was to work on my old belief system and find new beliefs that would be more beneficial to me, that would work for me, not against the desires of my heart.

Somewhere along the way, I started to really believe in myself and my ability to realize my dreams and have so much more in life. But this didn't happen overnight. It has taken many years of study, meditation, positive affirmations, belief in myself, and perhaps most important—*action*—to get to the place where I am today: a successful real estate investor, author, and entrepreneur.

I have made many mistakes in thinking I could get rich quick. Mistakes are inevitable in life but the key is to make fewer mistakes, with smaller consequences, and to learn from them. True wealth takes time to build and encompasses so much more than money, such as having a great balance in life of financial freedom, time for what really matters, happiness, strong relationships, and love. Success is about the total package. It does not matter how that package looks, whether it's wrapped in expensive fabric or plain brown paper. All that matters is what's inside.

Listen to Your Intuition

One of the most important lessons I've learned in life is to listen to my intuition. When you strive to be true to yourself in all areas of your life, your inner guide looks out for you. If you have a positive feeling about a business deal, relationship, or other situation, then move forward. If something doesn't feel right to you, ask yourself why—*and be open to the answer.*

Being true to yourself requires being truthful with yourself. Look honestly at your own behavior and why you are doing what you are doing in any given moment. Be accountable for the choices you have made to create what you currently have in your life. The more self-aware you are, the easier it is to hear and interpret what that little voice inside is telling you. Your inner self is looking out for you at all times, but you have to listen.

Be Teachable

You can't know what you don't yet know, so it does not benefit you to pretend that you know everything—to yourself or to others. You don't. There is so much to learn in this lifetime and so many great people to learn from. Appreciate every opportunity to learn and grow and recognize that others are in their own space too. Allow them to learn at their own pace while you learn at yours.

I have always been interested in investing, particularly real estate investment, but I didn't know enough about it in the past to pursue that dream. I was afraid to take the chance. So I clung to my seemingly secure life as an inspector in the oil and gas industry, even though I knew this was not what I was meant to do in this lifetime. It provided financial security and I didn't want to be poor for the rest of my life.

I finally realized that it was not actually security at all but a trap to keep me from following my dreams. I was certain there was a better way, so I started to look for it. I began taking those first tentative steps toward my dream—investing.

I made mistakes, and a few of my investments failed. I chased after the money, but I couldn't seem to keep it. I made one bad investment after another. Soon, my fear of making more mistakes pushed me right back into my comfort zone. Yet in my gut, I knew I had to keep pursuing the life I wanted. I have had to push myself over and over because I knew it was the only way I would get out of the rat race. I could not give up on myself. However, how could I get over my fears and take another chance without making the same mistakes all over again?

The answer was to become more knowledgeable. When fears stand in your way, and past mistakes keep you from following your intuition, the first step is to learn as much as you can about the situation. Many of my past mistakes were related to a lack of knowledge, particularly business and investment knowledge. Even though I had been learning about investing since I was 33 years old, I realized that I had learned just enough to make the investments but not enough to do it well. This is why learning must be constant, and why it is important to never believe you've learned everything you need to know about a subject. I got a late start, but it is absolutely never too late to get started on the right path.

So I read even more, took courses and networked with other investors. Armed with knowledge and the wisdom of past experience, I gave my dream another try. I am now a successful real estate investor in the United States and Canada and this success has weathered even the recent economic storms.

I continue to take every opportunity to learn and study from books, attend seminars and webinars, and pursue any other avenue I can find so that I am more knowledgeable and can make wiser decisions. Life is journey for me of constant growth and development. The more I know, grow, and experience, the more abundant and prosperous my life is.

Practice Positive Affirmations and Meditation

Of course, all the knowledge in the world doesn't mean much if your own negative thoughts sabotage what you are trying to accomplish through what you have learned. There is a spiritual, nonphysical aspect to each of us that can help create amazing abundance and prosperity in our lives if we know how to use it.

I have practiced using affirmations since I was 19 years old, and I've got it down to a science now. In fact, it basically is science—that of physics and vibrations, or energy. Simply think on what you want and be as specific as possible. Don't dwell on thoughts of what you don't want. Speak it out loud or write it down. The more time you spend thinking about the positive experiences, people, or possessions that you want, the more likely you are to attract these into your life. This is what the law of attraction is about.

Adapt your thoughts to what you want and draw on the connection of a higher source to create more of what you want. I focus on three goals at a time. As part of my morning ritual, I meditate and think on these three items that I want to manifest into my life, along with other affirmations and thoughts of gratitude for everything wonderful I already have.

Take Action

Sitting on the couch thinking positive thoughts is useless if you don't act on the opportunities you attract into your life. Knowing something in your head and putting it into action are two very different things. Small action steps toward your goals and dreams are better than no action at all. Be the turtle and follow through to the finish line.

You don't have to wait for an opportunity to present itself before you start taking action. If you want to be someone different, start acting differently. Take action steps to being, doing, and having what you want in your life. This usually means stepping out of your comfort zone.

For the longest time, I had so much knowledge that I wasn't putting to good use because of my fear of failure. With some of the mistakes I had made and the money I had lost, who could blame me for being afraid? But that's where the line is drawn between people who experience success and those who don't. Successful people are afraid too, but they take action in spite of their fears.

The problem for me was that growing up poor, I had a scarcity mindset which I had to overcome to achieve my dreams. My fears would leave me in a state of over-analyzing every situation until it was too late to take action. Eventually, I would grow tired of not doing anything to change my life, and I would go to the opposite extreme and jump in without completely doing my homework. This would often lead to failure, which only put me back where I started, over-analyzing the situation to death and not taking action.

The key, as with just about anything in life, is balance, which means taking risks to achieve your desires, but make them *calculated* risks. Risk is good but risk management is even better. Follow your intuition about an opportunity but do your research, including getting a second opinion from a neutral party whenever a lot of money is involved. Limit the time you spend thinking about it and then act.

Avoid the get-rich-quick schemes in favor of the stay-rich-longer strategies. At the very least, if you are going to take a chance on a very risky venture, don't put all your money into it. Spread out your risk among different opportunities so that if one fails, you still have other options going for you.

Use Failures to Fuel Your Success

At one point, I went from being debt free to $55,000 in debt, which was more than I made per year at that time. I had maxed out an investment loan with huge payments per month, and I was robbing Peter to pay Paul. The oil industry had become very slow, so my income as an inspector was drastically reduced. I couldn't make all my payments.

I did not go bankrupt. I worked extremely hard to get myself out of debt within two years while maintaining an excellent credit rating. I have been debt free ever since, outside of my calculated investments such as real estate, and I now have a passion to help others get out of debt. This failure led me to achieve my next big dream: writing a book. *The Wealthy You* is coming out this year and is a practical guide to the foundations of wealth based on what I learned through my experiences. I have also used my past mistakes to fuel another success: a series of iPhone applications that help people improve their credit, get out of debt, budget on the go, do positive money affirmations and access unclaimed money.

Look at the mistakes you've made in life not only as learning experiences, to avoid making them again, but as opportunities.

Have a Support System in Place

Some of the obstacles I've encountered on my path to success are trusting in the wrong people and not having an adequate support system. I have since realized how important it is to surround myself with people who are positive and supportive, with the intent to create long-term mutually satisfying relationships.

I acknowledge my shortcomings and recognize that I need the help of others to complement me. I am not a machine who can do everything perfectly. I believe we as people need to work together and draw on each other's strengths. In this way, we can help each other work through the challenges that block our path.

Whatever dream you are pursuing, make time to network with people who are at various points along a similar path. Not only will you learn from each other and be able to pool your unique talents and knowledge to help each other, you will also receive the kind of emotional and mental support you can really only get from someone who's either been there or is there with you right now.

Keep Dreaming

I have always been a dreamer. I daydream about everything and anything. I remember going to sleep as a kid, dreaming about what it would be like to have a million dollars, or better yet, 10 million dollars. These dreams brought me peace and hope for a better life one day.

Visions, or dreams, are very powerful, and the more you focus on them, the more likely they will become a reality. What you hold in your thoughts will create your life, so think about and envision the life you want and the person you want to become. Once you've achieved one dream, don't stop there. Dream bigger. Dream more.

Just don't forget to act on that dream, starting today. Vision without action just means you can see it when life passes you by.

Biography

Gerri Krienke

GERRI KRIENKE has worked as an inspector in the oil and gas industry for 11 years and is a real estate investor in the United States and Canada. She offers opportunities to partner with her on investments, particularly with people who want to invest but don't know how to or prefer to let an experienced investor take care of the particulars.

Gerri's book *The Wealthy You* is a practical guide to wealth and will be available in 2011. Also, see her iPhone applications that help people improve their credit, get out of debt, budget on the go, positive wealth affirmations and access unclaimed money. See her website for more details.

Contact Information

www.ProsperityGroup.com
info@ProsperityGroup.com
www.Facebook.com/TheProsperityGroup
Twitter @GerriKrienke

Chapter 14

The View from the Top

by David Sapp

My name is David Sapp.

I know who I am, where I came from, and where I'm going.

I own my mistakes, and I use them to move me forward, not hold me back.

I read somewhere that every true entrepreneur will try a huge number of projects that do not lead to success, and I believe that. I have lived that. Even as a kid, I was always trying to make my mark on the world.

I was a born entrepreneur, and as far back as I can remember, I wanted to make a million dollars and be my own boss. That desire started so early on, I can't tell you how old I was when I dreamed of my first empire. I did so many things to actualize my dreams that I can't remember all of them. I sold seeds, and I was convinced this would make me a fortune. I ordered things from catalogs that promised big returns for small efforts, and I believed in each and every endeavor.

At some point, I realized that although my desire to be successful was sound, my work ethic admirable, and the passion to succeed unmatched, the projects did not measure up. Awesome lesson learned. Evaluate the business plan inside and out before you invest.

My father raised me, with help from his parents. When I was seven, Mary came into our family, and she provided the motherly love that was missing. I think that not having her in my life earlier made me appreciate her even more once she arrived. My father was gone for weeks at a time for work, and although I understood why he wasn't there all the time to play with me and teach me things, I still missed him. He has taught me a lifetime of wisdom since my childhood. He was and still is my best friend. Understanding why he was gone taught me some very valuable lessons, however. You need to rely on yourself and figure some things out on your own. Even more important, I learned that you can't hold it against anyone else for not fulfilling your dreams; don't look for excuses to not do what *you* want to do.

I grew up in a Christian home. My grandmother instilled in me many core beliefs that embody who I am today. At a young age, I learned the power of prayer from my grandmother, and then later from my father and my mother. The story I am about to share is but one of many examples of God reaching into my life and providing for my heart's truest pure desire. For those reading this who do not have faith, I want to make one thing clear: I'm no more special to God than anyone else. He provides for all who seek His provisions, and my story is a small one of a healing He granted me, one that changed my life.

When I was somewhere around 11 years old, in the late 1970s, I suffered from severe allergies and asthma. I was allergic to everything, including dust in the air. It was debilitating: I wasn't able to ride my bike, pet animals, mow lawns, or be as adventurous as I wanted to be. One day I just got tired of being limited. That night, I got on my knees at my bedside, and I prayed; I prayed for what to a little boy seemed like an eternity—it was probably only 15 minutes. I prayed that God would allow me to breathe. I wanted to breathe the scent of fresh-cut grass, the smells of the cornfield, and most of all, I wanted to have pets. To this day, I really enjoy dogs and cats and all creatures. I wanted to crawl into caves and explore and see things I hadn't seen before. I prayed that God would allow this for me, as I knew deep in my core that I was meant to do these things. I was meant to be everything that I wanted to be.

I got up the next morning and announced to my family that I was healed, that I no longer had asthma, that I would never again wheeze with every breath I took. They didn't believe me, as I'm sure any family wouldn't. They basically patted me on the head and said, "Okay." I didn't let that deter me. I walked out of the house, got on my bike, and rode through a cornfield; I helped friends mow lawns; I ditched the bike and finally explored the big concrete tunnel that led to nowhere other than a road. Any one of these activities should have put me in the emergency room barely breathing.

But guess what? I was fine. I wasn't even stuffy. I walked up to my house at the end of that day and knocked on the door. I wanted my family to see that I was okay, that I really was healed. My grandmother opened the door, and what she saw was a very dirty little boy with twigs in his hair and a grin the size of Montana. It was then that my family believed I was healed. This is my take-away from that day when I was 11:

- Have faith in God.
- Don't let anyone tell you that you can't do something.
- Don't live your life based on what "experts" tell you.
- Push yourself and find out what you really can do—and then push harder and see where it takes you.
- Be passionate about having fun and achieving your goals.

I mowed lawns that summer and was as adventurous as I wanted to be. This was success for me, an 11-year-old in a small town in Indiana.

As I got older, my dreams and definition of success changed. I tried many things and had many jobs and successes that I earned with hard work. I was the youngest manager at the local Dairy Queen, and everyone was proud. Being the manager gave me my first official experience as a leader. I quickly realized that you can do more, accomplish more, and as a result, raise your bar of success higher, with a team. It was very clear that I needed to use my leadership skills to achieve my new definition of success. I needed staff, and I needed to lead them. I also needed to help everyone on my team be productive and have the tools they needed to achieve their own definitions of success.

If you are in a leadership position, hire thoughtfully. Hire employees who have solid work ethics and a desire to learn and grow within the position they are applying for. Do not hire entrepreneurs unless you need someone to work alongside you as your equal. They are like you—they will not be happy working for someone else. This is an easy mistake to make, because entrepreneurs are typically charismatic and confident, which are desirable characteristics to have on your staff, so be conscious of this pitfall.

To lead effectively, you need to keep your focus on the ultimate objective of your company. Be cognizant of the company objectives when you are creating a job description and assessing compensation. This isn't a parenting situation, or a buddy situation. Although every employee will bring something special to the job, "one size fits all" *is* the correct approach when setting expectations for your staff.

Too often, when objectives are unclear, distortion of job duties occurs, leading to staff conflicts. If a conflict arises, I suggest you address it, resolve it, and move on. Waiting for it to resolve itself can tear a good team apart. To keep these issues at a minimum, ensure that everyone you hire knows what is expected and knows the consequences of not achieving the expectation as well as the rewards of overachieving. Give your employees fair incentives to surpass their goals.

When I am putting together a team for any project, my role model is "The Donald." I admire his business acumen, his no-nonsense approach to obstacles, and his ability to regroup when necessary and forge ahead to new successes. Donald Trump is a perfect example of strong, effective leadership for current times, and I think future generations will look back and see the same admirable qualities that I see today. He is a born leader.

In fact, I believe that all entrepreneurs are born, not made. The true heart of an entrepreneur is not something that can be taught; either you are born an entrepreneur, or you are not. However, success is something everyone can achieve.

I know that I was born an entrepreneur, but that innate quality alone was not enough for me to be successful. I had to teach myself the skills of success. These are some of the key points I learned:

- Define your success.
- Define your personal values and live by them.
- Benchmark your projects to your own code of ethics.
- Give back to the community.
- Network within your industry.
- Understand that business is not personal and make the hard decisions.
- Remember that it's easier and cheaper to maintain your business relationships than to mend them.

The very first step is crucial: defining what success is for you. Without this definition, nothing you do will lead to achieving your dreams. Defining success is not the time to cheat on the test, phone in the performance, or short-change yourself out of the dreams you really want to achieve.

Think big.

Then think bigger.

Write down what you want to achieve. Think about it for a while. Pray on it. And after a day or two of mulling it over, and dreaming about attaining it, about reaching the top of the mountain, you need to claim it as your destination. So now you're "there." What then? What would be so different about who you are today versus the successful mountain-top dweller of tomorrow?

Write that answer down. You'll need to look at it from time to time to stay on track.

Let's say that your "mountain top" experience puts you in a financial situation that allows you to work more when *you* want, and less when *others* want, and it allows you more time to devote to what matters most to you: family, church, philanthropic events, charity. . . whatever makes you happy. You have cars, homes, vacations, and money in the bank.

But how are you different from who you are today?

Are you kinder? Are you happier? Do you deal with stress differently?

If you believe you will change when you are successful, then you won't make it out of the dream stage. You need to embody all the qualities *today* in order to achieve the mountain-top experience and *maintain* it. Did you notice the emphasis on *maintaining* success? Lots of people achieve success—keeping it is the key.

Achieving and living successfully starts with *being* a successful person as you define it. Start living on that mountain top today. Your perspective will change, and so will your future.

Biography

David Sapp

DAVID SAPP was born in Indiana in 1968. He is a self-taught computer technician and an accomplished artist. He has played piano and keyboards professionally in recording studios and opened on stage for Ty Herndon, Kenny Chesney, Montgomery Gentry, and SheDaisy. David has been in the financial community since 1997, entering real estate in 1987 as an investor, and becoming a full-time broker in 2004. He has used his acumen in both arenas to establish himself as a credit expert and to gauge the real estate market on buying homes and selling them for profit. David has documented $100,000-plus net earnings on many properties as flips.

In David's forthcoming book, he will share trade secrets about how credit actually works, how to use it, and how to turn bad credit into good, as well as how to buy and sell homes and make $100,000 or more every time, then use the proceeds to buy rental property with no mortgage and no debt, securing your retirement within 10 years.

Contact Information

MainStreetRealty@gmail.com

Chapter 15

The Most Resilient Parasite
AN IDEA

by Jérome Vaultier

What is the most resilient parasite? Bacteria? A virus?
An intestinal worm? An idea. Resilient . . . highly contagious. Once an
idea has taken hold of the brain, it's almost impossible to eradicate.
—Cobb in *Inception*

We all know that words have the power to change the world, and according to the greatest thinkers of our time, our world is the result of our thoughts. However, looking around us today, we may think something has gone really wrong with our thought process.

I know I felt this way when my world collapsed years ago, and in this chapter, I want to share with you how I built a greater, stronger, and more exciting world than I ever thought possible.

At the age of 25, I had it all. I was just about to graduate as a naval aviator at the top of my class, deeply in love with the woman of my dreams, and surrounded by a loving family. My future was promising, and I was unstoppable.

Or so I thought. I will spare you the details, but within a few months, I had lost my career, my girl, my friends, and half of my lungs.

The situation seemed desperate, but in retrospect, losing everything was the best thing that ever happened to me. Without these disasters, I would not be here today, sharing what I learned with you.

During my long road to recovery and my quest for success, I learned to change my thought process in powerful ways, helping me to become consistently, obsessively, and insanely persistent—the one and only secret to success.

One key to this secret is found in a remote corner of the Amazon jungle, where in the late seventies, a group of ethnologists discovered a group that had been living peacefully and quietly, away from what we call civilization, since the beginning of time. Composed of several tribes, this population had a unique characteristic.

They would never fight. The concept of war was totally unknown to them.

This mystery haunted the scientists for months. While human beings all over the world spent tremendous energy and imagination in the art of killing each other, these "primitive" tribes were behaving in a much more civilized way, without having even a single confrontation.

The enigma remained until the researchers began to study the people's language and made a startling discovery: These tribes didn't have a word for war. They simply could not materialize the concept or idea of fighting because they could not even name it in the first place.

Let's try it. Picture in your mind something you know exists, something you can feel or imagine but that doesn't have a name or a word to describe it. It is simply impossible, isn't it? One way or another, anything you can imagine you can describe somehow.

What if we could apply this discovery to our quest for success? What if we could eliminate what stands between us and the life of our dreams by getting rid of procrastination, fear, and the worst obstacle of all—the possibility of giving up?

Here is the hitch.

From the Book of Job 3:25 to *The Secret* and the Law of Attraction, from Tony Robbins to Matt Morris, the message is consistent: We will attract what we focus the most on. So the more we try to eliminate the words and associated ideas that describe our fears, the more we will focus on them and therefore attract them. It is a catch 22.

So the more you tell yourself not to procrastinate, the more you procrastinate. The more you try not to think of your fears, the more those fears start to become reality in your life, paralyzing you. The fear of failure becomes a self-fulfilling prophecy.

The idea of failing, of giving up, is indeed a resilient parasite. The more you try to eliminate the idea from your mind, the more you feed it and make it grow.

The solution to this conundrum struck me while watching an amazing movie based on the remarkable book *Enemy at the Gates,* by William Craig.

This book relates the battle for Stalingrad, a monumental human tragedy that took place in 1942 and became the turning point of WWII. What does this have to do with eliminating the option of giving up?

Everything.

While we can barely imagine what these men and women had to endure, there is a lesson to be learned. A shocking scene depicts the Russian troops relentlessly assaulting the enemy. Due to manpower shortages, these soldiers included women as well as men. Frozen, starved, outnumbered, and sometimes unarmed, they kept moving forward, one falling after another, but never even considering the possibility of giving up. Why?

The generals in charge had given the order to open fire on any soldier who stepped back. Any Russian soldier who tried to retreat for cover would be shot by his or her own men.

The concept of giving up was simply not in their minds.

To eradicate that most resilient parasite—the idea of giving up—you simply replace it with a more powerful idea.

Comparing a life and death situation with the quest for success may seem extreme, but is it really?

If being trapped in a life that doesn't fulfill you, working crazy hours for decades with no time left for your family and friends, not having the liberty to discover the beauty of this world and hoping that the "system" will be kind enough to provide you with a meager pension (and it probably won't) for you to survive on in your old days is not life threatening, *what is?*

The greatest achievers have one thing in common: a turning point. An event, most often a tragedy, that put their back against the wall, a situation so dire they had to take drastic actions and move forward or die (literally or metaphorically). They were engaged in their personal battle, won, and changed the course of their own history.

Why not apply this powerful approach to achieve our goals? Why wait until the situation is so painful or difficult to take the necessary action?

One word: Fear.

Although many people fear failure, even more deadly to our dreams is a fear of success. That's right. The old maxim is true: Be careful what you wish for.

This fear is tied to our need for security. Success requires risk, stepping out of our comfort zone. Although security is the exact opposite of freedom and the cheapest form of happiness, we still spend most of our energy trying to create it.

As Dwight D. Eisenhower said, "If you want total security, go to prison. There you are fed, clothed, given medical care and so on. The only thing lacking . . . is freedom."

So why do we work so hard building our own prisons? Why are we so afraid of taking that last step that often stands between good and great, caged and free?

Is it possible that there is a wrong kind of success?

Consider this: 80 percent of lottery winners lose everything within three years and wish they had never won. The tabloids are filled with stories of celebrities divorcing and going through the revolving door of rehab. People most of us consider to be examples of success often end up living totally unbalanced lives.

The reason for this was explained as long ago as 1807, when the philosopher Hegel wrote about "The Master-Slave Dialectic." One application of Hegel's theory is that the Master (we) relies on the slave (wealth, fame, etc.) to make his life easier and more comfortable, but there is a point where the Master depends so much on the Slave that he fears losing the Slave, and the roles are inverted.

In other words, with the wrong kind of success, the more we have, the more we fear losing it.

We may want to create wealth and success to free ourselves, but we often achieve the exact opposite.

- The new owner of a multimillion-dollar house has the stress of higher bills to pay.
- The musician who just released a successful album is immediately worried about the next one.
- The movie star propelled to the red carpet from the last block-buster is anxious about being picked for the next big project.

If you aren't self-confident enough to be absolutely convinced that you have what it takes to face any challenge, you will live in constant fear, no matter how successful you are.

Let's assume you have reached the point where you have done everything right and are just about to reach your goal. You may find yourself hesitating, finding excuses not to make that critical last step. You can't explain it, but the little inner voice keeps telling you, *something is wrong.*

This little voice is your intuition and usually your best adviser. It is telling you that more important than what you achieve is how you achieve it. Your instinct is telling you that you may be very disappointed by what you find at the top of the hill if you don't pay attention to the journey that lead you there.

The ends don't justify the means. The means *are* the ends.

Ask any successful entrepreneurs what they would do should they lose everything overnight. The truly successful will smile. The simple idea of the challenge is exciting. They may not wish for it, but they knew what they would do in that situation long before you asked.

Their secret is that they chase ideas, not money, and they always have. They are successful because they were prepared for success from the very beginning, because they *lived* their success long before they achieved the wealth or fame. Imagination is their only limit, and there is no room left for fear.

Easy enough to say, I know. Sometimes it feels like opportunities are few and far between, especially in today's economy. But they really aren't if you are prepared to attract them and recognize them when they arise.

Confucius said, "When the pupil is ready, the Master appears." In other words, be prepared for success. Do something, anything, toward your goal, without knowing the outcome, without *security.*

The opportunities of a lifetime will appear with much more power and imagination than you could ever dream of.

Retreat is not an option. By telling my friends, family, and everyone willing to listen what my goals are, I apply the Stalingrad strategy. The simple idea of my loves ones asking me about this project I had and having to tell them I had given up would be like a bullet in my heart.

When it comes down to it, success is just as resilient an idea as fear. The more you think about success, the more it takes hold in your mind. The more you take action toward making your dreams come true, the more of a habit this action becomes. Replace the idea of giving up with the idea of moving forward at any cost—and act on it.

You will find that true success is contagious. Once it takes a hold of your life, it is nearly impossible to eradicate.

Biography

Jérome Vaultier

After graduating at the top of his class as a Naval Aviator, JÉROME VAULTIER's military career came to an abrupt end. He turned this into an opportunity to become an entrepreneur and a world explorer. Dedicated to helping others reaching their dreams through financial independence, he created www.  directtrafficsystem.com. He also managed to keep his passion for aviation alive as a helicopter captain, flying all over the world for governmental and private organizations. Originally from Normandy, he now lives between the South of France, the Middle East, and North America.

Contact Information

www.directtrafficsystem.com
jvaultier@yahoo.fr

Chapter 16

The Biggest Myth About Career Success

by Bud Bilanich

I was really pleased to be asked to contribute a chapter to *The Art and Science of Success*. As a career success coach, I help people create the successful lives and careers they want and deserve. I'm happy to share my thoughts on success in this chapter.

First, a little bit about me. I was born a working-class guy. My grandparents on my mother's side were immigrants from Poland. That grandfather worked in a factory in the town where I grew up, near Pittsburgh. My father's parents were born in the United States but never went to school. My grandmother started work as a domestic when she was 10. My grandfather went to work in the coal mines of Central Pennsylvania when he was 8.

My hometown was a company town called Ambridge, so named because the American Bridge Division of U.S. Steel was headquartered there. My dad was an hourly worker for American Bridge for almost 40 years. My mom worked as a checkout person at a local supermarket and then as an office manager for a K-Mart store.

Neither of my parents got anywhere near a college, but education was a big thing in our house. All I heard growing up was "go to college," "go to college." I worked hard and got good grades in high school. I graduated from Penn State in 1972. I did a year of service as a VISTA volunteer, and then began my career as a training and development professional. I went to school at night to get a master's degree. It took two years, working full time and going to school full time, and I graduated with a 4.0.

At that time, I was working in the training department of large oil company. I worked hard, did a good job—and kept getting passed over for promotion. The reasons were vague: "You've only been here a little while," "The hiring manager thought the other person was a better fit," "You need to polish up some of those rough edges."

So I found another job, this time with a chemical company. I worked hard, did a good job, got good performance reviews—and no promotions. I was frustrated. In my heart of hearts, I knew I was as good as or better than people who were moving ahead while I was standing still.

I decided that maybe more school would be the answer. I quit my job and enrolled in a Ph.D. program in adult education and organizational behavior at Harvard. Once I got there, I realized that the same thing happens in academia as happens in business. The hardest workers and best performers don't always get rewarded and promoted. And that's the career success myth I want to bust here. *Good performance alone is not enough to create your life and career success.*

Once I broke free of this myth, I decided to figure out exactly what does make people successful. I got a notebook with a marble-designed cover and made a list of all the successful people in the companies where I had worked, all the people who got the promotions I didn't, and the people who had been role models to me in my life. I created a page for each person, writing down the characteristics I had observed in these people.

It was a long list. I started looking for patterns and groups of behaviors. When it was all said and done, I found seven distinct characteristics that the successful people I studied had in common.

They all:

- had a clearly defined purpose and direction for their lives and careers.

- were committed to succeeding; they faced obstacles and overcame them.

- had unshakeable self-confidence.

- were outstanding performers.

- knew how to present themselves in a favorable light.

- were dynamic communicators.

- were good at building relationships.

Once I finished my degree, I took a job with a very large pharmaceutical company in New York. I started applying the lessons I had learned from observing successful people—and I began getting promotions and good assignments. I became the confidante of several senior executives, and I began coaching up-and-comers in the company, teaching them the basic principles I had discovered by writing my observations in that marble-covered notebook. I also kept refining my ideas, making them easier for others to understand and apply. You never learn something as well as when you teach it. I became the most sought-after internal coach in that company.

Then I got cancer—and survived. I realized that I had an opportunity to reach even more people with my common sense message about life and career success, people I would never get a chance to meet while working one-on-one with executives in a very large company.

That's why I changed careers and became an independent career success coach. That's why I'm making everything I know about career and life success widely available on the Internet. That's why I blog, speak about career success as often as I can, write books—and this chapter. I want to help as many people as I can to create the successful lives and careers they want and deserve. I survived a cancer scare, and now I want to give as much as I can to as many people as I can.

All of this brings me back to the biggest myth about career success: the myth that good performance alone is enough to create the life and career success you want and deserve.

Good performance is not enough. It is merely the price of admission to the career success sweepstakes. Good performance is necessary for your success, but by itself, it will not lead to the success you want and deserve. I tell my coaching clients that in addition to becoming an outstanding performer, they have to be pretty good at all the other six keys to success I found through my research—and really good at two or three of them.

I've broken down the seven keys to success that I identified in my research into 140 tweets that I published in a book called *Success Tweets: 140 Bits of Common Sense Career Success Advice, All in 140 Characters or Less*. Here are a few tweets for each key to success.

Clarity

- Define exactly what life and career success mean to you. It's easier to hit a clear, unambiguous target.

- The mightier your purpose, the more likely you are to succeed.

- Don't focus just on making money. If you do, you'll be asking too little of yourself. Focus on how you can be useful in this world.
- Clarify your personal values. They are your anchor. They ground you. They center you. They keep you focused on what's important.

Commitment

- You're in charge! Commit to taking personal responsibility for creating the life and career success you want and deserve.
- Aim high. Set and achieve high goals—month after month, year after year. Do whatever it takes to achieve your goals.
- Stuff happens as you go about creating your life and career success. Choose to respond positively to the negative stuff that happens.
- Although other people and events impact your life, they don't shape it. You get to choose how you react to people and events. Choose well.
- Don't be afraid to fail. You fail only if you don't learn something from the experience. Treat every failure as an opportunity to grow.

Confidence

- Choose optimism. It builds your confidence.
- Everyone is afraid sometime. Self-confident people face their fears and act. Look your fears in the eye and do something.
- Four steps for dealing with fear: identify it, admit it, accept it, do something about it.
- Procrastination is the physical manifestation of fear and a confidence killer. Act—especially when you're afraid.

- Surround yourself with positive people. Hold them close. They will give you energy and help you create the career success you deserve.

- Jettison the negative people in your life. They are energy black holes. They will suck you dry, but only if you let them.

Outstanding Performance

- Master your technical discipline. Share what you know. Become the go-to person in your company.

- Become a lifelong learner. The half-life of knowledge is rapidly diminishing. Staying in the same place is the same as going backwards.

- Get organized. Organize your time, life, and workspace. Sweat the small stuff. Success is in execution. Execution is in the details.

- The better you feel, the better you'll perform. Live a healthy lifestyle. Eat well. Exercise. Get regular checkups.

- Good truly is the enemy of great. Don't settle for good performance. Today, good is mediocre. Become an outstanding performer.

- Care about what you do. If you care a little, you'll be an okay performer. If you care a lot, you'll become an outstanding performer.

Positive Personal Impact

- Create and nurture your unique personal brand. Stand and be known for something. Make sure that everything you do is on brand.

- Be visible. Volunteer for tough jobs. Brand yourself as a person who can and does make significant contributions.

- Demonstrate self-respect. Be impeccable in your presentation of self—in person and online.

- Be well groomed and appropriate for every situation. Always dress one level up from what is expected. You'll stand out from the crowd.

- Be gracious. Know and follow the basic rules of etiquette. Everybody likes to be around polite and mannerly people.

- Be courteous. It costs you nothing, and it can mean everything to someone else. It also helps you get what you want.

Dynamic Communication

- All dynamic communicators have mastered three basic communication skills: conversation, writing, and presenting.

- Conversation tips: Be warm, pleasant, gracious, and sensitive to the interpersonal needs and anxieties of others.

- Become an excellent conversationalist by listening more than speaking. Pay attention to what other people say; respond appropriately.

- Write clearly and simply; short words and sentences, first person, active voice. Be precise in your choice of words.

- Presentation steps: (1) Determine your message. (2) Analyze your audience. (3) Organize your information. (4) Design supporting visuals. (5) Practice.

- Practice presentations. You can control your nerves by practicing out loud. The more you practice, the less nervous you'll be.

Strong Relationships

- Get genuinely interested in others. Help bring out the best in everyone you know. Others will gravitate to you.

- Get to know yourself. Use your self-knowledge to better understand others and build mutually beneficial relationships with them.
- Pay it forward. Build relationships by giving with no expectation of return. Give of yourself to build strong relationships.
- There is no quid pro quo in effective relationships. Do for others without being asked or waiting for them to do for you.
- Resolve conflict positively. Treat conflict as an opportunity to strengthen, not destroy, the relationships you've worked hard to build.
- Be a consensus builder. Focus on where you agree with others. It will be easier to resolve differences and create consensus.

In this brief chapter, I've covered seven keys to creating your life and career success: (1) clarity of purpose and direction, (2) commitment to taking personal responsibility for your life and career success, (3) unshakable self-confidence, (4) outstanding performance, (5) positive personal impact, (6) dynamic communication, and (7) strong relationships. I've also provided you with a sampling of the career advice in my book *Success Tweets*. You can download a free copy of *Success Tweets* at www.SuccessTweets.com. While you're there, don't forget to download your free copy of *Success Tweets Explained*, a 395-page e-book that explains each of the tweets in *Success Tweets* in detail. It's my gift to you because I want to help you create the life and career success you want and deserve.

Biography

Bud Bilanich

BUD BILANICH, the Common Sense Guy, is a career success coach who helps his clients succeed by applying their common sense. He has been featured in the *Wall Street Journal, Success Magazine, Fast Company,* and *Self Improvement Magazine.* Dr. Bilanich is Harvard educated but has a no-nonsense approach to his work that goes back to his roots in the steel country of Western Pennsylvania. He is the author of 16 books on career success and a contributor to 6 others. He is a cancer survivor who lives in Denver, Colorado, with Cathy, his wife.

Contact Information

www.BudBilanich.com
Bud@BudBilanich.com
303-393-0446

Chapter 17

It's Never Too Late to Reinvent Yourself to Live Your Dream Life

by Dr. Joe Rubino

Just like so many other people, I felt trapped by my job. For me, that job was dentistry. Although it was financially rewarding (my practice grossed about $1 million yearly), after 10 years, it had become old. I no longer enjoyed the day-to-day challenges that accompanied running a successful dental practice. We had about 250 new patients each month, and I supervised seven other dentists, doing my best to be a painless dentist in a field where pain and discomfort cannot always be avoided.

However, my busy practice came with a huge overhead, which meant that I had to work day in and day out just to feed the overhead monster. Although I loved to travel, I could hardly manage to get away for a week or two each year with my family. And while I was away, I worried constantly about the practice, my patients' problems, and the constant headaches that go along with a staff of 15 people.

Meanwhile, day after day, my life was spent bent over looking into people's dark and sometimes smelly mouths, often causing them discomfort, if not actual pain, while they were wishing that they were somewhere, anywhere else! It was a stressful occupation to say the least. Moreover, I was totally out of touch with fully honoring my core values of love, creativity, contribution, inspiration, and freedom.

In short, I knew there had to be a better way.

That is when I discovered the realm of personal development. You see, I was intrigued by the idea that anyone could reinvent themselves to live their best lives in choice while honoring those values most important in their lives. In 1991, at the age of 35, I had become an extreme introvert. In fact, I had accumulated thousands of pieces of evidence over those past 35 years to prove that I was not very good socially, had few skills beyond dentistry, and was resigned to the "fact" that that was just the way it was. In fact, I was so introverted that rather than risk the possibility of having to speak with strangers, I took comfort in doing my continuing education through the mail. And although I dreaded the possibility of having to work in that profession for another 30 years before earning the right to retire and sit under a coconut tree on a secluded beach in the Caribbean, I believed that I possessed little chance of finding an alternative way to earn a living that would be both personally and financially rewarding.

I also intuitively had a feeling that I was playing small. I decided to summon up as much courage as I could muster and enter a one-year intensive personal development program. During this year-long program, I discovered that not only was life not working optimally for me because I was not fully honoring my most important core values, but that I had made up or bought into lots of negative, disempowering interpretations that truly did not serve me. I discovered that, much to my surprise, I could live from a declaration regarding the qualities that

I chose to be, rather than those qualities that no longer served me. The more I learned about how we all must take responsibility for attracting and manifesting whatever we wish to have show up around us in our lives, the more enthusiastic and hopeful I became that I could, in fact, reinvent myself and my life.

I immersed myself fully into a rigorous examination of who I had become and who I wished to be. By discovering my ability to live in choice, to develop the qualities that I wished to be known for, and to uncover and more fully develop my gifts, I took on the daily process of welcoming and embracing problems while looking for the gifts of growth that each contained. I completed my past by reinterpreting those decisions that no longer supported me, realizing that every painful experience had been a gift that added to my wisdom and empathy. I discovered further how my reactive emotional state of indignant anger had run my life by having me react to the words and actions of others as if they were personally assaulting and offending me. I learned that 99% of the time, being upset is about the person upset and only 1% about the person who is supposedly causing the upset. By reinterpreting each potentially upsetting event in the moment with empathy, forgiveness, and gratitude, I soon learned that I possessed the ability to empower my life rather than be at the mercy of external circumstances.

I then did a thorough inventory of my current situation. I identified exactly what was working well and what was missing that, if put into place, would enhance the quality of my life. I discovered that I was blessed with many gifts that I had no idea I remotely possessed. I discovered that I could write, I could learn to speak and inspire others, and I could learn to coach others to reinvent themselves to live their best lives as well. In short, my one-year intensive personal development program turned into an intensive ten-year program and a lifelong commitment to constant and never-ending improvement.

I decided to create a plan that would align with the written vision I had created for realizing my dream life. This plan involved replacing my mid-six-figure income as a dentist with an alternative source of income through network marketing so that I could be free to then pursue my new profession: being a life-impacting self-esteem, personal development, communications, and business coach. With the support of my coaches, I daily relished the opportunities that every new day offered for me to step into. Within 18 months, by following the personal development principles I was learning about daily, I was able to build a six-figure residual income through network marketing and begin full-time my lifelong quest of being the best I could be with the intention of championing others to be their best.

Over the last 20 years as a life-optimization and business coach, having coached more than 1,000 individuals to live their best lives, I learned that success is not getting everything you ever wanted. It is being in pursuit of worthwhile goals that honor your values while loving the process. Contrary to how most people see success—life will be great when some event happens—true success is falling in love with the daily process of learning, growing, and experiencing while in the pursuit of an empowering vision. I've learned that there are two components critical to attaining success in life: a burning desire and a positive expectation. It is not enough just to want something badly; it is necessary to see our success as inevitable if we are to generate the self-motivation necessary to do those things that will put us firmly on the path to achieving that success.

I discovered that personal reinvention and elevating one's self-esteem require a three-step process: healing and completing the past, assessing what's so in the present, and designing an inspirational and compelling future vision in choice. When the negative self-talk that limits most people is effectively managed, and one develops the ability to create empowering interpretations that support his or her success moment by moment, especially in times of upset, one can attract those people and realities that are consistent with one's energy and thus create the basis of a dream life.

When one has the courage to envision that dream life and then the self-motivation and positive expectation to act and manifest it deliberately, miracles happen. By acting in alignment with one's commitments rather than what might be most convenient in the moment, one can take daily action in the direction of achieving one's vision on purpose. Of course, as soon as we make commitments, problems are sure to arise that can derail us from these commitments, causing us to take the path of convenience and return to the status quo. Those who are successful know that each problem contains within it the seeds of success needed to break through any challenges. By embracing, welcoming, and breaking through problems, we develop greater personal power, more self-confidence, and the courageous ability to do whatever it takes to achieve our goals and manifest our vision. This process of falling in love with personal development and welcoming challenges is key to be the best we can be as we overcome obstacles and seize our personal power en route to achieving our visions.

Leadership always begins with a decision and is followed by a declaration. In other words, leaders possess the courage to act in accordance with the goals and visions they create while inspiring others to join them in the pursuit of those visions and create visions of their own. Leadership is *not* what you acquire as a result of having achieved a certain income, title, or position. It is a place you come from as a declaration that guides your decisions and actions.

When you are the source of everything that shows up in your life and in your business, your actions will be in sync with this self-declared leadership role. The elements that characterize leadership include a clear and well-spoken vision that serves as an inspirational guiding force for yourself and others; a specific action plan that answers the question, "What exactly will it take to manifest this vision?"; an enthusiastic contagious belief level that causes others to join the cause and act, motivated by a positive expectation of success; an authenticity and genuine humility that comes from a true commitment to contribute to others and a commitment to ultimate invisibility—that is, getting out of the way and allowing others to step into *their* own power. This is an ability to make others greater than yourself, empowering them through example with a commitment to seeing a possibility for them that they might not yet clearly see for themselves. This is what it means to be an inspiration to others.

The primary ingredient essential for achieving success in every area of life and for manifesting one's dream life is high self-esteem. Your misinterpretations of events damage your self-esteem and run your life. Freedom comes from reinterpreting your past with compassion for your humanity and that of others. Forgiveness paves the way for self-esteem to flourish. Only you can diminish your self-esteem, and only you can restore it. Freedom comes with nonattachment to whatever another says or does.

I invite you to fall in love with the personal development process. Welcome each day as another opportunity to learn and to grow in self-esteem, personal power, and experience as you honor your values and commitments, live your self-declared life purpose, manifest your gifts, and create the success you desire for yourself and others.

Biography

Dr. Joe Rubino

DR. JOE RUBINO is an internationally acclaimed personal development trainer, life-changing success and life-optimization coach, and best-selling author of 12 books available worldwide in 23 languages. He is the CEO of The Center for Personal Reinvention, an organization that has impacted the lives of more than 2 million people through personal and leadership development programs, providing participants with tools to maximize their happiness, self-esteem, communication skills, productivity, and personal effectiveness. To subscribe to his complimentary newsletters; to learn more about championing your self-esteem, communicating more effectively, life-impacting personal or group coaching, and transformational courses; or to read about his books, visit his websites.

Contact Information

www.CenterForPersonalReinvention.com
www.TheSelfEsteemBook.com

Chapter 18

Live the Uncommon Life

by Justin Tillman

Paint Your Horizon

What is an uncommon life? It is the manifestation of a predetermined vision transformed into a physical reality. Here is a universal law. You have everything inside you right now to create and build the life that you want, through the power of your mind, body, and spirit. We are designed to feel with our heart and manifest with our body.

A perfect example is a 5 year old. At that age our imagination is limitless. Our actions are 100% driven by our heart. If we felt like building a ginormous castle that sat on the top of the sky accompanied by talking dragons and powerful wizards, we did not think, Wow, that's a dumb idea. We didn't ask for someone else's opinion to see if it were possible. We just did it.

Then as time progresses, we begin to learn words like probably not, unlikely, too risky, dangerous, stupid, foolish—the list goes on and on.

We start picking up behaviors and social norms. We listen to authority figures like our parents, teachers, and people in our community. We accept their limiting beliefs at face value, without questioning the legitimacy of their suggestions, because we believe they understand how the world works. We begin sculpting our lives through a pessimistic lens. We do not want to stand out for the fear of being ridiculed or looking foolish. Our actions, which where once lead by our heart, have now been domesticated by the comfort zone of our rational mind. We inevitably water down the very tool that will set us free: our creativity. That kid-like enthusiasm that was very much alive in many young adults today has now died. Many are programmed to live a common life.

Now, I'm not saying that the people closest to you we're trying to keep you from living an uncommon life. If anything, they were giving you the best advice they could. They encouraged you to follow the path of the common not because it is fun, but because it is practical. And the path of doing what you love and getting paid to do it is considered an impractical reality to obtain.

The way I see it is that if you're going to live an uncommon life, you are going to have to do what most people would consider risky—go for it anyway. Your life is a masterpiece waiting to get painted; it's just up to you to use the brush. It is your job as the artist of your life to take as much time as necessary to think about the kind of picture of your life you want paint. As Morpheus said to Neo in *The Matrix* "Just let it all go: fear, doubt, and disbelief." You've got to free your mind. Give yourself permission to revisit that kid-like enthusiasm. Only this time you are more powerful than when you were a kid. You have grown wise with experience and have already overcome many challenges up to this point. You have the ability to acquire all the resources you need by creating a clear vision of what you want and setting your mind and body on a mission to getting it.

So for the first exercise, sit back in a quiet place and ask yourself some simple but powerful questions that can help you paint your picture. What is your idea of a good life? What top 100 experiences do you want to have before you die? Whom do you want experience them with? Where would you live? What do you want to accomplish? How do you want to give back? Keep running wild with more questions and answers to these questions. There are no right or wrong answers because you make the rules.

Find Your Plane

Today many people are not living their purpose because they are afraid to be who they are. They believe that who they are might not be good enough. So they let their God-given talents lie dormant inside them. Due to this belief, many find themselves stuck in an emotional purgatory, a place where there is an inherent disconnection between where they are (common life) versus where they want to be (the uncommon life). Where you are now has everything to do with the vehicle you are using.

Think about it like this: If you are heading from New York to California, would you rather walk or take an airplane? The obvious answer is to take a plane. The same is true when heading from the common life to the uncommon life—you want to get there the fastest possible way.

There are two important rules when it comes to finding the plane that will help you take off to your dream life. One, it's got to make you feel alive when you're doing it. Two, you have to find a way to serve others through a profitable business in which you can use your uniqueness. Let's face it: Dreaming is good, but living the dream is better. And the dream life is likely going to cost you money. Don't get stuck on money as your main driving force, but don't become disillusioned because it is unmistakably relevant. Remember: Money doesn't make the world go round; it just pays for the entire trip.

So here are some questions that can help tip you off to finding your purpose. What are you naturally good at? What activities do you find yourself kicking people's asses in regularly? What can you have a two-hour conversation about without feeling bored? What common clues keep reappearing from your past? For instance, since college I've been pulling together and writing ideas about how to inspire people to live their dreams and do what they love. Years later, while cleaning my office, I would find these dozen of notes and word documents on my computer and still feel the same. Last but not least can you see yourself doing this activity for the next 5, 10, or even 20 years from now?

Once you have found your purpose, it's time to turn your dream life into a reality. You need to find a problem that you once had but overcame and help other people benefit from your solution.

Were you once bad at keeping a good relationship but now have a meaningful and fulfilling one? Can you coach and show other people what do so they can have a relationship that lasts? Were you once out of shape but now have rock-hard abs. Can you develop a fitness program that will help people lose weight? Were you once broke but now your balling? Can you develop a step-by-step guide to help people make money? Here's the point: If you want to live life on your terms, you need to sell a product or service people need or want. If you don't, it's like trying to get a plane to take off without any wings.

Take off with Action

When it comes to personal development and learning how to improve my life, I would consider myself to be a pretty avid reader. I would read, read, and read some more. But when it came down turning my vision into reality, I never really committed myself to the action of getting sustainable results. I would frequently waste time getting

LIVE THE UNCOMMON LIFE

distracted by shiny rocks that glimmer but never seemed to find any gold. I was fickle, and this was a recipe for disappointment.

Each time I restarted, I felt an unsettling feeling inside me that I needed to rush and catch up for the years I had missed out on. But then after a week of going at an unsustainable pace, I would eventually let go and get sick of even the thought of writing content. Then like a domino effect, I would stop another discipline, and another, and then another.

I'm a little embarrassed to say that it has taken me over four years to get going with my personal brand. I would start, stop, start, stop, over and over again, but I would never get enough traction to take off. Then one day, I decided enough was enough. I was tired of only living a life of potential. It was time either to put up or shut up. I had to find a way to become consistent. I had the desire. I had the drive. But something was still holding me back.

I finally discovered what it was. The reason I and so many others in pursuit of the uncommon life fail to take action consistently is that we fail to establish a compelling enough reason to be consistent in our action. We depend primarily on willpower to carry us through. But the truth is, if we rely solely on our willpower, it will eventually fail us.

Let's look at three examples to gain more perspective on this concept.

Example 1

Picture this: You are standing on one side of a bridge, and on the other side is a 100 dollar bill. To get it, all you have to do is walk across the bridge and grab it. How much willpower would you need to go and grab it? Not much, right?

Example 2

Let's say six hours later, that same bridge is covered with a blaze of fire that stretches 1 1/2 miles long. And the base is only about three feet above a sea of hungry sharks. The will to get across has greatly diminished, right? A hundred bucks is probably not worth it anymore.

Example 3

On the other side of the bridge is a person you love more than anything else in the world, passed out and lying on the very end of bridge, with only minutes to live before the bridge collapses. Would you find a way to get over there in time no matter what the present dangers might be?

The reason most people fail with their goals is their lack of compelling reason to take action. When the sky is blue, the sun is out, and they feel 100% up to it, they act. Like in example 1.

However, the true test of your commitment to succeed is shown when things aren't so peachy. Someone close to you passes away, your significant other dumps you, and you feel like the world is conspiring against you. Suddenly, the path no longer seems convenient. This is where most people stop taking action and give up. Their personal story becomes more important than living the uncommon life.

The only true way to be consistent in action regardless of what is happening outside you is to make your why bigger than any fear, doubt, or anxiety that you may have about moving forward. You will take as much daily, weekly, and monthly action as necessary to reach your goal. When a person reaches this level of intuitive congruence with their purpose, circumstances will never hinder progress.

The question you must answer for yourself is how will you get to that level of desire? And another simple but powerful question: Why do you want an uncommon life?

For me, the answer is time. Why? Because tomorrow is never promised to anyone. We assume we will wake up tomorrow because that's what we've been doing for however long we've been alive. This earth-shaking reality struck me when my mother passed away to cancer at the young age of 61. I remember for many years how we'd talk about going to live in Paris for a while so that she could paint, display, and sell her art. We spoke of living in California because we believed so deeply that we're born to be stars. We had a vision, a passion, to live an uncommon life and were on the verge of action. Then she became sick and was taken from me. All our congruent goals and dreams are now just a memory inside me today.

You simply can't afford to waste time if you want to live the life of your dreams. You have to go after it today.

You have to ask yourself, If you passed away today, would you have said or done more? Would you have lived a fearless life, where you went after what you valued most? Would you have spent time with the people you wanted to spend it with? Traveled and learned the languages you wanted? Truly become the best person you could possibly be? If the answer is no to any of these questions, it is time to reconnect with the reason you are here on this earth.

Remember: There is only one right type of action, and that is daily strategic action. Even if it's just for 30 minutes a day, always be pushing the ball forward. You have to keep progressing. Do it inch by inch and it's a cinch.

If you want take off of the runway of the common life and head straight for the uncommon life, you've got to take daily action toward you dreams, whether it's convenient or inconvenient. If you make the commitment to see it through to the end, the price will be worth the reward. Never let anyone fool you: Success does happen overnight; it's just a combination of many nights.

Cheers to your uncommon life.

Biography

Justin Tillman

JUSTIN TILLMAN became an entrepreneur at age 20 and ran three different businesses in college. He is the recipient of the Dream Award 2010 from the Emanuel Foundation, and became one of largest joint venture brokers in the personal development community in less than two years. Justin is also the  CEO of Theuncommonlife.net, which inspires people to find their purpose and make money doing what they so they can live life on their terms.

Contact Information

Theuncommonlife.net
Justin@theuncommonlife.net

Chapter 19

You Too Can Succeed!

by Godfrey E. McAllister, Ph.D., DTM

I can still hear the thunderous roar of applause at the Annual Awards Banquet as hundreds of people sprang to their feet in recognition of one of the greatest salesmen of their time, who despite the odds had again shattered his own world record. What is really great about this memory is that I am the person who received the tumultuous applause.

Born in Guyana, South America, I had recently migrated to Jamaica and was successfully recruited by the international conglomerate American Life Insurance Company (ALICO). Competing with weak Jamaican dollars in an international U.S. dollar arena against thousands of ALICOnian colleagues in over 60 countries, it seemed impossible to everyone that I could succeed in becoming ALICO's worldwide #1 agent—that is, to everyone except me. At the end of year one, I was declared #1 personal accident insurance salesman in Jamaica. At the end of year two, I was declared #1 in the Caribbean region. By the end of year three, I was declared #1 in the world. In year four, I was again #1 in the world, this time breaking my own record. In years five, six, seven, eight, and nine, I maintained my worldwide #1 position, each year breaking my own record. As I converted successes into being successful, I was invited to give my first motivational speech, "Dare to Dream . . . Then Become Your Dream!"

Who in the world does not want to be successful? I want to be successful. You want to be successful. The question is, How badly do we want to succeed, and how high a price are we prepared to pay for success? Did I have a price to pay for my success, and if so, how high was that price? I can assure you, it was not easy, especially when you consider that I had only recently migrated to Jamaica. My success had as much to do with the enormity of the opposition to my success as it had to do with the enormous effort I decided to make to overcome that opposition. I share all the details in my book *You've Got All It Takes to Succeed*.

According to *Dictionary.com*, "*Succeed* is to accomplish what is attempted or intended." That is simple enough. Yet, for many, the achievement of success is anything but simple. I am proposing that if you have the fundamental required abilities; the desire to succeed in achieving a specific goal; and the ability to leverage the advantages in your environment, you will be able to identify or create the necessary opportunity in which to invest your focused mental and physical energy and effort for as long as it takes to succeed in attaining your goal. Join me on this journey.

Principle #1: Before you can succeed, you must have a goal, intent, aim, or objective. In the absence of a goal, we automatically succeed, but only because if you aim at nothing, you are sure to hit it. It really does not matter what your goal is as long as it is practical. Your goal does not have to be something that someone else has already done. It could just as well be something that no one else has done. But it must be something that *can* be done, and something that can be done by you.

Your abilities and skill-set are therefore critical to the formulation of a viable goal. If you are 4'6" tall, excelling in American Pro Basketball may not be a viable goal. If you routinely faint at the sight of blood, becoming a medical doctor may not be a viable goal. However, if despite the improbability of achieving your goal you are convinced that your goal is attainable, then prove to the world that you can not only dream, but that your impossible dream can be attained. Your goal must therefore be specific, definable, quantifiable, and measurable. Your goal must be aligned to a performance time frame, even if this time frame has to be subdivided into short, medium, and long-term performance periods.

Principle #2: You must apply focused, unidirectional, and sustained mental and physical energetic effort in order to succeed. The successful student has studied intensely. The successful athlete has trained rigorously. The successful comedian has spent numerous hours in serious preparation. Henry Wadsworth Longfellow declares:

> The heights by great men, reached and kept,
> Were not attained by sudden flight;
> But they, while their companions slept,
> Were toiling upward through the night.

Principle #3: Psychologists now concur with the Bible that, "As a man thinks, so is he." Thoughts have been electromagnetically and chemically identified and analyzed and are no longer perceived to be vague phantoms of the inner recesses of our minds. We know that we react differently to our wide range of thoughts. Thoughts of love and affection result in specific reactions in our body, whereas thoughts of fear and anger produce opposite reactions. The now-familiar word "psychosomatic" was first introduced to the medical community in 1818 by Johann Christian August Heinroth. Our thoughts and emotions influence our physical structure, and vice versa, to a lesser extent.

Subconsciously, our thoughts are influenced by the information and other stimuli that invade us through our physical and spiritual sensors and receptors. Guarding our thoughts is therefore a full-time lifestyle undertaking that will force us to pay careful attention to what we concentrate on, look at, listen to, and enjoy. Failing to systematically marshal our thoughts will impair our ability to be successful.

Words are our vocalized thoughts. It is out of the abundance of our heart and mind that we speak. There is power in the spoken word. God states that He will judge us on the basis of our words. Contrary to traditional thinking, our words can hurt and our words can heal. With our words, we can conquer, destroy, or build others, and ourselves. When we guard our thoughts, our words will be harnessed, and our actions will fall in line. The constant repetition of any action will form a habit. Habits then acquire a driving force of their own and commit us to ensuring their longevity. Having taken control of us, these habits become our character—and it is our character that determines our destiny.

Principle #4: A popular omission in most discussions of success and failure is the role of our spiritual energizer. You are both physical and spiritual, and based on irrefutable evidence, it is arguable that the "real you" is spiritual. However, even at a minimum, allowing for a spiritual influence in us, we should not ignore the contribution of the spiritual to our success or failure. Whether or not we are conscious of it, our spiritual component relates to, and draws on, one or more spiritual sources for its energy.

The devil is one such source, and we have heard of many who have "sold their souls" to the devil in exchange for huge material and temporary success. On the other hand, a major maxim in the Christian faith is "I can do all things through Christ who strengthens me." Reliance on our spiritual strength is a critical component in the success formula. The good news is that there is a choice of sources, and each of us must make our own choice.

Principle #5: You must make full use of the opportunities that come your way. An opportunity is the converging of a series of events, factors, and circumstances around you at the "right" time, which, when acted upon and taken advantage of, provide the needed launch pad from which you are propelled into your next great success. William Shakespeare said, "There is a tide in the affairs of men, which, taken at the flood, leads on to fortune. Omitted, all the voyage of their life is bound in shallows and in miseries."

It is important to realize that a genuine opportunity is in part created by you through a series of general and specific preparations for self-readiness for that opportunity. Kate Middleton is now Catherine, Duchess of Cambridge, because she seized an opportunity that would not have existed had she not attended the expensive "Ivy League" school in which Prince William was enrolled. Whether we in part create opportunities, or whether they are "thrown in our lap," they are useless to us until seized and exploited. In our pursuit of success, we must formulate the physical, mental, and human environment that we believe will be most conducive to facilitating our success, and then consciously create it.

Principle #6: Persistence and perseverance are essential to success and require more than just energy and hard work. They require an act of the will and a determination that no price is too high to pay, and no time is too long to actively wait to achieve your goal. Ordinary people have dreams and wish they could accomplish things. They even begin the journey toward success. Then when the going gets rough, the weak and feeble in character and spirit stop going. The difference between successful persons and failures is seldom the lack of opportunity, nor the willingness to engage the process, but rather, it is the determination to stay the course. It helps if the journey to your goal includes what you love.

> Success is failure turned inside out—
> The silver tint of the clouds of doubt,
> And you never can tell how close you are,
> It may be near when it seems afar,
> So stick to the fight when you're hardest hit—
> It's when things seem worst that you mustn't quit.

Principle #7: Desire brings all the other success components together. It is the catalyst in the science of success. Desire is translated from the Greek word *epithumia*, which is also translated as "lust." It was used of Jesus, and it is used of every successful person.

In one of my books, *You've Got All It Takes to Succeed*, I responded to the frustration of being unable to find an adequate definition of desire by creating my own.

> To desire something is not merely to want it. To desire something is not merely to wish you had it. To desire something is not merely to like the idea of having that thing. To desire something is to become totally and completely obsessed with the thought of having that thing to the point that you are convinced that it is attainable, and to the point that you believe that you will attain it, and as a result, you consciously and sub-consciously unleash all your mental, physical, social, emotional and spiritual faculties and resources in the relentless pursuit of the materialization of the object of your desire.

> Desire therefore is not a passive word. Desire is not a feeble expression of interest. Rather, desire is the starting point of all achievement, and the one ingredient without which our lives will forever be marred by the morass of mediocrity.

Finally, of the many laws that govern our existence, the "law of attraction" is arguably the most directly linked to our success. Think of two very senior citizens that you know. Tell me which you prefer. Is it the miserable one who daily talks about her arthritis, back pains, neck cramps, and botched opportunities? Or is it the one who, though enduring the discomforts that sometimes come with age, is cheerful, positive, humorous, and full of mini-history lessons that your lecturer may have overlooked? You might say that you are attracted to a specific person, and sometimes you can't even think of a good reason. The person, however, should be taking all the credit for deliberately attracting you. It is the attracter that attracts the attracted. Just as you can be attracted, so you can attract.

What is true of human relations is equally true, even though less obviously, for opportunities. We attract things and opportunities to ourselves based on the mental vibrations that we transmit through our thoughts, expectations, attitudes, words, and actions. Think of this process as sowing and reaping. If we sow negative thoughts, expectations, attitudes, words, and actions, we will reap negative results, degrading relationships, failures, and poverty. When you sow positive thoughts, expectations, attitudes, words, and actions, you shall attract to yourself positive results, productive relationships, and prosperity. As a matter of fact, it will seem that all the forces of nature and God himself have conspired to bring you the success you so richly deserve.

Biography

Godfrey E. McAllister, Ph.D., DTM

DR. GODFREY MCALLISTER is a Distinguished Toastmaster, international motivational speaker, and author of books on motivation, consumer advocacy, and America's Christian heritage. Dr. McAllister is available to speak at your special event on almost any subject, including "Conquer through Creative Communication," "Secrets of Successful Selling," "Fear Fosters Failure," "To Be or Not To Be . . . Sucker or Suckee," "Rise from Your Slump . . . and Succeed," and "Dare to Dream . . . Then Become Your Dream." His mantra is, "Whatever you consciously conceive and ardently believe, you will inevitably achieve!"

Dr. McAllister offers a unique satisfaction-guaranteed professional fee condition. To book Dr. McAllister or request his "One Sheet," see his contact information below.

Contact Information

Themotivator@gmail.com

727-279-6868

Chapter 20

Success Comes Before Work Only in the Dictionary

by Betty Wong

26.2 miles is a long, long way!

I had reached the halfway point of the Honolulu Marathon and was catching my breath on the curb at the water station, thinking: Why am I doing this, and what have I gotten myself into?

Other runners shouted encouragement as they passed me. "Don't quit. Don't sit too long or you will stiffen up. Keep going!" At first, I was tempted to get up and smack those people! Trouble was, I was just too tired to get up. So a few moments later, I decided instead to make it to the finish line, at any cost. I was going to finish. I was going to succeed.

Later I thought about what had made my desire to succeed stronger than the desire to stay on the curb. Success is the achievement of a goal or desire. It's always a very personal decision since we each have our individual goals and desires. Goals and desires come in many forms.

Hit a hole in one in golf? Bowl a perfect game? Lose ten unwanted pounds? Find your life partner?

Success also depends on our point of view. If desire is in the eyes of the beholder, success also looks different to everyone. What you may envision as success today may become just another day at the office tomorrow.

It depends on how you perceive it. The importance of our differing perceptions struck me after my first marathon. How do you get to the finish line of a marathon? Some say it is the same way you get to Carnegie Hall—practice, practice, practice. For a marathon, it is taking one step at a time.

You register for the marathon, show up at the start line when you're supposed to, and run 26.2 miles to the finish line. It's what I did to successfully complete my first marathon in Honolulu.

Everyone can achieve success. Others may call you a success even when you may think you are not.

I did not have a coach or a mentor and hadn't even trained. I put on my running shoes and running outfit, toed the start line, and followed other runners for 26.2 miles. After more than eight hours, I crossed the finish line. Several days later, with my blisters freshly bandaged, I was finally able to walk again and go to work. After all the congratulations and accolades were over, I felt empty and somewhat dissatisfied. I even lost track of my finisher's medal.

Most non-marathon runners wonder why you would want to put yourself through all of that. Everyone has his or her own real reason, and we often do not share the real reason with people. Reflecting back, I believe my dissatisfaction was because I really had no valid reason for running the marathon.

As a new arrival in Honolulu, working on a project for my new employer, I was alone. The only people I knew were colleagues working on the same project. Although I was the proverbial fish out of water at first, project team leaders Russ and Shirley drew me into their atmosphere of support and togetherness. I soon decided I wanted to be Russ and Shirley when I grew up. Confident and self-assured, they seemed to be experts at everything they did. I ran the marathon primarily because these people whom I so admired would be running. Unlike me, Russ and Shirley trained. They successfully completed the marathon and then several more.

Signing up for the Honolulu Marathon was just my going along with the crowd. My "why" for running the marathon was not big enough to give me the incentive to put forth more effort to run it the right way.

How about you? You may have all the tools you need to achieve success. Yet having the right tools is often not enough.

My greatest tip for success is to have a compelling "why" to help you overcome the inevitable challenges you'll face on the way.

For several years after the first marathon, I had several "what if" moments. What if I had trained? What if I had trained with someone or had a coach? I probably could have had a richer, more rewarding experience if I had just approached the race from a different perspective.

Once you have a compelling reason, you also need a process to achieve success. You must have a system.

The key to success is to take *action* by implementing the system you have chosen.

You may have the belief and the positive mental state to succeed, as well as the necessary resources such as money, time, a system, and a team. You also need a good catalyst. All the money and desire in the world are worthless without *action*.

Ten years after my first marathon, I learned about an organization that helps move you from the couch to the finish line of a marathon. I thought this program could provide an opportunity for me to run one for real this time.

So after seeing the program advertisement, I took action, determined to make this marathon experience different from the first. I signed up to run the Houston Marathon, paid a registration fee to join the organization, then showed up for the first group run and meeting looking for guidance and leadership.

Leadership involves taking one or more people from one point to another point. A good leader motivates his or her team members to perform well. If team members are not motivated by a leader, each team member must be self-motivated. People can lead themselves. Many find it easier and more effective to be motivated and feel accountable to a leader.

At our first group run, we were assigned to a subgroup based on our individual running pace. Experienced marathoners led each group. Subgroup leaders had used the program and anticipated the obstacles we would be facing. We ran with our group and discussed our challenges afterwards. The leaders offered advice and instructions for the upcoming week.

The training program system included weekly training group runs and individual training days. After each weekly training group run, all the subgroups gathered into a large group for a presentation on a running topic. The larger group focused all the runners on achieving a common goal: completing a marathon. We were accountable to our subgroup leaders to accomplish our individualized training. The training program focused on helping us complete intermediate running milestones, which included increased mileage every week.

With the system and coaching in place, I just needed to execute the program. As always, there were challenges to overcome. The road to success is never smooth or straight, and is fraught with detours, potholes, and barriers. Sometimes you get lost.

Learn to face challenges and do not let them deter you.

Rather than spending time with family and friends, runners are out on early morning runs and going to bed early. Others may not understand the time and effort needed to complete marathon training and not sympathize with what you are trying to achieve. Marathon training also means running in rain, snow, heat, or cold so we can be prepared to run in any weather.

Unfortunately, runners usually contend with injuries. Blisters, shin splints, and black toes were part of my routine. I learned lots about bandages, orthotics, and specialized running shoes, and eventually found the best equipment for me. In many respects, these obstacles were not challenges. They were just learning experiences that helped me prepare for marathon day.

Naysayers are likely to tell you that you cannot complete the training and finish the marathon. It requires faith in yourself, the program, and your leaders to move forward.

When you get toward the end of the race, don't make the mistake of listening to the negative, whining people around you. There will be groups of people, here and there, who are complaining of how tired they are, and that they can't go any further. Do what I did: find someone who is running ahead of you with a positive mindset and healthy pace, and fix your eyes on them!
—Steve Borgman quoting an unidentified veteran runner at the 2010 Chicago Half-Marathon

I stayed with the program and did everything the group leaders advised us to do. After several months, we were ready to run.

My Houston Marathon experience was definitely different from my Honolulu experience. Prior to the Houston race day, I told people I was training for a marathon, so my friends and family cheered me along the route. When I crossed the finish line in Houston, I was totally thrilled by my accomplishment. I celebrated with my family and friends. After all the celebrating concluded, my thoughts were on what race I should do next.

What was the difference? What had changed? I believe it was the "why." My reason for running the marathon was not just to finish. Instead, I wanted to properly train and immerse myself fully in the journey of completing it. I deserved that finisher's medal.

After the Houston marathon, I found my Honolulu finisher's medal. Both medals are now proudly displayed on my success wall, and I have come to terms with my first experience. It was not a failure. It was just the first step on the road to the successful completion of many more marathons. Now I have run at least one marathon in each of the 50 states of our great country, which allowed me to go places I never would have visited otherwise.

You need to determine what success you want to achieve. Why do you want to achieve such success? Focus on the "why." Determine the steps necessary to achieve the success and find a leader to show you the way, someone who has obtained success in the same endeavor.

Then take *action*.

After you achieve success, enjoy the fruits of your labor and plan the next achievement. See you at the next race!

Biography

Betty Wong

BETTY WONG is an investment fund manager with a private equity firm as well as an entrepreneur with businesses in commercial and residential real estate and Internet marketing. Additionally, she is a practicing attorney helping families overcome divorce, child custody, and guardianship challenges.  She has argued and won a case before the Supreme Court of Texas. Ms. Wong challenged herself to run a marathon in each state before the age of fifty. She completed the last state marathon the week before her fiftieth birthday.

Contact Information

www.desirablerealestateassetmanagementservices.com
info@desirablerealestateassetmanagementservices.com
9203 Hwy 6 South, Suite 124-146
Houston, Texas 77083
281-536-0101

Chapter 21

A Sense of Balance

by Anand Ferco

I find myself often asking what success is and how one measures it—if one does at all. Over the years I think I have zoned into this simple but useful definition: success is the balance one has in his or her life. Balance of money and time; balance of oneness and being busy; balance in material wealth and emotional wealth; balance in action and words. Success is often measured in monetary terms, but what I have found true more often than not is that when measured against this monetary pole, success does not get measured in terms of happiness, family, or, once again, balance. The truly successful people in this world are those who have not only topped the monetary pole but have also excelled in the other facets of life.

The website DailyOm came up with this the other day: "The thing to remember about the world, though, is that it ebbs and flows, expands and contracts, gives and takes, and is by its very nature somewhat unreliable." The only constant in life is change, and the only reliable aspect of life is you and your role in it.

Additionally, I have always been a firm believer in information dissemination, or continual training. Truly vibrant and successful leaders have never held onto their knowledge base; instead they pass it on, knowing that our wealth lies in everyone's wealth. I enjoyed doing this at university and at our family-run plastic recycling company, and I have found it invaluable in training the next leader, the next department head, or the next intern. Anyone who doesn't understand, or doesn't want to, in my experience has deep-set insecurities—which are common to all of us, but the ones who tackle this on head on are the next generation of leaders.

More and more, as the days pile into months, and the months stack up into years, I find myself really taking on board the theory that you are the most, if not the only, important person to listen to. After all, who do you listen to the most? Your own voice—even your best friend or closest relative does not talk to you as much as you do. So don't you think what you nourish your mind with is important? You have choices every day, and the choices you make today will affect your future, so when faced with a choice of what to feed your mind—TV or a good book that will give you tips on personal development and skill—which one do you think you should pick? The question actually is which one do you pick more often than not?

Driving forces are important. Defining or knowing your driving force is probably more difficult, as you probably already know, so let me give you some insight into my driving forces. Now, I have always loved traveling and felt that it not only made me more worldly, more attractive to others, and generally a better story/life teller, but also made me who I am today. In other words, I believe without a doubt that the best form of personal development is traveling this amazing earth we have been blessed with. I did this through university by taking on temp jobs and working weekends so that I could get on a plane to Sweden or Portugal or wherever the cheapest deal was at the time.

Once I got settled into my life in Zimbabwe, hyperinflation (highest in the world at the time) and instability (in economics and politics) kicked in. They say that every cloud has a silver lining and that everything in your life is aligned with your perspective on it. I could have taken the common stand of "life sucks," "it's their fault," "what can I do, I am the victim here" (which was easily done when a loaf of bread skyrocketed to Z$1 trillion), but I was blessed to have a family and a dear friend who was always so bubbly with life that I thought she was drunk most days, and so we walked the path not taken by many. On this path, we said, okay, we are in this situation in Zimbabwe, and things are not working they way they do in other countries, so what silver linings can we find? Guess what we found. Airfares on the national airline were so cheap (1/10 the normal airfare at times) that it was foolish for us not to travel while we could.

Zimbabwe's economy has now changed; for one, we have dollarized to the U.S. dollar, which means that inflation isn't the most important thing to worry about and the average guy on the street can plan his future and save money every month—something that was impossible to think of a few years back, when saving money meant losing money through rampant devaluation. But I meet friends nowadays who say things like, "I didn't use that opportunity to go to Singapore or South Africa or wherever because I could not see past the dire situation." Now that things are stable, they still can't go because the prices to fly to Singapore or South Africa are so expensive, it's not within their budgets. If your eyes are open, some doors are open, and if not fully open, they are ajar if you are willing to see them. I have faith that the friends who were in my life at that time were a gift; they showed me a way to keep traveling even when others were tied by the shackles of "real life." I simply accepted that everyone's "real life" was slightly different.

My paternal grandmother used to say this until the day she passed away: "Those who travel will reap the benefits." There is more truth to this statement than I thought when I was young. In the past few years, I have volunteered in Thailand, lived in a monastery and been ordained as a novice monk, hiked for days on end with severe acute iliotibial syndrome up to the base camp of Mt. Everest—and you want to know what I found? I am leading my team (recycling plastics to ensure a better future for the next generation) in ways I didn't think I could, all thanks to these "extracurricular" activities.

The simple equation is that personal growth and development translates to better leadership at work and at play. Family elders want me to spend more time with their kids, work colleagues want to bounce ideas off me, and friends come to ask questions that allow them to learn, but mostly I am learning from them. Why? I choose to feed my mind with positive thoughts, worthy authors, and challenging ideas, and my travels have always put me in a position where I am surrounded by such.

Let me spell out a few steps anyone can start with. You have probably read or heard them somewhere or another, but I'm here to tell you again and ask you to actually do them. Trust me on this: No successful person has gotten to where they are based on pure luck. They were ready when opportunity came, and they acted. This applies to stay-at-home mothers, to business leaders, to anyone who knows they have a hidden gem in them somewhere. So let's start:

1. Write down what you hold close to your heart. What is important to you? Please don't think you have to follow in the footsteps of tycoon Donald Trump or saintly Mother Teresa—this is *you*. So if that means being a role model for your family, being a leader in your community, or being an inspiration to your nation—write it down. Nothing is too big or too small if

it is important to you. Ideally write these down where you will see them regularly.

2. Write down a life list. This is something I learned before, but now I fully understand its importance. A life list is a list of things you want to experience during your life, like crossing Sydney Harbour Bridge or tandem skydiving. You can always keep adding to your list—it is truly endless, so write it in a booklet or something that you can always go back to, and check them off as you do them!

3. Whatever your position or station in life at the moment, do your job as if you own the business. Do not sit there and blame your boss, your co-workers, or your incompetent subordinates and team members. Trust me, it leads you nowhere of true value. So stand up, raise the bar, and be the best you can be at whatever you do. The amazing thing, whether you believe it yet or not, is that pride in your work, striving for excellence, and being accountable for everything you do has a way of paying you back—I call it karmic career building.

4. Write down your own obituary, or better, an introduction to yourself. Imagine you are about to be introduced on stage—what few lines do you want people to know or remember about you? And yes, this is ego stroking, but it's also what you are aiming for in your life.

5. Take five minutes a day of quiet time. I cannot emphasize this enough—if I had a dollar for every time someone asked me how I fit it all in my day, I would own my own island by now! And the answer is that nine times out of ten, I do it by taking quiet time to listen to myself, removing any distractions. (One out of those ten times, I fit it all in simply by good schedule management.) In the beginning, you will hate it, because you

will be amazed at how much noise our minds are preoccupied with—the aim is to remove all of this and be quiet. It takes patience, practice, and time, so start today. Place this book down next to you, take a deep breath, and close your eyes— every time a thought comes into your mind, gently remove it and continue. Over time the stillness your mind gains will make you more effective as a person and able to achieve more in the same 24 hours that everyone else has. Please don't think that the wealthier people of this world have 25 hours in the day, because they don't!

Never let the beatings of life leave you down because at the end of the day, what truly counts is whether you got up. This was taught to me firsthand by my dad, one of few men of steel, who has been down and back up more than a rollercoaster ride. I saw that a man's true legacy is not if he succeeds or fails in the generic terms we know, but if he is the one who keeps his cool in an argument, gets back up again after huge financial losses, and is still there for others even when he's at his lowest point.

I now know that helping others will always be the way forward and the true steps toward success.

Biography

Anand Ferco

ANAND FERCO was born and educated in Los Angeles and brought up in Portugal, the United Kingdom, and Zimbabwe. A 32-year-old oxymoron, a business-oriented environmentalist, Anand is the director of Polywaste Plastics. He has also cofounded committees and been active on various high-profile  committees within Zimbabwe, including an experts subcommittee for government strategy on post-inflation waste-management solutions. He spends much of his time supporting causes, volunteering to help children with cancer, and traveling overseas to raise education levels of those less fortunate.

Contact Information

anand.ferco@gmail.com
P.O. Box ST1000, Harare, Zimbabwe
263 77 241-7171

Chapter 22

You Can Do Anything You Want...

by Ayn Ulm

• • • if you know how to think. This is true, and my hope is that you will find, as I share my life experiences, challenges, and successes, that nothing is impossible for *you*.

So how do we obtain right thoughts for success? We want a success attitude.

The only thing that can hinder success is giving in to fear and its many masks, which deceive even the "elect." The way to overcome obstacles is to learn to identify masks of fear and uncover their hold on you. For example: "I'm too old now to do such and such."

FEAR is an acronym for False Evidence Appearing Real. It is a *suggestion* that comes to mind, appearing to be our thought, and it can keep us from reaching our goals. We learn from experience, and the learning process teaches us what life is all about; we are always on another journey simultaneously—that of living our lives.

The journey is the goal, for we find that as we obtain whatever we seek, it does not really satisfy; but obtaining the desired result does give us confidence to move forward toward what our hearts call on us to achieve next in this journey of life.

It has been said that success is an attitude. A state of thought. Earl Nightingale says in *The Strangest Secret* that "we become what we think about" (www.earlnightingale.com). Through a process of self-discovery, we must become aware of how and what we think about so that we can change how we think and have a more abundant, successful sense of life.

Attitude is more important than the past, than education,
than money, than circumstances, than what other people think or
say or do. It is more important than appearance, giftedness or skill.
It will make or break a company, a church, a home.
—Charles Swindoll

Looking Back

I grew up the oldest of six children. Our mother raised us as Dad was usually gone. We had very few material possessions, so I learned to think more about ideas rather than things. I was always a dreamer; I always had music playing and was either singing or dancing. I learned to be resourceful, and mother taught us to be honest, reliable, and responsible and to have a strong work ethic. I wanted my brother and sisters to prosper. As I grew up, I kept the desire to help others—that was always my *mission* wherever I worked, but I needed to learn how to set and reach goals for success.

The pivotal point in my life that allowed me to begin moving forward was an awakening I had of my true spiritual identity and of the unlimited possibilities I had in life. This became the foundation for much progress through an enlightened sense of being, and it became the basis to build on from that early childhood desire to help others.

My career provided a wonderful opportunity to help people. As a job developer, I worked with people who were out of work due to the economic situation. Plants were closing down, and these people were definitely in need. I found, however, that the training these people were being given was inadequate to enable them to get back to work. To solve the problem, I envisioned myself teaching small groups what they needed to know. I approached my boss and told him about the challenge I was having placing people on jobs and told him if he would bring the training into our division, I would teach the workshops. He agreed, and then my challenge was what to teach them and how. I understood they had a lot of skills that would transfer to other jobs, but I had to teach them how to adapt and get the jobs in the first place. I searched resources and located material that informed about principles of success and how to set and reach goals as well as how to find, get, and keep a job. I also found many activities to help them think differently—to be aware of their strengths and weaknesses—gaining confidence as they moved forward.

One of the videos I located was by Lou Tice, and he discussed self-talk and looking at goal setting in present tense (www.thepacificinstitute.com). This was an "Aha" moment for me. I loved the video and used it with all the groups. The program was a success, and I gained confidence in my abilities to help others. Later I had the opportunity to obtain and use his complete program on goal setting in training sessions with the Welfare-to-Work Program.

Envisioning what you want and supporting this vision with affirmations is to me *the single most important key in achieving success.* Life is success in and of itself, but without goals, we do not feel successful.

Goal setting in the future tense suggests a lack mentality, and this is a negative foundation.

My next career opportunity required leadership in a supervising capacity. To me, *leadership means inspiring others to be all they can be.* A leader must be caring. Leadership requires the practical application of all the principles of success for oneself as well as for others. In the marketing manager position of an adult education program, I led a team of recruiters to make money for the school. When the team had originally taken over the program, it had been projected to fail. We worked on a mission to serve the people; we encouraged each other, reached our goals, and far exceeded the expectations of the school in our successful results.

One person I hired was the first African American to work for the college. When I was training her for presentations, she seemed insecure, and I encouraged her to be herself and showed her how to accept her success. She worked with goal setting and affirmations, and then she far exceeded anyone else who had ever worked for the college before that time. It was such a privilege and an inspiration to have worked with her and to see her succeed. No limitations here!

With the Welfare-to-Work Program, there were many challenges and many needs of the participants. We worked with goals and affirmations with great success. A mother who had no home or clothes for her children was transitioned into an apartment and provided clothes and food in one week after we worked with her. An individual came by and watched a video on self-talk and affirmations on the way to take the pre-GED test; after taking the test, she got her GED right away. Great results.

We need to learn to affirm to ourselves daily what we want to see happen and to do so in the *present tense.* We learn to set goals on an *abundance* basis rather than on lack. (For more information on this, read *The Abundance Book*, by John Randolph Price.)

Success Principles Taught and Practiced

Vision—Define what you want to do, then see yourself doing it *now*. Learn to write affirmations to yourself, seeing yourself enjoying the vision. How does it look? What does it feel like? Are you enjoying it? It all starts with an idea. The idea must take place within you before you will allow yourself to reach your goal or vision. (Read *You'll See It When You Believe It*, by Wayne Dyer.)

Self-Esteem—Do you see yourself as worth it? Is the goal worth it? You are as your creator made you, and you must love yourself. God is first, and you and your neighbor are second in the requirements for the self-esteem needed to soar and sing in victory. Whitney Houston's song "Greatest Love of All" is about the love that comes first. You cannot love others if you do not love yourself—you will have no love to give. Forgiveness is essential in learning to love yourself and others. All champions must find that space within that allows them to be champions.

Fact vs. Fiction—You must learn distinguish between the truth and a false suggestion of fear. Walt Disney had his first character stolen from him before he created Mickey Mouse. Did that stop him? No. He knew where the idea came from, and he knew he had another idea, so he moved forward and became the successful cartoonist he was, sharing Mickey with all of us. Any thought or suggestion that comes to you telling you it can't be done—no matter how forceful it might be—is fiction. Nothing can stop you *but* you.

Work—It does seem logical that to reach a goal or vision, you will need to work toward that end, and doing so requires a working *commitment*. Working spasmodically is not sufficient since reaching any goal usually requires work at regular intervals.

Perseverance—The real test comes when one must say, "I will do this work and stay with it until the goal is reached." This may be a hardship and require much sacrifice, but the determination to get the job done must take precedence over other options for use of your time and thought.

Faith—This principle relates to self-esteem, for if you do not believe it is possible to reach your goal, you will more than likely not allow yourself to reach it. You must place faith in the principle of abundance in action within yourself.

Inspiration—There will be days or blocks of time when you do not feel like doing anything toward your goal. You must learn what inspires you *to do it anyway.* For example: listening to music, reading inspiring books or articles, talking to mentors, and so forth. Gratitude is a necessary quality at this point. What are you grateful for? *To express gratitude moves your thought past the fear to another level, which allows you to move forward. Remember prayer.* (Read Gerald G. Jampolsky's *Love is Letting Go of Fear.*)

Goodwill—To be truly successful you need to have a spirit of goodwill toward others. You must want to see others blessed and happy and not do anything intentionally to harm or undermine others in reaching your goal. For example, Hitler had many of the principles, but he seemed to miss the mark when it came to goodwill toward others. Remember, you must "love your neighbor as yourself." (Read *The Gentle Art of Blessing,* by Pierre Pradervand.)

Association—This principle is of utmost importance in reaching your vision.

1. You need to identify and associate with those who will encourage you and inspire you to keep working.

2. You must determine that *no one* will keep you from reaching your goal. Sometimes discouraging people are very close to you, and you must learn when and if to discuss your goal with them.

3. Associating with good reading materials and audios as sources of positive feedback is helpful too. (Read *Power of Intention,* by Wayne Dyer.)

Note that these principles are qualities of thought *we already have.* Every time we have reached a goal of some sort (to stop smoking, for example), we have used these principles. Fear may have tried to slow you down or come into your thoughts as a suggestion ("You're never gonna do this, so why try"). You may have been tempted, but you persevered toward reaching your envisioned goal.

In summary, we must first decide what we want—envision the goal—then support our goal with affirmations and be diligent in fulfilling our desire with work, sacrifice, and patience. This is the way of thinking that must be done *to do anything you want.* In the end, you and others will enjoy the benefits of your success.

The remarkable thing is, we have a choice every day regarding the attitude we will embrace for that day. We must develop and maintain that attitude of *success consciousness* every day and let our enriched lives attest to our sincerity.

Biography

Ayn Ulm

AYN ULM is a global career facilitator/instructor and a life coach. She has successfully transitioned many unemployed workers into new career oppor-  tunities by using success principles in workshops and one-on-one coaching sessions. Described as a "champion motivator," she is also a singer, who has performed all over the Southeast. Ayn lives with her husband, two parrots, and a dog in Anderson, South Carolina.

Contact Information

http://patsiayn.angelfire.com
unique13@bellsouth.net
321 Hembree Road
Anderson, SC 29625
864-222-3440

Chapter 23

Birthing Success

by Tanya MarCia

I overheard her praying. In a raspy voice just above a whisper, she told God she was grateful that she'd never really wanted for anything. She told him that she had grown tired and was ready now. She had lived a good life. The next morning, sitting on the side of her bed eating her breakfast, she slumped over. As her daughter slapped her face shouting, "Momma! Momma!" she repeated, "I'm all right. I'm all right." And took her last breath. Annie B. Monroe, my great-grandmother, died two months shy of her 101st birthday. If one is blessed to be healthy and live one hundred plus years, I believe they know a little about success.

Annie would be the first to tell you that the secret to success is that there is no secret. Born in 1886, she knew that the same things that determined success in her day are applicable today. She had a passion for life and declared in her youth that she would live 100 years. Her faith in God, her wisdom, and her level of integrity made her an icon of leadership in our family, in the coal mining community where she spent her early adult life, and throughout the state of West Virginia. She was a strong advocate of education and self-discipline. She dedicated her life to excellence and serving others. She believed that being active preserved one's mind and body, and that rest was essential.

My great-grandmother was a midwife long before it was fashionable for women to have careers and before blacks had the right to vote. She handled the responsibility of saving and preserving life with no more than hands-on experience and a fundamental high school education. She caught babies until she was in her mid-80s, and is credited for having delivered over 1,000 children. Her most shameful testament, and her most proud, was that she only lost one. With tears in her eyes, she would tell us that the baby was in trouble, and she had done everything she could. The doctor wasn't able to make it in time.

She stumbled into midwifery without intent. Standing beside Dr. Anderson during his rounds on a pregnant neighbor, she heard him tell her friend, "When your time comes, call Annie. If she needs me, she'll call me." That began her career as a midwife. Working as an unofficial apprentice alongside Dr. Anderson, she learned the skills to deliver babies. He would call on her for assistance because she remained calm and focused in a crisis. Despite her initiation into the world of midwifery being accidental, she developed a passion for ushering babies into the world. Well into her career, she was awarded a license for her extensive experience through a grandfather clause when more stringent requirements were instituted for lay midwifery practice.

Passion was at the heart her love for the art of midwifery. She would encourage us to follow our hearts and do what we loved long before the adage was a part of pop culture. I recall watching her pace back and forth in front of the living room window, waiting for a frantic husband. Barely five feet and stout, her frame was bound in an old-fashioned corset taut under a starched white dress exclusive for birthing babies. A mangled truck would screech into the driveway, and a nervous husband would whisk Grandma away, little black bag in tow. Off limits to the hands of curious little girls like me, it clanked with tiny vials and shiny accoutrements for bringing babies into the world. Days later, Grandma would return home tired but never weary, a glint in her eye, and a smile in her heart. Sitting around the kitchen table, we listened while she cast a spell with a story of the miracle of life and the events of her journey into the mountains to catch a babe.

Back then blacks lived separate from whites. The word "segregation" didn't exist; that's just the way it was. In the coal mining community, the railroad track marked the line of separation, a line one should never cross if one's skin wasn't the right color. If you were black, and especially if you were a black woman, venturing deep into the mountain hollows in unknown territory was a life-threatening risk. When a baby was coming, Grandma gave no thought to skin color or what lines should or should not be crossed. A baby was on the way, and she intended to welcome that baby safely into the world. She stepped out in faith every time she left the house with focus and clear intent and no thought to being in harm's way. She was "the midwife" and renowned throughout the state. Husbands and family traveled far to fetch her to catch their babies. She delivered white and black babies alike and never incurred an incident that threatened her well-being.

Born to a black woman and a white slave owner, my great-grandmother was allowed to learn to read and write at an early age. She taught her husband to read during their courtship. She emphasized the importance of education, especially to the girls in the family, as a means of self-reliance. "Never depend on a man to take care of you" was her mantra. All eight of her children were college educated, which was no small feat, especially in the early 1900s. Each year a child was to enter college, Granddaddy would sell a plot of land to cover the expense. They belonged to a select few of blacks who owned property, and this fortune placed them in a position to take advantage of the opportunities that knowledge combined with skill could bring. The issue was never if her children or grandchildren would attend college; it was where.

Self-mastery and discipline were essential to living under her roof. Excuses were never tolerated, and whining was not allowed. Grandma Monroe was a subscriber to "just do it" before Nike was a thought. She believed if you worked long enough and hard enough, you could accomplish anything you set your mind to do. However, just doing it was not enough. You had better "do it well or not at all." She would admonish her children with "bring home an 'A' or don't come home," which instilled a code of excellence in each of them. She encouraged her children to be their best selves. Each one honored her declaration by rising to the height of his or her chosen profession.

Having a spirit of service was core to her beliefs. Her passion for catching babies extended far beyond the moment the child came into the world. During the time she practiced midwifery, it was believed that a woman should stay in bed for nine days after giving birth. Grandma would stay with the new mother for over a week cooking, cleaning, and caring for the mother and her family. Most times the family was unable to pay for her services, so she came home with jars of apple butter, or a chicken, maybe with a sack of potatoes as a token of their appreciation. A family's inability to pay never stopped her from attending a birth and being away from her own children to tend to someone else's. Being of service was her calling, and it was never about the money. She was dedicated and committed to her craft and helping anyone in need.

Her definition of health was defined by one's ability to care for self and remain active. Her declaration to live 100 years had the stipulation that she be fully capable of caring for her own needs and living independently in her own home. No one in our family can recall one day that she was ever ill with even the slightest of maladies. In her favor was the fact that she had lived half her life before the invention of prepared food in cardboard boxes and microwave ovens, before gyms with stationary bikes and treadmills, and before ozone layers torn from smog and pollution. Her food was wholesome and home grown. It didn't need to be fortified with vitamins or preserved with chemicals and additives. Water was her energy drink. She had no concept of exercise as we know it. Without the luxury of machines and gadgets, everything she accomplished in a day's work was done with manual labor and a bit of elbow grease. She went to bed with the chickens and rose with the sun. Sundays were sacred and days for rest. She lived a life of balance and harmony, cornerstones for sound health and integral to growing old with grace.

Asking for the secret to success is like asking for a pill to lose weight. It's just not that easy. But my great-grandmother taught me that the keys to a successful and fulfilling life, regardless of your definition, are simple and timeless. Common disciplines repeated consistently over time will yield the results of a life fully lived. Take a risk by exploring new territory. Never be afraid to step out in faith. You may discover a love you never knew existed. Have a passion for living and for what you love to do. Strive to do your best in every endeavor. Imagine that everything you do is stamped with your name, and never do a thing that you wouldn't be proud to attach to your signature. Find a way to contribute value to the lives of others. Remember that health begins in your mind, with the ideas and beliefs you feed yourself. Honor the body you've been given with a balance of activity, rest, and nourishment. Make learning a lifelong habit.

I've spent thousands of dollars on personal development seminars, weekend and week-long workshops. I've read more books on leadership, business, and success than I can count. I've been trained and mentored by millionaires and billionaires. But there was no need for me to ever look past my upbringing for the steps to success. There was no need to look outside my home to find a heroine. Nothing compares to the legacy of my great-grandmother's life of love and service, and its ripple effect into the lives of everyone who met her. I honor her memory by living a powerful and bold life, fully self-expressed. I honor her with being authentic and true to what she taught me. I honor her by sharing her success and birthing her story.

Biography

Tanya MarCia

TANYA MARCIA is a published author, professional ghostwriter, and certified copywriter. She writes for people on the move with powerful messages to deliver and inspirational stories to tell. She is sought for her exceptional ability to paint pictures with words that inspire bold action. Tanya  is dedicated to empowering others to live a purpose-driven life, a "why" worthy of their dreams fully self-expressed. Tanya is married to the love of her life, Fritz, and they are the proud guardians of a delightful coyote dog, Ginger.

Contact Information

www.writerstouch.net
Tanya@writerstouch.net
505-867-4414 (office)
505-688-0870 (mobile)

Chapter 24

A Child of Africa

YES, WE CAN, TOO!

by Colette Bowers

Born and raised in Zimbabwe, I am privileged to live in one of the most beautiful countries on the African continent, with picturesque landscapes and sunshine and blue sky for most of the year. Zimbabwe is also home to the Big Five and the mighty, breathtaking Victoria Falls, aptly named *mosi oa tunya* (the smoke that thunders). However, even with all its beauty, our country has been one of the most challenging environments in which to live.

The last decade has left an indelible mark in the livelihoods of Zimbabweans from all walks of life. Simple things that other nations generally take for granted, like turning on a tap for running water, switching on a light, or going to the supermarket to buy bread, became a luxury. Empty shelves in the supermarket became commonplace, as well as there being no fuel at the pumps for our vehicles. Our currency, the Zimbabwe dollar, weakened, followed by a collapsed banking system. Jokingly, we all became millionaires overnight. During this time, many entrepreneurs were born out of necessity, as the pay earned through a single job was just not enough to make a living, compounded by the fact that the currency itself wasn't worth the paper on which it was printed by the time payday arrived.

Health services deteriorated, with skilled doctors and nurses seeking greener pastures elsewhere. Endless lines became the order of the day—for medication, basic commodities such as bread and milk, and wages. Inverters and generators brought light and some semblance of normality into homes for those who could afford them. For the majority, though, candles flickered in the still dark nights, and trees were not spared, for they had to keep fires burning for cooking, to provide warmth and give light.

However, *we made a plan* and we survived! Thankfully, we have come through the worst of this trying time and are much stronger for having experienced this, as characters are built on the backbone of adversity. Because every single day posed a challenge, our network of friends and associates became our sources of strength and support. Through this, relationships were built that will last a lifetime. If we could manage these challenges and somehow be successful during this period, there was every reason for us to be successful in anything else.

For too long, Africa has been described as the "deep, dark continent," home to war, conflict, and disease. Such a narrow perspective needs to change, given that Africans have a rich cultural heritage, and Africa nests some of the most influential people, who are making great strides in all areas of life. Most Africans have fought hard for their success, having confronted trial and controversy, compared to their counterparts in the more privileged countries who tend to have things much easier.

As the youngest in a family of four children, life as a child was fairly easy for me. Being spoiled and usually getting my own way meant that

I didn't have to compromise in too many situations. As a fairly average family, we weren't born with a silver spoon in our mouths, but our parents made sure we didn't go without, and love was always overflowing in our home. We grew up with a family closeness that most families don't have the pleasure of knowing or understanding. My siblings are my best friends, and I'd be lost without them. Through all my crazy ideas and various business ventures, they have always been there to support me. Sadly, with the economic meltdown in the country, the average Zimbabwean family has been split, as relatives left in search of more stable environments. As a typical example, my parents moved to South Africa; my brother, Alban, is based in the United Kingdom; my sister Loreen is in Australia; while Bernie, my other sister, and I remained in the country.

My parents have been true role models and taught me that as long as I put my mind to it, I could do anything. And this has seen me through most of my endeavors. Little did I know growing up just how important this statement was: "If you put your mind to it!" Now I know that's exactly where success starts—with one's mindset.

Qualifying as a chartered accountant in 1989, I went into the corporate world and worked with figures behind a desk for a further seven years. I soon realized this was not my passion, and my ladder to success was leaning against the wrong wall. And I was good at what I did. But I've also now learned that good is the enemy of great. We all prefer to stay in our comfort zone, 'cause that's where we are, well, the most comfortable! Although being a chartered accountant did make for a good background education, I knew there was more to life than looking after someone else's finances and making someone else rich.

My next venture was buying a food franchise in South Africa, and this was a real eye-opener into a "traditional" business that really doesn't work. We were told that it would take about five years to make a profit, and yet we still made the investment. Needless to say, the franchise business lasted only about two years and ended up being a very expensive lesson in life. I am now a co-owner in a successful medical company, supplying implants to patients who require total hip and knee replacements. This, in itself, is quite challenging because most international supply companies steer clear of doing business in the country, as Zimbabwe struggles to find its road to democracy.

I have always seriously believed that network marketing is the business model of the future, but I couldn't really get passionate about nutrition, makeup, and plastics. Finally, I found the company and the industry that I could get passionate about—travel! And life will never be the same.

The best business tip I ever heard was "Never quit. Never ever quit!" Perseverance is the key to everything because, I do believe, good ideas will eventually fall on good people. It's not about how many times you fall down; it's about how many times you get back up again, and the latter should always be just one more time.

My definition of success is rather simple—never having to make a decision based on time and money ever again. To have the financial and time freedom to follow my passion, to do what I want, when I want, and spend time with the special people in my life. Because life is too short to not be doing what you love with the ones that love, support, and celebrate you.

Leadership for me is the ability to lead others down a road that they would not normally go down, with the map and tools to help get them where they want to go, to work with people, building relationships along the way that actually mean something. Leaders need to be trustworthy, passionate about what they do, enthusiastic, committed to excellence, supportive and encouraging, remaining positive no matter what comes their way. A leader's vision should be bigger than that of the people they lead. To communicate effectively is definitely one of the most important characteristics of being a leader and a lesson that is so often overlooked in all areas of our lives. Lives would change immeasurably—not only financially but emotionally too—if we could all communicate better with each other, and this has got to start with the youth.

My favorite quote of all time has to be the one from Margaret Mead: "Never doubt that a small group of thoughtful committed citizens can change the world. Indeed, it is the only thing that ever has." Reiterated by Zig Ziglar: "If 2 or 3 agree on a common purpose, nothing is impossible," it shows that it doesn't take an army of people to make a difference in the lives of many.

My first role model was Oprah Winfrey, a woman who overcame so many obstacles in her life to become the powerful woman that she is today. She continues to positively affect lives on a daily basis. However, a recent role model is Marc Accetta. Little did I know that when I met Marc Accetta and his company team in London that it would change the course of my life forever.

We don't know what we don't know. This is one of the short, but powerful, messages I took home after seeing Marc Accetta at one of his live speaking events. Marc gets to the very core of what makes us tick. He is the missing link between the current education system and success in life. While formal education is important and necessary, the information that Marc shares with you leaves you thinking, "I wish I had known this 20 years ago!"

It's my passion to get this education to as many of the youth as possible. I look at my 15-year-old son, Gino, and I am positive that he can have the future that he desires, knowing that he is now being equipped not only with a formal education, but also with the *right* education. The current education system doesn't teach the skills we need to know to be successful in life, such as leadership, communication, and goal setting. If we could just get this education to the minds of the youth, we could change a generation.

Knowing that this was just what we needed back home, I decided to approach the company speakers when they were travelling to neighboring South Africa. Starting with one of the most inspiring speakers, I have had the honor of seeing Johnny Wimbrey present his seminar *Think and Win Big*. It took eight emails before Johnny finally said yes to coming to Zimbabwe, but I never gave up, and the impact he has had on our lives will be felt for a very long time. From that seminar, I have seen lives change right before my very eyes, and knowing that we had a little something to do with that is such an amazing feeling.

Johnny taught us to go back to our dreams, and one of the stories close to my heart is that of my sister, Bernie, who in her twenties had a passion for fashion design. Life took over, and her dreams of designing took a back seat. Now, more than 20 years later, after being inspired by Johnny's words, she has started her passion once again. Bernie recently participated in a local fashion show with designs that could grace any catwalk in New York, London, or Paris.

With Johnny as our first official event, and quite by accident, our events management company Sapphire Events was born. Sapphire Events has now given us the opportunity to rub shoulders with inspiring speakers such as Jefferson Santos, with "Your Breakthrough in 2011," and most recently Marc Accetta and Matt Morris, who spoke on the "Art of Leadership" and the "Art of Persuasion." Together with these amazing speakers, we have been given the chance to impact so many lives around us, particularly the youth, and we are so thankful for this opportunity.

Success is not about *leaving* wealthy but about *living* wealthy, and being wealthy is not just about the money. It's about living a good life, with a purpose, with good relationships, and making a difference—just one life at a time.

Success is a choice. Success is an attitude. And we have the choice to decide our attitude every single moment of our lives.

Biography

Colette Bowers

With a bachelor of accounting science (Honors) degree and qualified as a chartered accountant, COLETTE BOWERS is now following her passion of having an impact on the lives around her by assisting in equipping them with the skills that are so vital to being successful in life, focusing  especially on the youth. As one of the owners of Sapphire Events, she plans regular inspirational and motivational events, ensuring that the participants' lives will never be the same. Colette resides with her son, Gino, and lives by the motto "Making a difference, one life at a time."

Contact Information

colette.bowers@gmail.com

17 Autumn Road, Rivonia, Johannesburg, South Africa

+27 11 5633883

+27 72 3647655

55 Borrowdale Brooke Village, Borrowdale Brooke, Harare, Zimbabwe

+263 4793778

+263 77 2235091

Chapter 25

My Vertical Success

by Cecilia Matthews

*D*efining "vertical" success is easy, as compared to defining "worldly" success. Why? Well, for one, the two run in opposite directions to each other.

The latter focuses primarily on financial and material wealth, as though this is the only road to success. The first one, on the other hand, pledges love, peace, joy, abundance, prosperity, and freedom. Vertical success differs from worldly success in that it has been designed and programmed before we came to this earth. From day one, we are wired and connected by an invisible line to this vertical success, so we are born already successful.

Even though we can't see it, it is real and available to all of us.

No matter under which flag we live, which culture we come from, or which religion we follow, it is everywhere. This vertical success is God, and from my heart and soul, I would like to share with you my personal experience.

Before I go on, let me mention that I'm not a religious person, an evangelist, or a church lady by any means, with the intention to preach, persuade, or change someone's personal and religious beliefs. I define this vertical success as the awareness and understanding of our own spirituality and the relationship and connection to the Source who created us. The sooner we acknowledge it, the faster and freer we are going to grow and develop the universal Master Plan designed for us.

But due to the world and its emphasis on the physical and material, the value of the spiritual gets suppressed and dismissed, leaving us only the choice to go horizontal.

This awareness has been present and real to me for as long as I can remember, since my early childhood. On my own, I conversed with God, hiding in a small closet, every time something or someone bothered me. It was my little secret. How nurtured and powerful I felt every time He spoke to me.

Seeking to connect with God from that time, and after moving to this beautiful country from Colombia, I was exposed to other church denominations and religions, very different from my Catholic upbringing at home.

It was fascinating the diversity and the luxury they displayed. In college, I purposely enrolled in a world religion class, curious about how the rest of the world viewed God. Even though most of them talked about the same God I knew, their contradictions and the conflict of interest among them totally confused me and uninspired me to join them, so my interest declined.

My career and studies became my priority and focus, and although I lacked nothing, and everything on the outside looked nice and normal, an emptiness inside of me kept growing and growing like a tumor, suffocating me and dragging me down.

After two decades of "soldier discipline"—collecting degrees, attaining possessions, and working continually—how dare I feel so lost, confused, and depressed? Determined to find out if all this was part of my life plan, I took on a relentless mission to find God on my own. No one came to my door; no one beat me up with a Bible or dragged me to a revival meeting to help me find Him.

I knew where I had kept Him quietly for so long: inside my closet.

I spent hours, weeks, months, and years studying, reading, and listening to Him and His Word, with the hope that He would provide me with all the answers that the world could never offer me. Little by little, He started showing me how He operates, and how simple it is to follow Him. He welcomed me back after I had disconnected from Him.

This was fifteen years ago, and ever since, I have wasted no time in making up for all the time lost with Him.

I know today that absolutely everything I experienced and passed through in my life was part of His design for my vertical success. Not only did He fill my emptiness, but He also brought out the greatest happiness, peace, joy, and freedom I've ever experienced in my entire life. Along with that came the many rewards, victories, and successes that have taken place in my life from that time, such as the godly and loving relationship I share with my husband of 20 years, where we have become as one—"mashed potatoes," I call it—as He planned.

I gained freedom by attaining so much knowledge and wisdom in learning how to heal my body naturally when conventional drugs failed me. By the way, healing was not on my goal list. It was on His.

And in my finances, my vertical success surpassed what we know and believe here on earth. Imagine debts disappearing before your eyes, just by asking, and a daily harvest, based on all the seeds planted for so long. The list is too long, but I'm sure some of you get my point. Some may consider it magic, but it is real!

We don't need to wait for a catastrophe, a terminal illness, or an accident to "conveniently" access our vertical success. Why wait? He is our insurance and protection plan. Why not enjoy and use it while we're on this earth?

Remember, He gave us 10 straightforward rules to go by, and His formula is simple: believe, have trust, have faith, and obey.

He is my greatest divine mentor, the One we all wish to have. I'm also grateful for the "spiritual" earth mentors He put in my life, like my unbelievable mother, whose amazing spirituality and wisdom have touched every aspect of my life, who taught me about giving, loving, and respecting. My husband, whose leadership and fearless work ethic have inspired me and others to achieve the impossible, and my gorgeous cats, are the best mentors I've ever had in the "unconditional love" department. These animals were part of His Plan for me, and I couldn't be happier.

Regardless of whatever circumstance happens during your life journey, don't ever give up. Always forgive yourself first, laugh, and make every day count.

No matter who you are, where you are, or what you've done, remember God is the only One who would never reject you, or question your appearance and life experience. So you have nothing to lose or risk, and He doesn't mind if you go back to where you came from.

This vertical success is a lifetime work in progress, exciting and challenging, but made easy by His love and gift to us. I couldn't imagine walking today without Him, in this lost and troubled world we live in, where injustice and lies are fed to us daily. He is the best weapon we have for survival. And wouldn't it be a dream come true to have all children exposed to this vertical success since birth? How then would the future world look? Unimaginable: no lies, no thieves, no killers, no hunger, no wars.

And what if we all glue the broken world together with love, by stretching our arms wide to reach our brothers and sisters all around the globe, to join us as a family of one? All this is possible if we are willing to do it.

My life today can be described as Heaven on earth. No matter what challenge, circumstance, or adversity hits, He is always there to take care of me. Somehow my world has shifted a lot, and I don't fear it anymore.

Allow me to invite you to explore this rewarding path to your vertical success, where all possibilities and dream are within reach. You will not be disappointed.

Biography

Cecilia Matthews

CECILIA MATTHEWS is an entrepreneur, an intuitive, a natural healer, and a health coach with over 25 years of research in health, wellness, personal development, and spiritual growth. She graduated with honors and a multi-major degree and now uses her true gifts and talents to help people and animals heal naturally and quickly.

Cecilia first uncovered the power of our bodies to heal themselves through her own experience with challenging and chronic physical conditions. Now she creates customized programs to help her clients get results, giving them the ability and knowledge to take their health and healing to the next level.

Contact Information

www.MyVerticalSuccess.com
cecilia@MyVerticalSuccess.com

Chapter 26

In Times of Struggle, We Often Become the Most Resourceful

by Mikkel Pitzner

If you think you can . . . or think you can't . . . you're right.
—Henry Ford

When you hear the stories of self-made successful people, you will often find similarity in how they went through some struggle, got to a real low point when they decided they were not going to take it anymore, and decided that they would pull themselves out of the rut once and for all.

For me, this happened quite recently. It was an experience where the pendulum of my financial situation went from the one extreme to the other. You may be suffering from the same economic crisis the world is still trying to recover from today, and I would like to bring you some hope that you can change your situation.

You can say I was born with a silver spoon in my mouth, but I was not necessarily handed a lot of spending money as such. Certainly my highly successful self-made father had provided a framework in which we did not need anything materially growing up.

This, however, did not prevent me from getting into a situation of overextending myself financially when I became a young adult and bought my first house in 1991. The house was absolutely fantastic, but the financial burden of the mortgage gave rise to huge stress, especially at each quarter, when payments were due. My own income was still too small to support what it took.

I kept on struggling with this burden, and some years I made greater successes than others and the financial pain decreased. In spring 2008, certain turns of events led to a financial windfall that made me very well off, and by summer that same year, when I decided to sell my house and move abroad, I was hugely rewarded by the appreciation my house had gone through during the 14 years I had owned it. You might say that this was my first struggle through a situation of hardship when I landed in a beautiful spot. That summer I was on top of the world and had a very healthy bank account.

I felt like a king. Life was good, and I was on a roll, spending money fast and almost believing I could walk on water. I bought loads of art, a top model Ferrari, and customized super expensive Ducati motorbikes (yes, plural).

I felt an obligation to put the large amount of money to work in order to grow it further, and I felt nothing could go wrong. Yes, I have to admit I wanted more (pure and simple greed), but mostly, because of my upbringing and mindset, I felt obligated to do so rather than just have the money sit in a bank account doing nothing. I accepted a high-risk profile and placed my money into various investment positions, some of them very fancy and technical, such as highly geared currency swap positions, which basically means you borrow loads of money to be invested on top of your own money in order to reach even greater results quicker.

But then the bubble burst. The financial crisis set in with great force especially around September 2008, and although my investments were spread over many different modes, spanning various owned businesses, partnership businesses, stocks and shares in many different industries and sectors, in order to spread and reduce the risk considerably, the crisis was so severe that no matter which of my money placements I looked at, losses across the board were a reality, especially my currency swap positions, which had been so heavily geared that I faced the brink of bankruptcy by the year end.

At the height of my investment positions, I had debts to the tune of approximately 6 million dollars, so when the crisis showed its ugly teeth and that year's financial tax report had to be tallied up, my net worth was hugely negative exiting that year. Had I sold off everything that I had in my name including the last shirt off my back, I would still have been left with a huge debt load. This was not good and certainly no fun at all.

The banks I had been working well with up till then, and that months earlier had loved me so much and pushed to lend me even more money, suddenly were not so friendly, demanding repayments and realization of the stocks, and so forth. My other businesses either added to the losses or remained stagnant, providing me with no improvement.

I had no money coming in, loads of obligations, no access to money, a business that continued to lose money, and I had bills to pay. The banks were not accommodating nor showing empathy. My father had died a few years earlier, and his wealth had been placed into a trust fund from which we children were getting nothing.

It was a dire situation. The pain grew, and stress ran on red alert constantly. The burden became excruciating, and a way out seemed impossible. Everywhere I turned, the world economy was in shambles. Even some of the greatest AAA-rated banks had cracked, countries were in default, entire industries on the verge of disintegration. Bankruptcies among companies and people went sky high, and no improvement in the world economy was in sight. I reached a point where it seemed like the only option was quite simply to throw in the towel.

Enough! Enough! Stop this pain!

Then it happened. A turning point. Something inside of me said, "No, no way you can give up. Screw the banks. Screw this situation. You can do it. Pull yourself together and find a way to get through. Show them. Show them all."

Someone once told me that when you are in a real fix, pressed up against the wall with nowhere to run, it is actually not that bad at all because it makes you realize you cannot escape but just have to face the enemy and fight your way through. As human beings, we try to avoid the pain and steer around it, but usually you will find that the greatest rewards are through the pain, whether as part of your personal development and growth or related to financial breakthroughs. It is through the pain that we often move, progress, and transform ourselves the most to a better and stronger situation or indeed to a better and stronger version of You.

I cleaned up my positions as much as possible and demanded that the banks hold on a bit with other positions. I ramped up activities and business where it seemed we could make some headway, sold off the company that was bleeding and robbing my time, energy, and focus. I sold off inventory that I could realize at acceptable levels. I reinvented myself into a new role of consulting in a field that I had never worked in before nor ever had any experience in, and I embraced calculated risk, offering myself for free in order to place myself in a position that could aid me in my quest for success and prosperity.

By May 2011, I managed to pay off all my bank and credit card debts, leaving me completely debt free. My million-dollar home is not burdened by a mortgage. I have no super high-risk investments in my portfolio. My companies are growing and making money. I am not quite back financially to my peak, but I am getting there. I know that my new setup entails way less risky positions; I have much more lucrative avenues of future revenue streams; and perhaps more important, my outlook on value has changed dramatically, improving me much as a person to the benefit of those around me, my family and myself.

And I still have most of the art, the Hummer, the Ferrari, and the Ducatis, although I have put most of this up for sale—want to buy them?

Unless success is accidental, such as winning a big lottery, I believe it starts with a decision. The decision that you will go out there and do whatever it takes and will not falter or give up before you have gotten your result.

But to support the decision you really have believe that you can do it. You see, if you don't believe, you are actually just giving up beforehand, and your internal communication will tell you that you might as well not take any steps toward improving your situation to an extent that will make any real difference. And unfortunately, it seems that although human beings have proven incredibly resourceful when really needed, we also all seem to have a gene that makes us look for excuses for not taking that step. That's why most people never take any action but just accept their daily routine with their ordinary job that they possibly do not even like that much.

And remember: Even if the mountain seems too overwhelming or the road you need to go is immensely long, remember that a marathon starts with just one step, the first step. But don't wait around. Don't wait for that perfect moment. Perfect moments do not come by often by themselves. You have to create them yourself by doing.

To aid you in your quest in finding the strength and mental flexibility, you should fuel up with the right fuel. Not only do I mean that you should have a healthy fit between mind and body, but also that you should continuously fuel your brain with great sources of inspiration. There are loads of motivating success stories out there available in many forms, not least the success stories of others who have made it to big results overcoming great obstacles and challenges along the way. By fueling up, you accumulate a lot of knowledge and inspiration that will help you model others who have made it before you.

Remember also to give yourself a little bit of credit and celebrate the small successes along the way to remind you that you are getting somewhere and that it is worth it to push through.

Be open to look for success in unusual places or through unusual paths. When in June 2008 I decided to leave my home country of Denmark and move to the United States, and simultaneously decided to make changes in my career, I actually found a need with a local company near where I moved to and addressed the company's CEO, demonstrating that they had that need.

I then offered to take care of this role for *free*—something that was hard to say no to. Nine months later this company was so pleased that they voluntarily offered me $75,000 for the work and $100,000 to continue another year. The subsequent year, the offer for yet another year amounted to $170,000.

What's more, the provision of my services is on a consultancy basis with variable hours, which means that I choose my own working hours and how many hours I put into it. In other words, I am basically my own boss and remain free to do whatever else I wish, run my own businesses next to this, have other clients, and accrue other sources of revenue and income too. The services were also in an area in which I had never worked. To achieve extraordinary results, be prepared to reinvent yourself. I acquired the skills I needed from the continuous fueling of my mind over time with resources, books, and knowledge wherever I could find it.

The new world has made it possible to find avenues to use whatever small skill or specialized knowledge you may possess and to amplify that to get your message out there, earning you noticeable returns in a very short time. And it can be done with very little monetary investment.

Remember also that many opportunities present themselves if you look, perhaps especially in times of crisis. You may possess skills or knowledge that could help others, that they would be willing to pay for. Put yourself out there and serve others and you shall be rewarded.

So to recap, my recommendations for anyone who wishes to instill and achieve success:

- Decide to make that change.
- Believe that it is possible and that you can do it.
- Fuel up yourself along the way with supporting materials.
- Celebrate your small successes along the way.
- Model success and successful people.
- Act. Take that first step, and do so now.
- Look for success and opportunities in unusual places.
- Reinvent yourself.
- Most important, serve others. Give generously and you shall receive—this is very much the order today in the new world.

In closing, instill in yourself the best possible habits. By making them your lifestyle, and by the compound effect as described by Darren Hardy in his book *The Compound Effect*, your changes today will adjust your trajectory and will yield great results in your future, far bigger than anticipated.

Winning is not a sometime thing; it's an all time thing. You don't win once in a while, you don't do things right once in a while, you do them right all the time. Winning is habit. Unfortunately, so is losing.—Vince Lombardi

Biography

Mikkel Pitzner

MIKKEL PITZNER is a serial entrepreneur; professional board member in Denmark, Sweden, and the United States; social media expert and consultant; small-time investor; and dreamer extraordinaire. Mikkel is a partner in the unique marketing and trailer rental company Freetrailer,  which currently operates throughout Denmark and Sweden, with more countries to come.

Originally from Denmark, Mikkel used to run what became the fourth-largest car rental company and a leasing company he doubled in size, as well as owning and operating the largest limousine service company in Denmark, which he managed to grow 3200% during the first year of ownership alone. He also successfully ran an import and distribution company for scuba diving equipment. Mikkel currently resides in Florida with his wife, Olga, and nine-month-old son, Gabriel.

Contact Information

www.mikkelpitzner.com
mp@mikkelpitzner.com

Chapter 27

Change Starts in the Mind

by Rev. Dean Decastro

One of the critical factors of success is the ability to change oneself. What are some of your personal problems that keep you from achieving success in every area of your life? Is it procrastination? Indecisiveness? Perfectionism? Inconsistency? Lack of confidence? Before you can change your life, you have to change yourself.

Zig Ziglar said it best: "Before you can have, you got to do; and before you can do, you got to be." The late Jim Rohn echoed this philosophy of success when he defined success as "something you attract by the person you become." A preacher once said, "Your talent is your reputation before men; your character is your reputation before God."

Changing one's weak character is not easy. But it is possible. And it is also simple. It's as simple as reciting the first five letters of the English alphabet: ABCDE.

Real change requires an inside look. Permanent changes come from the inside out. It is important for us all to know how our programmed beliefs and judgments of an event create reactions that are actually sabotaging the positive change process.

Let's take a look at the ABCDE starting point for personal change.

A the activating event or situation

B the belief, or our inner perception of the event

C the consequent emotions and behaviors

When reading the alphabet, we don't go from A to C without passing through B. Any event or circumstance (A) is powerless in itself to produce an emotional response (C) until it has been evaluated (B). In other words, it's not what happens to us that causes our problems; it's our interpretation or opinion of what happens to us that determines our thoughts, feelings, actions, and responses.

D deleting the old programming that's causing our problems

E exchanging the limiting beliefs with the sound beliefs that are in alignment with reality

The old computer adage GIGO (garbage in, garbage out) applies just as well to our brains. Our brains are like tape players. We have the ability to record new programs over the wrong programming. Let's illustrate with a practical example:

A (activating situation) Minister whose church is not growing

B (belief) I am a worthless person

C (consequent emotion) Low mood, perhaps even depression

Eleven years ago, my wife and I started a bilingual Asian church in New York City. The church has been growing slowly but steadily; however, often I would feel depressed when I compared my current one-hundred-member church with the over-a-thousand-member church that I had previously led.

The ABCDE system of change made me realize that it was not the current size of my church that was causing my depression and unhappiness; it was my evaluation that I am a worthless person. As a Bible-believing Christian, I am responsible for disputing and deleting this wrong belief and exchanging it with the following belief: "My worth as a person is not because of what I do but because of who I am. In Christ, I am highly favored, greatly blessed, and deeply loved."

The Power of Thought

The first three letters, ABC, underscore the importance of our belief system. Never underestimate the power of thought. According to Dr. Caroline Leaf, a psychologist who has researched the science of thought for many years, every time you have a thought, it is actively changing your brain and your body—for better or for worse. In her book, *Who Switched Off My Brain?*, Dr. Leaf clearly illustrates how the latest breakthroughs in neuroscience prove that you can break the cycle of toxic thinking; you can break unhealthy patterns.

In numerous studies over the last several decades, scientists from both quantum physics and neuroscience have clearly shown that thoughts are things. They create energy and messages that are even transferred between human beings. A great book that describes how we transfer our energy, positive or negative, to others is the *Hidden Messages in Water*, by Masaru Emoto, a world-famous scientist. His book describes over twenty years of research and experimentation on water crystals.

For instance, Dr. Emoto took two pitchers of water and placed them in separate rooms. One pitcher was exposed to beautiful music like Bach and Mozart. The other was exposed to Acid Rock. He describes other experiments where he talked to one beaker of water lovingly and to another harshly. In both the above examples, the soft music and loving words produced beautiful crystals, and hard music and bad words produced ugly crystals. This book provides the scientific evidence to support the truism that our internal perception of what happens to us actually shapes our reality.

The Definition of Insanity

The letter D points to the choice we have in deleting the wrong programming that's impeding our success in life. As human beings, we were given the power to choose what we should think. We can use the power of our will to override old dominant habits and create new ones. We can literally change any area of our life and create the future we desire.

People who don't want to change their limiting beliefs have problems with pride. A good definition of insanity is to keep doing the same thing again and again, expecting a different result. As the saying goes, "If you keep on doing what you are doing, you will keep on getting what you are getting." If you stick your head in the sand and ignore things that you have the power to change, you can't blame anyone else when they don't turn out right!

In his best-selling book *Good to Great: Why Some Companies Make the Leap . . . And Others Don't*, business leader and author Jim Collins compares two growing giants, A&P, the largest retailing organization in the world in the 1950s, and Kroger, a small value-based chain of supermarkets also thriving in the fifties.

As technology began to progress in the tumultuous sixties, both companies, very traditional in approach, saw that the world was changing around them. Each company conducted research, built expensive tests, and hired expert analysts to forecast the future.

They both reached a similar conclusion: Because of the way the world was changing, convenience was paramount. People would want to do as much one-stop shopping as possible: food, toiletries, pharmacy items, prescription drugs, and so on.

In a stunning lapse, A&P basically ignored this information. Kroger, on the other hand, acted on it and implemented the "super-store" strategy that we now take for granted. By 1999, Kroger had become the leading grocery chain in the United States, generating profit eighty times that of its one-time competitor A&P!

Theological Evidence Behind the System

The last letter E (exchange) challenges us to find the "true north" principles that will replace the wrong and limiting beliefs.

As an ordained minister for over 30 years, I firmly believe that the Bible contains the North Star that will guide us through the dark forests of life. The truths in the Bible give me hope that change is possible.

I grew up in a dysfunctional family. As an illegitimate child, I was programmed for failure. People told me that I would not amount to anything, that I would not accomplish anything. But thank God, my faith in the Lord Jesus Christ turned my whole life around.

Today, I have been serving the spiritual and emotional needs of people for many years. I have been happily married to my beautiful and talented wife for over a quarter of a century. Through several book writing projects, my dream of being a writer is becoming a reality. God showed me a system of success that I can share with the whole world through the Internet.

I still struggle with the old and stubborn programming in my subconscious mind. But with the ABCDE system of change, I have learned to diagnose the limiting beliefs that are causing the negative emotions and behaviors in my life. I then quickly confront and chal-lenge the perceived lie and replace it with a verse of Scripture or a truth more in harmony with God's Word.

The Law of Attraction

Physically you are what you eat, but spiritually, you are what you think. "As he thinketh in his heart, so is he" (Proverbs 23:7). One of the most neglected verses in the Scriptures that teaches the importance of our thought-life is Proverbs 4:23: "Keep thy heart with all diligence; for out of it are the issues of life."

It's my own personal opinion that the *heart* in this verse refers to our emotional mind, which is the subconscious mind. The wise king Solomon exhorts us to think about what we are thinking about, because all the results in our life, whether they are good or bad, flow from our thought-life.

Almost all success literature mentions the law of attraction. This law simply teaches that we become what we think most of the time. The great apostle Paul may have implied this principle in the latter part of Romans 7:25: "So then with the mind I myself serve the Law of God; but with the flesh the Law of sin."

In the next chapter, Paul mentions the mind that's governed by the Spirit of God and the mind that's governed by the sinful nature. Putting the two scriptures side by side, I believe we can fairly conclude that with the mind that's controlled by the Holy Spirit through the use of the Scriptures, we will be attracted in the direction of obeying all the laws of God.

But if we allow our sinful nature or the flesh to control our minds with ideas that are not in harmony with the Scriptures, we will naturally be influenced to obey the law of sin. In other words, what we believe will determine how we behave.

For instance, if we fill our minds with the truths about God's unconditional love, it seems effortless for us to love even the unlovable. But if we keep dwelling on sinful thoughts like hostility, sexual lusts, greed, and so on, it's just a matter of time before we will act on those wrong thoughts and impulses.

Conclusion

No matter where you are today or what decisions you made yesterday, there is hope. Change is not always easy, but it is possible. It starts in your mind. Your mind could indeed make you well and successful. The ABCDE model of change is the foundation by which you could build a successful life. You're only a thought away from realizing the life of success and total fulfillment you truly deserve. The choice is yours. The time is now. Think about it!

Biography

Rev. Dean Decastro

REV. DEAN DECASTRO specializes in motivating and supporting people to make the changes they desire to live their best life. He was born and raised in the Philippines and has been an ordained minister since 1978. He got his formal theological education from the Philippines and the United States. Pastor Dean is a gifted communicator, writer, counselor, and Bible teacher. He is married to Dr. Angelina Decastro, who heads the Asian psychiatric in-patient program at Bellevue Hospital in New York City. Pastor Dean and his wife founded the Great Commission Bible Church in Jamaica, New York, with a vision of transforming people's lives with the good news of Jesus Christ. The Decastros are both fluent in English, Mandarin, Fookienish, and Tagalog, and can also speak some Cantonese and Spanish. They are both dedicated to helping people deal with their personal problems.

Contact Information

www.ChangeStartsintheMind.com
www.BalancedChristianLiving.org

Chapter 28

Success through Mental Martial Arts

by Roger J. Aston

My story begins at age 13, when I was riding my bike through my hometown, Birmingham, England, and saw a van advertising a martial arts school not far away. Even the Asian-style lettering on the side held a fascination for me. I had no interest in team sports but wanted to learn something different, so I followed the van to an old church hall that had been converted into a dojo. In I went and saw the huge empty tatami (mats used for practice). I was so taken with the whole atmosphere—the posters, photographs of judo (the gentle way), aikido (harmony way), and other martial arts. Even the clothing (judogi) fascinated me. I enrolled, and the commitment cost me all my wages from my out-of-school job. It took a month to raise the cash to buy my first judo suit. I was on my way. Little did I realize that the philosophy and disciplines I would learn would influence the rest of my life.

Wednesday afternoons I went to the dojo, where all the other students were adults, bigger and stronger than I was. This was serious stuff—people were being thrown all over the place, strangled, choked, and suffering pain in arm locks. While everyone seemed to be having a good time, I was way outside my comfort zone, armed only with my endless enthusiasm.

In a class of only six, the principal sensei (teacher) was a small but solid Japanese man named Kenshiro Abbe. He was a master of judo and several other martial arts, and one of only a small number of Japanese to introduce and promote the arts in Europe. This man was in every respect to martial arts as Nureyev was to ballet or Elvis to rock & roll. He helped form the entire foundation of my learning. I also studied with two other martial arts legends: Senta Yamada, master of judo and aikido, and Masamichi Noro, aikido master, who went on to promote the art in France.

Dr. Jigoro Kano, the founder of judo, said, "It is a training for life." It is this philosophy that I hope will be of great insight in all areas of your life as it has been in mine. It is not necessary to practice the martial arts to understand this teaching.

To begin with, the martial arts were devised for ordinary people to achieve extraordinary results by study and application of learnable skills. This is the key to all progress. I have found this to be true over the last fifty years.

The Japanese have a word, "kaizen," which means continuous improvement, a good habit to form in all our endeavors. As life is constantly throwing new challenges in front of us, we need to find good solutions to move forward. Even finding the fortitude to keep moving can be a problem at times. I believe that the foundation of principles found in martial arts will give you the resources to be, do, and have almost anything you desire, even if realistically you probably can't have *everything* you desire.

The philosophy is at one level just a collection of words. My hope is that you will internalize the words and give them meaning for you. Make them part of your being, unconscious components of all you do. Imagine being able to live your life with a refined mental program that has infinite capacity to produce great results at will any time and every time it is called upon. This is the essence of martial arts thinking. You will learn to see beyond the superficial and the apparent.

The order of all achievement starts with vision followed by focus and only then action. Throughout these steps, the constant must be a good attitude. Let's look at this concept a little more: vision or ideas form the basis of all achievement. It's where we decide what we want and see it in our mind's eye. Some of us find this easier than others because we tend to process thoughts with a bias toward the right side of our brains; that's me—lots of ideas. However, the next part is hard for me because it involves the left brain to focus and produce a plan to follow. Only then is action worthwhile to execute the plan, taking us toward our goal. It is not unusual for people to spin off on a tangent into all sorts of unplanned activities that just seemed to come along. Not to stifle spontaneity, which can be fun, but you have to recognize when it prevents the real goal from being achieved.

Life always moves towards the new; whatever your vision, you will have to learn something new. Choose to be the best you can be. Master your subject, then go further to a position where artistry and creativity are the hallmarks associated with whatever you do. By looking for more, you may well discover more than you were looking for. Step out of your comfort zone. Leave behind stability and get into the action zone. Motion has its own magic as learning and progress accelerate. Make your moves with style and elegance to stand out from the crowd. Use your imagination and uniqueness on every idea, pursuit, or ambition. Engage your whole brain—only this will enable you to be the Da Vinci or Einstein in your field.

Many people are continually reliant on the primitive part of the brain, the reptilian area that is there to facilitate fight or flight in life-threatening circumstances. Because so many are under constant stress, they are unable to break free and move the center of activity to the frontal area of the brain; they remain cut off from their imagination and creativity. If you have constant stress, do all you can to eliminate it before you attempt to move forward.

The world is not full of black belts. Many start the journey but lose their way for a variety of reasons, just as many in life lose their way and never see the success they set out to achieve. Be prepared to stay the course when the going gets tough, which it inevitably will. I well remember in martial arts the periods when nothing seemed to go well, and I did not seem to be getting anywhere. Eventually I broke through to a new level of understanding again and again. This can't be forced or hurried—it has to be experienced. You can no more buy or inherit experience than you can a black belt. Keep at it and all will be revealed.

There once was student who was desperate to emulate his master. He said, "Master, how long will it take me to be like you?" The master replied, "10 years." The student was not happy. "No, master, you do not understand. I will work and study so hard. How long will it take me? The master replied, "20 years." Finally the student said, "Master, I will work and study harder than any of your students ever before. How long, please?" You have probably guessed the master's reply: "30 years." You see, in some things, we need to recognize that there are no shortcuts, and that excessive effort is not the answer. Focus on the important and banish the rush and urgency whenever possible. The payoff will be a higher level of confidence to control events; success will become an expectation, and guess what? The universe will join you along the way.

Falls along the way of life are just like being thrown in the martial arts—possibly unpleasant, sometimes devastating, but always a chance to learn more, although not always at the time but when we are ready to process the experience. If you become defensive and consumed by fear, you will find yourself in a place that is hard to recover from. The mind and body close down. It's called depression, and it stifles progress. Do all you can to avoid that response to any problem—it can steal years from you.

As you apply the principles, your unconscious will recognize how you are directing it and will produce great solutions for you. Remember that what we call intuition is much more than a random thought from nowhere. It is the unconscious mind giving us an insight based on the sum of our learning and experience to date. Learn to recognize the small voice from within with its fleeting message. Capture it, trust it, and act on it as part of your plan. Easier said than done, you might be thinking. To access this great resource more often and at will, the first step is to relax. Just as in the martial arts, no action is wise under stress and tension. Remember the translation of judo—the gentle way—and aikido—harmony way. Tension and stress are out. Meditation and emptying your mind are in. I urge you to study and learn more on the subject. It will be a key part of your personal growth.

As I progressed with my martial arts, I began to learn about combination techniques. Sometimes an initial attack on an opponent does not go according to plan. Well, that's life, of course. The answer is to follow up with a second technique without pause or hesitation to guarantee the outcome. This means in all that we do, we should be prepared with a plan B. Flexibility in the mind and body are key. It may be that you are just a minor adjustment away from success. Life is dynamic, moving all the time—stay with it.

We all have a story to tell, and mine is no different in that I have had good times and bad; indeed, the bad were dreadful. My dear father died after suffering for three years. He was only 46 years old. My mom worked so hard, but we had very little in those days.

I have had two great businesses that were very kind to me. On the surface life was good. I was in the wrong marriage, however, and it did not survive the tragic death of my middle daughter in a road incident at just 13 years old. Divorce, estrangement from my 9-year-old son, loss of home and business followed. Loss of spirit, confidence, and self-esteem lasted for a long time.

I now have a wonderful wife who contributes so much to balance in my life. She is very different from me—coming from the heart is her major strength. We are a great team, and in all that we do, we come as a package: two for the price of one. My son is fully restored to his place in the family, and my eldest daughter has a lovely family and a successful business.

Life is always a work in progress, and I have many goals to work on. My project at the moment is to create a planning tool to facilitate the coming together of both sides of the brain to create great results for people. I am calling this the Da Vinci planner for the moment. I believe the genius is in people. There is someone to solve every problem in the world—they just don't know it yet.

You are one of those people. Just keep in mind the following principles of success, and you will live your dreams:

- You can achieve the unbelievable.

- Respect others in all your endeavors.

- Step out of you comfort zone no matter what.

- Trust you unconscious mind, your intuition, to provide great answers.
- A fall is an opportunity to learn and begin again.
- Commit 100% every time to your goals.
- Keep going. Put yourself in the contest—not defensively but with confidence.
- Remember the sequence: Vision, focus, action—with a great attitude to make it work.
- Think in combination moves. Be ready. Be flexible to fine-tune ideas and actions. You may be closer than you think
- Free yourself from routine and fear. Doing so is the only way to break through to creative imagination.
- Relax and be kind to yourself. Have fun.

Biography

Roger J. Aston

ROGER J. ASTON is a student and master of martial arts, and a practitioner of NLP and Erick- sonian hypnosis. He is also a coach, an author, a seminar leader, an entrepreneur, a musician, and an artist.

Roger would be pleased to work with you to create your vision of a great future, develop a plan to focus on, and encourage you to take massive action toward your success. For coaching or to find out more on forthcoming projects, articles, and information, you can contact Roger via his website.

Contact Information

www.rogerjaston.com
info@rogerjaston.com

Chapter 29

Extraordinary Ordinary Women

by Victoria Rei Ristow

Some of my fondest memories are of a time when I was two years old. My uncle Jack was a young man, and he set me on our dog, Lady, to ride her like a small horse. She was a gentle black Labrador, who was patient while I pulled on her tufts of fur to hold on and ride bareback. My uncle was kind and gentle, too, wanting to play and have fun and hear my squeals of delight with being such a "big girl."

My grandmother Sophya would care for me and dress me up. I delighted in her cooing over me and being so happy with my presence as she held me in her lap.

These were happy times. The few and far between happy times, when I was not only safe, but also delighted in simply being there with my uncle and grandmother.

There were many other memories, though, that were full of fear and terror.

At two years of age, I was locked in a closet, in the dark for an unknown number of hours. My mother put me there because I had spilled a milkshake she had given me. She left with my sister to visit an aunt. After some time, the aunt asked Mother where I was and why I was not with her for the visit. When mother finally confessed, the aunt insisted on returning to our apartment with Mother to let me out of the closet.

Until then, though, I remember beating on the door over and over again to silence, and screaming at the top of my lungs, until I could scream no more.

When they finally arrived, so did the police. The neighbors downstairs had called them after hearing my incessant screaming and crying. My mother was told by the police that they would take us girls away from her if they were called about even one more incident.

This must have started Mother's paranoia. So we moved a lot. My mother wanted to keep us away from her mother. We only were able to play at our aunt's house, when mother would leave us to be babysat. Mother feared her mother would take us away from her.

I could not understand why my sister was allowed to visit our aunt and uncle for the whole summer, alone. We, her sisters, were not invited or allowed for some unknown reason. This went on for several years.

I later learned that this aunt was not really my aunt, but only my sister's aunt. Our mother had married several times. This aunt later told me, when I became an adult, that she had to blackmail our mother to get time with my sister for the summers, as she was really my sister's grandmother. The blackmail was to not tell the police about mother's continued abuse, nor tell my mother's mother where she and we were.

This environment of walking on eggshells, not knowing when we would be moved, or when we would be hit, beaten, or locked in a house or closet for being "disobedient," was all part of what I and my siblings lived with daily.

There are four of us, all from different fathers. And we all came through our tough childhood differently. We found individual methods of coping and growing up. Our health and well-being levels vary depending on how long we had to live with Mother.

As I got older and studied psychology in undergraduate school, I realized my mother was mentally ill and later became an alcoholic, probably to self-medicate. She never sought treatment, not admitted to her bizarre and harmful behaviors to us or others. She just kept running, and moving.

Mother's undiagnosed and untreated mental illness worsened over the years. Eventually, most of could not relate to her anymore and shut her out of our lives.

Despite this kind of childhood, I somehow kept a bright outlook, knowing my life could be better. I dreamed of being loved well and having a happy life. Where my optimism came from, I do not know.

Subsequently, I studied addiction, psychology, counseling, and healthy communications, and I facilitated groups while putting myself through undergraduate school. It is said if you want to learn something, then become a teacher on the subject. I participated in group self-awareness weekend seminars, group counseling, and individual counseling. All to become a healthier someone and to avoid becoming like my mother.

I wanted desperately to break any cycle of abuse that the psychology books say gets handed down from generation to generation. I did not want to pass any kind of dysfunctional life onto my children. However, all that did not stop me from marrying addiction, or mental illness self-medicating with addiction. Fortunately, we parted ways as I became healthier emotionally. Yet my pattern of giving and giving and not receiving support or healthy care from my spouse continued. I was developing my own emotional intelligence, healthy relationship behavior, and ability to communicate, yet I was not receiving healthy relationship behavior in return from my intimate others.

In my journey I learned that the pattern of life I was experiencing was called co-dependence, a pattern in which children grow up shaped to give but not receive good from others. We do not know that we are drawn to "takers" who do not have the capacity or desire to give and take, as in healthy relationships.

My siblings had not kept in contact. We all chose to live on far sides of the country. When communications were reinitiated, it was too painful, because we would talk about our common experiences of childhood abuse. We avoided each other because of that, and it is sad that we could not be close, as other families are.

This journey of recovery has been, at times, lonely. It takes courage to separate from the dysfunction of biological family, and going it alone to find new friends, and chosen family. Since we do not trust ourselves during the emotional recovery, we often choose not to have intimacy, emotionally or physically, particularly after having tried and only getting more abuse or neglect from the unhealthy partners we chose.

Daughters of abuse are taught to give and give, but not receive, even more than sons are because it is a woman's role to nurture and give in our culture. We are not taught to expect or insist on receiving healthy reciprocity from all our giving, nor how to perceive another's ability to be safe and healthy for us in any kind of relationship.

Most of us are in our 50s or 60s before we understand that we were raised in role reversal to be the parent while yet a child. After finally stopping the abuse and neglect we endured again during our own marriages, we do not know how to have safe, healthy intimate relationship. So we stay single.

Yet in this journey that we daughters take, a few of us know and pursue, wholeheartedly, our health and well-being. We decide to learn from our parents what *not* to do, and instead read, go to counseling, increase our self-awareness, and participate in self-development of healthy thinking and lifestyle.

Of all the women I have interviewed who have this type of background and yet have pursued health and well-being, all of them have had to take the journey alone, without any support from their families. In many cases, families continued to reject them or not communicate with them.

Eventually, though, they become change agents in their own lives, and then also in the lives of their biological families. And they are the *only* ones in their families who have chosen the path to wellness—emotionally, physically, and spiritually.

To be this kind of change agent is a hard and challenging task. It takes endurance and holding onto ideals and goals unwaveringly, often in the face of hostility toward us as committed wellness change agents, for ourselves first, then possibly for others.

The extraordinariness of these ordinary women is that they make an incredible difference in their lives and in the lives of others—family and friends—converting very damaging behaviors and thinking to healthier behaviors, thinking, and practices. They teach themselves how to teach others to treat them with respect and reciprocity while continue to be giving. Giving is still important in relationships, but a healthy balance also involves reciprocity. Giving is done out of love and kindness, which comes from heart and spirit.

However, predators, takers, also like love and kindness, and they prey on those who give it out of ignorance and naivete, those who aren't yet able to perceive people who intend harm or are harmful in their repeated actions.

Recognizing and staying clear of predators, and their harmful behavior, is essential and probably the hardest lesson for co-dependents to learn. This piece of wellness is usually the last piece to be understood.

Success in my world is learning to pay attention to and trust my feelings. Ralph Waldo Emerson wrote that "Self-trust is the first secret to success." Learning to be trustworthy to myself, in my own perceptions, behaviors, and spoken words, is the challenge of developing emotional and social intelligence. Then practicing expecting and receiving healthy behaviors and words from others is next. This leads to having a healthy support circle for ourselves.

Those who teach and write about healthy behaviors and better communication styles to successfully solve conflicts or problems, are among those who teach us better ways to think about and live our lives: Stephen Covey, Sr. and Jr., John Bradshaw, Al-Anon, Marianne Williamson, Nelson Mandela, Debbie Ford, Jack Canfield, Zig Ziglar, Louise Hay, Daniel Goleman, Bill and Hillary Clinton, Thunderbird School of Global Management, Elisabeth Kübler-Ross, Deepak Chopra, Leo Buscaglia, Gerald Jampolsky, David Hawkins, Dan Baker, Wayne Dyer, Oprah, and NAMI for family (National Association for Mental Illness). Developing a healthy circle of chosen family and friends is essential to having wellness in our lives.

The challenge and the strength is to "Find and follow the good."

To be a change agent in one's life or a leader on any scale, it is critical to initiate and maintain relationships. Trust is a family, local, regional, and world issue. As Stephen Covey, Jr., writes in his book, *The Speed of Trust*, trust can reduce the time to get anything done successfully. Developing trust is essential to successfully developing relationships.

Successful leadership or being a change agent requires highly developed emotional and social intelligence, as defined by Daniel Goleman. Skills of wellness in relationships require us to develop our own emotional intelligence, then expand to developing social intelligence to successfully identify those who are healthy enough to have in our inner circle. Social intelligence is also needed to know how to deal with others in many other relationship capacities.

Successful relationships require these skills. And successful lives and work require successful relationships.

Biography

Victoria Rei Ristow

VICTORIA REI RISTOW is a successful mother, wife, graduate student (twice), and champion of wellness in relationships and in self. Professionally, she has applied both master's degrees—an MAEd and an MBA—in the industries of disability case management and domestic and international business development.  Her successes include negotiating contracts never before done, expanding areas for trade, company growth to 700%. As a mediator, she has persuaded many parties, with varying interests, to agree on plans and benefit entitlements successfully 98% of the time. All while being a successful agent for healthy change in her family and among her friends. Her treasures are her husband, daughters, and close friends. She is Blessed.

Contact Information

www.extraordinary-ordinarywomen.com
vrei06@gmail.com
9420 E. Golf Links Rd, Suite 218
Tucson, AZ 85730

Chapter 30

Success: Work Hard, Follow the Leaders, Have Fun!

by David S. Velasquez

There are many definitions of success, and success means something different for everyone. There are many ways to measure it, tangible and intangible: from finishing school to getting a great job; from climbing a corporate ladder to being entrepreneurial and working for yourself; or from finding your personal relationship with the Lord, to being a good spouse, parent, sibling, or friend. In our society, many measure success in terms of amassing financial wealth and independence, even though financial wealth means something different to everyone. So, the big question is: What if success is relative, and everyone is, or can be, successful in one way or another?

For me, and for most people, what we call success changes over time. I've learned that success is a journey. Each step along the way, every leap and each stumble, every opportunity and every failure, changes the playing field and how we view or measure success. We can be very successful in one area and unsuccessful in others. Success is really independent of how others measure us and ultimately a very personal matter.

Only about 4.5% of US households are millionaires; 14% say their parents were wealthy; 90% of millionaires are college grads. Millionaires say they got there through hard work, smart investing and saving, being frugal, and taking risks—41% say luck has something to do with it. I believe the numbers speak for themselves, which I first realized while reading *The Millionaire Next Door*. I've found the steps for success are hard work, lifelong learning, seeking leadership to learn from and listen to, and duplicating their successful habits. None of this should be drudgery; have fun!

I've been most successful when I've had good leadership, but I don't see myself as a great leader. I think I'm probably a good #2, but I have always had great leaders, mentors, and role models—even when they didn't know. Leaders demonstrate courage, knowledge, competency, and an ability to listen better than their protégés. I learned this in the Army: "Leadership is the process of influencing people by providing purpose, direction, and motivation while operating to accomplish the mission and improving the organization." Leaders take measured risk on their own but are generally more risk averse and prudent with others.

Here's my story. I've survived a traditional modest upbringing, a near-fatal car wreck in my 20s, and a divorce and a broken neck in my 30s. I rather coincidentally landed two back-to-back careers that provided many diverse experiences, strong mentors, and a foundation that allowed me and my wife to become millionaires in my late 40s. I know money isn't everything, but in this world, it sure helps everything else.

Today, five years later, with world affairs and the economy still in question, we're positioned to live comfortably on various investment income streams. I'm more excited than ever about having time to live a more purposeful life, the potential of building multi-generational wealth, and trying to help other people break out to the next level of their success. For those who know me, there aren't many secrets. Many of those who know me may not even see me as successful. I do have my faults and feel rather typical. I provide my story here in thanks to the many that have helped me feel relatively successful, and in hope that it might inspire others to celebrate their successful lives.

Today I live where I was born and raised with my four sisters by wonderful parents, in San Antonio. Teresa, my wife of nineteen years, and I stay happily married and well grounded with our humble upbringings, and I try to be a good role model for my daughter, Veronica, and my many nephews, nieces, and other relatives. Mom and Dad were my first mentors, and today, I still learn much from them every day. I think they should have their own chapter—I'm so thankful I'm back home and get to see them regularly, and at minimum, for Sunday barbacoa breakfasts!

I graduated from McCollum High School with a fantastic group of people that are some of the best people anyone could know. I'm so lucky to have McCollum friends! I worked nights and weekends at the local grocery chains after the eighth grade and through college, went to summer school every summer, and managed to escape getting caught or into too much trouble for all the crazy things we did. I wasn't unique—we were just raised to work hard in our community. I have always been lucky to have fantastic teachers who inspired me, like Joan Clark and Morris Bundict, to name two of many. My friends and co-workers helped me decide to go to college and study electronics engineering. Since Trinity University was in town, cost the most but provided the best financial aid, and allowed me to keep that great job at the H.E.B. grocery store chain, it was the best choice. There was no big plan, and in fact, I was fairly naïve growing up—it was just serendipity. At Trinity, it was tough being a below-average student and running out of money quickly in my first year. Freshman ROTC adventures with Ron Toupal led me to a three-year ROTC scholarship and, upon graduation, a career as an Army officer.

Clearly my Army career provided many life-long friends, leaders and mentors—too many to mention, but I cannot understate the value of this career in terms of the responsibility and profound leadership to which I was exposed. As an electronics engineer, I had a very nontraditional career on the business side versus the classic tactical side of the military. I had great assignments, and twice, I went to graduate school full time while in the Army and learned with some of the military's best and brightest.

While at the US Naval Postgraduate School, in Monterey, California, I broke my neck in a flag football game on Army-Navy Day, 1987. The injury is still aging my body faster than normal. Luckily, the neck injury was not crippling, and with the help of my classmates, I graduated on time. I learned how teamwork and trust are probably the most important key in achieving success, but it doesn't hurt to be lucky (pardon the pun!). At my professional home in Fort Gordon, Georgia, where Teresa and I met, I relearned three of the greatest tips for success from Col. Bill Guerra and Jim Carey: Work hard, play hard, do right. At the Army Command and Staff College in 1992, I learned by being around the best and the brightest Army leadership. The majority of my classmates came with fresh experiences out of the 100 Day War, Desert Storm I. Life happened fast. As Teresa and I left for Germany, we consolidated our debts by refinancing her car and selling mine. I was 34 years old, we were $12,000 in debt, and loving life!

Teresa and I had a great time in Europe. Her job there helped us get out of debt, enjoy living in Europe when the exchange rates were not favorable, and start a modest investment habit. Veronica traveled to Europe ten times in three of her elementary school years, and I'd stop over to see her about every three months on my many return trips to the United States during our three years in Germany. Army peers helped me get stationed in Orlando, Florida, where Veronica lived, upon return, in 1995. There were more circumstances, but suffice to say, once there, I took advantage of a 15-year retirement option the Clinton Administration offered the military, as part of their now infamous balanced budget initiatives, and started my second career, with then the largest employee-owned research and engineering company in the nation, SAIC.

The career at SAIC, coupled with my income streams from Army retirement and rents from prior homes, allowed us to save and invest significantly. After 10 years, the SAIC founder retired, and the company went public in the second largest stock market initial public offering of 2006, behind MasterCard, creating many millionaires. I was 48 years old and one of them. It was funny that Teresa and I didn't really know what to do differently once we realized we'd met one of our major lifelong goals. So after about three months, we decided to just keep doing the same thing—working, saving, and being ready to take care of those we care about when prudent.

Outside the financial windfall, I've been only modestly successful but more fortunate in my second career, relative to my peers. I've worked in areas such as command and control, modeling and simulation, electronic commerce, information assurance, and cyber defense—all technical disciplines. I've usually been proficient (and lucky) enough at most tasks, and passionate enough about the mission to contribute to the great things fantastic SAIC people do every day. I worked hard and have had many chances to learn so much from both seniors and subordinates alike. Every missed opportunity opened a new door and a new opportunity. Reuniting in 1997 with my high school classmates had made me long for home. So in late 1999, a near layoff led to a better position, and the company moving us from Orlando, back home to San Antonio, where Teresa also grew professionally. Ironically, it was Dad's simple advice to walk in to the local offices that led to the job that moved us home to San Antonio, and to a chance to give back to the community I'd grown up in, but been away from for over 20 years.

I support my high school alumni nonprofit, MAST, which hosts an annual softball tournament to raise scholarship funds. I volunteer on the board of directors of a (now) 3 billion-dollar credit union, SACU. That role gives me access to great business leaders from whom I still learn. They inspired me to complete a leadership-based executive MBA in 2004. The combination of the credit union experiences, now in its eleventh year, and the EMBA education simply opened my mind—my mental box—to a broader and deeper way of thinking and understanding of my purpose, my gift, and whom and what I value.

The journey hasn't been perfect. I've had failed investments and debtors stop paying until legal action made things right. I've learned that while I like rental property income and deductions, I dislike the landlord role. I learned from those experiences and survived the market crash of 2007 fairly unscathed. At the time of this writing, I continue working, mainly out of loyalty to my work teammates and the mission, and to fuel multiple diverse streams of income.

In 2008 I was inducted into my High School District Hall of Fame, ironically, a trigger event that made me feel successful. In 2010, an MBA classmate invited me into a financial social network with other success-minded friends and great leaders. This social network led me to tell my story in this chapter, and as a gift, provided us both the reason and the means to reconnect with friends and family, and share our future successes directly. I've learned that opportunity doesn't knock—it sneaks by, and you have to be open minded and aware enough to jump on it when it's around you.

There is more to tell, but even more left to do. Going forward, we know that even taking much less risk, more success is imminent!

There is truly an art and a science to achieving success, regardless of how you define it. The art of success is focused on knowing yourself and finding your purpose in life. It's about knowing where you're going. The science of success is more discrete and measurable. The science of success is focused on the means you employ, such as being at the right place at the right time, with the right people; setting goals; and taking action to make the best of the obstacles you're dealt in your life.

Biography

David S. Velasquez

DAVID is a native of San Antonio, Texas. A lifelong learner, he has a BS in electronics engineering and three master's degrees, including an executive MBA. He was a self-made millionaire before he was 50, as a retired Army officer and disabled veteran, and is currently a mid-level manager at a high-tech Fortune  300 company, a credit union board director. He and his wife, Teresa, travel in a financial social network with family and friends.

Contact Information

www.DTVAssociates.com
dvelasquez@satx.rr.com
210-558-7766

Chapter 31

Briarley's Story

by Briarley Nicholson

$\mathcal{I}$ grew up on farm in Bindura, Rhodesia, with my parents and two older brothers and our beloved animals. We lived in an old farm house with a fenced garden and had great fun playing with boxes, building forts, climbing trees, riding motor bikes, building tunnels in cotton bales, and splashing through mud in the back of a truck. It was a healthy outdoor upbringing.

We had a very simple lifestyle, and my dream in life back then was to grow up and become a teacher, just like my mum. My mum taught at the local district school, Bindura Primary. Bindura is a small mining town, situated 80 kilometers north of Salisbury (now Harare). Our weekly outing was a trip into town to get groceries and to meet friends for tennis at the local country club. I attended Bindura Primary School and even opted to board in the hostel from the age of five, on a weekly basis, to be with my friends.

As time went on, we lived in a war zone, with the liberation struggle in our country. We had to learn to shoot guns and dash to hideaways, and we had to travel in a convoy for safety. Dad had to go on police reserve duty for weeks at a time, and Mum, my two brothers, and I would sleep in the passage, Mum with a gun when we heard strange noises outside. One Christmas Eve, we lost our home to a terrorist invasion, where they poured petrol over our house and set it on fire. Thank goodness we were in the city with our grandmother, so we were safe while our belongings went up in flames. Our animals escaped.

At the age of 11, while my parents were at a school function and I was sleeping in the hostel, a young drugged man got into my room, locked us both in, and jumped into bed with me, forcing himself upon me. Luckily I managed to get up, and friends hearing my screaming knocked the locked door down. All was okay, but from a young age I learned that I was a survivor and could face life. I learned to deal with my nightmares, and with many fear factors, and I learned that circumstances can be put behind you, and you can look forward to growth.

Life from then on was fun, hard work, confusing, growing up—and I just got on with it. I was always encouraged to do my best. I was no A student, and studying was hard for me. While I loved sports and my friends, I had trouble understanding what was wanted from me at school. I got my grades and moved to another school, where I excelled with the praise and encouragement I received in a different system. Here I started to learn leadership skills and became a prefect, the captain of my house Sabi, and head of the school hostel. University was out of our budget, and I had *no* desire for further studying whatsoever.

I was encouraged to work through my school holidays to earn money of my own, which I gladly did. I learned very quickly how to work hard and to save whatever I could to pursue my dreams.

After hours spent with grandparents and listening to their stories of travel around the world, I discovered a new desire and began to dream: I wanted to travel the world. My mother encouraged me to do everything I wanted before settling down to get married, as she wished she had done more. That was enough motivation for me. I formed my motto—"Never regret anything in life; learn by it"—and I identified my dreams. My mum's regret became my inspiration—to make it happen. As our currency was already devaluing in "real" terms, I needed to move to the United Kingdom to earn some hard currency to realize my dreams. From Zimbabwe, with one year of work experience, I moved to South Africa to earn a currency that could buy my first ticket abroad and set my goals in place to get to London.

It took me 18 months of working two jobs to get my first air ticket abroad. I then moved into a house with 13 others to save money and build my finances to travel the world. London itself was a huge experience. Looking back, I wish I had taken far more advantage of courses and seminars back then, but more education was the last thing I wanted. I just wanted money to travel the world. I worked three jobs, secretarial during the day, bar work on two nights of the weekend, and sales on the weekend days. I just kept going and saved my salary and survived off the other incomes.

I bought a backpack and traveled through Europe, to the Greek islands and Turkey, to the United States and Asia and Australasia. I lived my dream. I realized that when you set your heart on something, it can be achieved, no matter what. I learned to save, keep out of debt, yet go for my dreams. It was a lot easier than I had ever imagined and wow, so much fun.

I returned home, after falling in love, when I was 26 years old. It was wonderful to be back in our beloved Zimbabwe, and I got back into the corporate world, in finance, as I knew I had to learn about figures. However, boredom set in, and I felt empty. I had achieved my dreams, but I had not yet set new ones.

My new dream was to marry and have a family, but I was soon frustrated with lack of ambition and progress. I parted from my partner to build my life again. Heartbroken but determined to get more from life, after an introduction to Tony Robbins courses, my vision changed, and a new dream formed—personal growth and development. Mastery University with Tony Robbins. This was way beyond my reach with our devaluing dollar; however, with a change of everything, including having to find work with a foreign income, I took the leap of faith with commission only, and my life has never been the same.

I could now see my dream on the horizon, and *nothing* would stop me pursuing this. Not only did I travel around the world for the program, but I went beyond and attended Leadership Mastery. There were times when I barely had a cent to scrape together, but I signed up, and I just believed and put in the hard work. I achieved, and now I always believe. As soon as I have no goal set out, I find the days disappear with little to show. I have learned that to achieve success, I must master the reason behind it all.

Both Anthony Robbins and Robert Kiyosaki have been my mentors for years. As they traveled the bumpy road to success, they have had severe pitfalls, yet they have managed to pull through these and climb the highest mountains and share their stories. Neither was given a silver spoon. They have done everything themselves. My new mentor is Matt Morris. He has also created his success himself, and he's sharing his story with the world. I have the utmost respect and gratefulness to these people. There are many more, but these are my greatest mentors of life.

My greatest tip for success in life is to take the time to dream and identify what you really want to accomplish, then find the driving force behind your goals, the reason, or the why, you want to achieve them. When you have a sincere reason, you will not even see the challenges along the way, as you will always see beyond them to achieving your goal. My mum gave me a poster as a child. It said "If you can imagine it, you can achieve it. If you can dream it, you can become it." This is so true. We need to imagine that we have already accomplished our dreams.

Success is satisfaction with your own personal growth, with who you are and the life you are leading and the inspiration and effect you have on others. To be able to look into the mirror and say, "I love you—congratulations" for the difference you have made in your life and in the lives of others—and to mean it with sincerity.

The three prongs on the key to open the door to success are belief, action, and follow-through.

My personal steps for success are as follows:

1. Focus on personal growth. Feed yourself constantly with positive stories. Read and learn from those who have done it. Apply their tips and techniques every day.

2. Spend time with yourself. To identify your path ahead, allow yourself to dream and take the time to set up a MAP (Massive Action Plan) for your progression.

3. Be accountable and honor your word, even to yourself. Do what you say you are going to do and follow through constantly. Get up when you fall down.

4. Find your passion, have integrity, and help others as much as you can.

Some of the roadblocks I have experienced are discouragement and negativity, especially from those close to me; fear; financial lacking; not being intelligent enough; and lack of confidence. To overcome these hurdles, I started teaching others about attitude and fear. I started doing life coaching to help others identify and achieve results, which helped me tremendously to face my own fears and to "walk my talk."

I realized that when you really want something, no matter what it is, you will find a way financially to achieve it, if enough will is there. Hard work becomes fun if you are passionate about it.

In the process of helping others, I learned how to lead by example and to guide others to become leaders. Leadership is being the leader that all leaders look for. In this process, I strengthened my confidence, integrity, sincerity, compassion, and developed even more of an understanding of human behavior and how to bring out the best in people to develop both themselves and those around them.

I am still growing and learning, always reaching for the next dream. As the old saying goes, "Winners never quit, and quitters never win." Or my mum's version: "If at first you don't succeed, try, try, and try again—until you succeed!" This has been invaluable in my life. No matter what happens to you on your road to success, *never ever* give up. The impossible may take a little longer, but it's always possible.

Biography

Briarley Nicholson

BRIARLEY NICHOLSON is a financial advisor and personal life coach, currently living in Zimbabwe, where she was born. She is also the director of her own company, The Transformation Centre. Briarley is passionate about making a difference in people's lives, helping them believe in themselves and succeed in life.

Contact Information

www.thetransformationcentre.com
http://briarley.worldventures.biz
briarley@thetransformationcentre.com

Chapter 32

It All Starts with This...

by W. David Medina

I have definitely had quite an interesting time on this big blue rock. I went from being horribly bullied to becoming a black belt. Long hours of piano and music lessons turned into playing the lead in the high school play, a professional music career, and a trip to a reality TV show. I went from being awkward in elementary school to graduating with honors from an ivy league university. I was never good enough to make any of the sports teams in school. but I ran my first triathlon at the healthy age of 41. I used to sell Christmas cards and lemonade to neighbors and eventually ran a multimillion dollar business as an executive for a Fortune 50 company on Fifth avenue in New York City, and I have run my own company full time for the past 12 years.

If I were to look back and try to define the reasons for my success, there are many lessons that I am very grateful for. My hope is that I can share a little bit of that with you, and if it helps you out, I would be deeply gratified and hope that you can pass it on too. Just promise me that you'll get in touch with me and let me know, okay? Great.

Now with any type of success, there is also the process of experiencing failure. And boy, did I have plenty of that. Sometimes it seemed as if I couldn't get the right answer no matter what I tried. What kept me going? What is it that allowed my tolerance level to be high enough for me to wake up and do it all again the next day? One word.

Passion!

Musicians must make music, artists must paint, poets must write
if they are to be ultimately at peace with themselves. What human beings
can be, they must be. They must be true to their own nature. This need
we may call self-actualization. . . . It refers to a man's desire for
self-fulfillment, namely to the tendency for him to become actually in
what he is potentially: to become everything one is capable of becoming.
—Abraham Maslow

Passion is what defines me. It's who I am. It's what I do. It's how I walk through the world. So I guess my question to you is, what is your passion? I know you have more than one. I know that sometimes we can't spend enough time with our passion. To me passion is the reason you get up in the morning. It's the reason you do what you do, say what you say, and be who you are. And you know what? My hope is that you spend every last stinkin' minute that you can muster with your passion. It's a great place to be.

Sometimes people ask me how they know if something is a passion for them. To me, the questions I then proceed to ask are:

1. What would you do if you knew you couldn't fail?

2. What would you do anyway if you knew you would fail?

3. What would you do if money were no object?

4. What would you do if you knew you were not going to get paid for doing it?

5. What would you pay to do?

6. What dreams do you still have to accomplish?

Abraham Maslow, the great psychologist, told us in his hierarchy of needs that after we are done taking care of our basic needs, such as food, shelter, and safety, that at the top of the list is our need to express ourselves fully and completely, to self-actualize. He didn't characterize it as something that would be nice to accomplish, but instead classified it as a need—along the lines of food and shelter. I couldn't agree more. Maslow also says, "If you deliberately plan on being less than you are capable of being, then I warn you that you'll be unhappy for the rest of your life." Ouch.

> *Everything—a horse, a vine—is created for some duty. . . .*
> *For what task, then, were you yourself created? A man's true delight*
> *is to do the things he was made for.*
> —Marcus Aurelius

I learned early on that I had a passion for martial arts. And what's funny about that is that I did not know it until I was mercilessly bullied every day! I was bullied because I was short, because I was Asian, and because I was shy. I used to pass by a karate school on the way to church every Sunday, and I convinced my parents that I needed the lessons.

The training was hard both physically and mentally. I was asked to do things that were way out of my comfort zone and that also confronted many fears that I had. I was expected to defend myself against other people who were bigger, smarter, and stronger. I was also asked to help keep the school clean and perform other small but important tasks. Was I good at it when I started? Absolutely not.

I made many mistakes, some of which hurt *a lot* more than others. The burning desire I had to reach my goals allowed me to own those mistakes and become smarter because of them.

I still train to this day, and I now own a very successful martial arts school. I have also given presentations to many groups, clubs, and organizations, and at international seminars. I have been inducted into the Martial Arts Hall of Fame and have received a Ph.D. for my studies, contributions, and experience.

Because I was bullied, I found something that I love and adore, have been an ardent student of for almost my entire life, and that gave me skills to contribute to others. The best part is that I have genuinely helped out kids that were bullied too. Talk about a silver lining!

The Three Armies can be deprived of their commanding officer,
but even a common man cannot be deprived of his purpose.
—Confucius

I also have a passion for the business world. I will admit that I am the ultimate consumer. I love to shop and see what new things are out there. I love the value I receive from different companies, people, and products. I wanted to learn how to bring amazing products and services into the world and provide value.

I was accepted to a top-tier business school, and I was taught by very talented professors. My training was rigorous to say the least. Not only did I have to learn the material, give oral presentations for every class subject, and dissect what seemed like a million case studies, but my grades were also based on how I competed against my classmates. Everyone I sat with in my classes had an active interest in not only learning but also making sure I got a lower grade than they did. Yikes! And many of these students were naturally brilliant. Talk about swimming with the sharks. But you know what? I truly believe that I was blessed with the opportunity to be where I was. I made the decision that I was going to honor this blessing and go at this opportunity 100% and nothing less. I was less attached to my outcome and more attached to my efforts. My gratitude and passion propelled me through school, and I came out an honors graduate on the other side. Amazing. Thank you.

It is better to strive in one's own dharma than to succeed in the dharma of another. Nothing is ever lost in following one's own dharma. But competition in another's dharma breeds fear and insecurity.
—Krishna

After my studies, I began to work for incredible people in amazing companies. I worked on Fifth Avenue in New York City as an executive for a Fortune 50 company. I was in charge of a multimillion dollar business that serviced thousands of customers across the United States. I was in meetings with the CEO of our publicly held company, and I had to make sure our resources were being wisely put to use across the country. My challenges were humungous to say the least. I knew this experience was as big as it gets when it came to running any type of business.

Every minute of every day was extremely challenging. I had to learn fast and get up and running even faster. My bosses were as sharp and talented as executives come, and their demands and expectations were extremely challenging. I knew that with the challenge was a fantastic growth opportunity for me personally, so I made the decision to again go at it full bore. I'm glad I did, because the education that I received was *priceless*. Thank you.

This above all: to thine own self be true, and it must follow, as the night of the day, thou canst not then be false to any man.
—William Shakespeare

One fateful day after my New York stint, I was approached about purchasing and taking over a failing company in my hometown. The business was a failed franchise that no one wanted to purchase. While doing my due diligence, I was amazed at how bad the business was being run, or in this case, not being run at all. In my judgment, there was massive room for improvement, and my instincts told me to move forward. My challenges were quite daunting, but I knew in my soul that the business could work.

I had to negotiate with several companies not to shut off the utilities. I had inherited just a few of the old clients, but it was not enough to sustain the business. Many of the clients had issues that were unresolved and needed attention. There were several costly commitments made by the previous owner that needed follow through. The business needed systems, policies, and procedures that would help stand it up on its feet.

I threw my entire being into making the business work, and to my surprise, I shattered previous sales records for the company in under 60 days—60 days after that, I surpassed my goal for the year.

Twelve years later, the business is still going strong and continues to make a difference in the community. Thank you.

A ship is safe in harbor, but that's not what ships are for.
—William Shedd

My family is my passion. I look forward to being with them every day. And yes, my wife is a saint for putting up with me. A real saint. A really, really, really big saint. Thanks, honey. And I am utterly and completely wrapped around both my daughters' fingers. After being with my kids all day, I still rush home every night to try and catch them before they fall asleep. Crazy, I know. I love you, Maria. I love you, Kenzie. I love you, Riley.

I absolutely must give a shout out to my father, whose passion enabled an entire generation to live the dream of growing up and living in the United States. He was the first one in my family to make the hard struggle of emigrating from the Philippines to the United States, then proceeding to bring his family and extended family here. His strength, fortitude, and hard work enabled me to be born a U.S. citizen. Thanks, Dad. I love you. I love you, Mom. I love you, Aaron. I love you, Sarah. I love you, Auntie Honey and Uncle Jamie.

So for me, passion either puts you in the game, or not. You could be really good at doing something, but if you are not passionate about it, you're probably not *really* doing it. And God forbid if you ever have to compete with me if I'm really passionate about it and you're not.

Now get out there and start spreading your passion and talents. There are people waiting on you—including me!

Biography

W. David Medina

W. DAVID MEDINA lives in Philadelphia, Pennsylvania, where he was born. He is an honors graduate of the Wharton School of the University of Pennsylvania. He is also a former contestant on Ed McMahon's *Star Search*. David is a former executive for May Company in New York City, and the current owner of Medina Kenpo Karate in Springfield, Pennsylvania, which specializes in families, kids with special needs, and kickboxing. He is actively involved in coaching, consulting, speaking, playing tennis, and competing in triathlons.

Contact Information

www.wdavidmedina.com
www.medinakenpo.com
w.david.medina@gmail.com
1-888-598-6563
1-610-543-0544

Chapter 33

Grateful Farm Boy

by Mike Pawlowski

Humble Beginnings

My story of success began on a 150-acre ranch in northeast Washington. The closest town, population 400, was 14 miles away. I came from poor beginnings financially, but rich in freedom, independence, and ingenuity. My parents taught me the value of money and hard work, integrity and commitment, and a zest for life.

Summers were filled with many fun activities: harvesting hay, stacking bales in the barn, herding cattle on horseback, building or mending fences, picking wild huckleberries, fishing, swimming, and best of all, riding my motorcycle. Putting up the hay and gathering firewood were family events. The four of us mowed, baled, trucked, and stacked 30–35 tons of hay in a few short days. We often worked by headlights until 10 p.m. to get the last load in the barn before the rain ruined the hay. This was a season when neighbors helped neighbors.

All families volunteered to help whoever had bales in the field when the rain clouds were coming. During late summer, we packed into a 1962 flatbed truck and headed to the mountains. We would cut, split, and load three cords of wood in one day. Upon return home, my dad, brother, and I would unload the truck (after dusk) while Mom prepared dinner. We gathered 12 cords of wood each summer; only a few pieces remained by the end of spring.

Winters were spent shoveling snow, feeding the cows and horses, chopping ice in Deep Creek so the animals could drink, sledding, snowmobiling, and bringing in firewood to heat the house. After completing homework, my brother and I would shovel paths to the woodshed, shop, barn, cold cellar, and mailbox, often by moonlight or porch light, sometimes unable to keep up with freshly falling snow. Once the paths were clear, we'd grab our Red Flyer sleds and race to the barn. It was like a homemade toboggan run with vertical sides cut two to three feet deep in the snow.

From these humble beginnings, I learned family values of teamwork, helping neighbors, honesty, perseverance, resourcefulness, and self-confidence. They are woven into the fabric of my soul.

After enlisting in the Navy, I discovered I possessed a knack for leading people. My passion for leadership was founded on one basic principle: improve work conditions and processes affecting my people, the command, and ultimately the Navy. Years of leading and observing people led to the success principles shared in this chapter.

See the Big Picture

My most rewarding moments came while serving as Main Propulsion Assistant onboard the USS Harry S. Truman, a 98,000-ton nuclear-powered aircraft carrier. I led 120 men and women responsible for operation, maintenance, and repair of the ship's distilling plants, electrical generators, and main propulsion turbines. During weekly training, I proudly explained how their daily efforts supported the ship's mission. I touted the fact that the ship could not function without the services they provided. Without steam, we could not launch F-14 Tomcats, take hot showers, or have clean laundry. Without propulsion, we could not leave port, or more important, return home. Without electricity, nothing on the ship would operate. Without drinking water, we could not survive. From this foundational understanding, I fostered teamwork and pride in a clean, highly-functioning engine room.

During main engine training, I recruited the help of an F-14 pilot to explain how the steam we produced was used for launching aircraft. He detailed why the ship's speed was frequently varied to launch and recover different size aircraft. Hearing it directly from a pilot was very effective at reducing animosity my sailors felt toward the Air Department. The frequent changes in the ship's speed caused increased wear and maintenance on propulsion equipment. This sometimes led to feelings of resentment by the mechanics having to repair more equipment. Some people (employees or sailors) are quick to assume that they have the hardest job or the most difficult working conditions. It's funny how this belief often goes both directions. You can build a more cohesive company by informing separate departments how each affects the other and how both are vital to the company's bottom line.

Seldom did I encounter a sailor whom I could not motivate to put forth his best effort once he understood how it directly contributed to the command's mission. You can apply this concept at all levels of management in any company, large or small. Nearly everyone comes to work with the intention and desire to perform well. Sometimes their desires are derailed by reaction to a negative person, inefficient process, or seemingly unnecessary requirements.

Empower Your People

As a leader, you should create an atmosphere in which employees feel safe in bringing issues to you or their supervisor. This empowers your people to seek ways to improve processes, internal or external, affecting their productivity or work conditions. Why is this important? If something negatively affects their productivity (or work conditions), morale will suffer, their effort will weaken, productivity will further degrade, product quality will degrade, product cost will increase, scheduled deadlines will be missed, and your customers may seek service elsewhere. In the Navy, this equates to a ship that is unable to fully accomplish its mission and may cost lives during the ultimate test of battle.

Empowerment is a powerful tool. Each time a sailor presented an idea, I would listen to how she thought it would improve safety or reliability or save time. Then we'd discuss how to implement the idea and what new resources or authorization may be required. Once the idea was implemented, she saw firsthand if it yielded the expected improvements. Her success was shared within the division, thus encouraging others to bring ideas for improvement or innovation. This positive effect feeds on itself. Each person feels like a valued member of the command and contributes directly to its success.

Focus on the Possible, Not the Impossible

Besides sharing the positive successes through your command (or company), another key to building an environment of creative, dedicated sailors (or employees) is to react positively to unexpected events and seemingly bad news. Do not blame the person who may have caused the event, and certainly not the one who reported it to you. Remain calm, listen intently, think clearly, and decide whether this issue requires your immediate attention and intervention, or whether your folks can devise and implement a course for correction with simply your approval. Then spend your time ensuring they have adequate resources and informing your boss in a manner that will assure his confidence in a successful outcome with limited impact.

When involvement is necessary, focus your thoughts on ideas for correcting an unfortunate event and getting your work group back on track. Don't focus on *possible* negative impacts or outcomes. Rumors will spread, and pretty soon the negative will come to fruition. Instead remind your people how they successfully overcame similar challenges in the past and relay your faith, trust, and confidence that they will succeed this time.

I recall vividly one night that was particularly embarrassing but led to an important discovery. It was shortly after midnight. I had just laid down for sleep when my phone rang. It was a report that my guys had overfilled a potable water tank, and the water was flowing into the executive officer's stateroom. The XO was second in command. I dressed and reported to his stateroom to find him standing in two inches of water. I could see surprise and disappointment in his eyes; he saw my disappointment and embarrassment. I did not react by yelling at my people but instead rallied everyone involved to clean it up. After investigating, we discovered that the level gage for that tank was malfunctioning and needed to be replaced. The XO didn't yell at me and neither did my boss. Both had witnessed many improvements in personnel performance and machinery condition throughout the engine room and had confidence we would prevail again.

Communicate Expectations and Standards

Clearly understood expectations for performance and behavior are vital to a company's success. Making your standards visible throughout the company is a positive, effective communication method. During my first department head tour, I developed the following leadership philosophy that sustained my success in later years. You may use these or develop your own. Most important, be yourself!

Vision

Provide trained, credible, combat-capable forces ready to fight and win!

Teamwork

- Exercise mutual respect up, down, and across the chain-of-command.
- Break down barriers to communication. Cooperate within and between departments.
- Each person onboard is vital to protecting the nation!

Knowledge

- Knowledge is power.
- Lack of knowledge causes uncertainty.
- Uncertainty leads to mistakes.
- Mistakes lead to personnel injury, equipment damage, and more work.

Immediate Action

- Don't delay taking action.
- Have courage to stop and correct someone doing something unsafe or wrong.
- Be a part of the solution, not part of the problem.

Efficiency

- Whatever the task, strive to improve efficiency and reduce waste.
- If you know a better way, *speak up!*

- If a subordinate does speak up, *listen!*
- Don't complain if you have made no attempt to improve the process.

Problem Solving

- Bad news, unlike good wine, does not age well.
- Promptly notifying your chain-of-command (supervisor) when problems arise ensures that the maximum amount of time and best resources are available to solve the problem.
- Always be honest in your appraisal of the situation, no matter how bleak it appears.
- Everyone makes mistakes. Don't make the same one twice.

Pride

- Take pride in your working and living conditions.
- Pick up trash, whether on the ship, on the pier, on base, or in your neighborhood.
- Report material and equipment deficiencies, whether in your department or another.

Reduce, Reuse, Recycle

- Reduce supplies used for a task whenever possible.
- Reuse that grocery sack; don't take one if you don't need it!
- Set up recycling hubs throughout your company and your neighborhood.
- Keep your eyes and ears open for ways to enhance recycling.

Safety and Fun

- Be vigilant about safety for yourself and your shipmates, both on and off the ship.

- Always observe and adhere to written procedures and use sound judgment.

- A positive attitude, even in the darkest hour, is contagious.

Honor, Courage, and Commitment

If you ever doubt a course of action, measure it against these standards and you will find yourself on solid ground.

The above principles were written for application in the Navy. A few words have been adapted for your understanding and use in a civilian company. Most important, they must come from your heart. In the eyes of your people, you must practice these standards of conduct yourself.

Give Thanks

One can think of the Navy as a very large company. The secret of success depends not on the size of company in which you work, but on how you engage people throughout the day. See the positive aspects of other people and the beauty of life (flowers, trees, mountains, and sky). If you are constantly bemoaning your job, belittling your co-workers, and berating your boss, you will attract similarly negative people into your coffee-break discussions. Topics will be mostly complaints about company policy, parking spaces, or the manager that everyone hates. Notice how few good things happen to members of this group.

Conversely, the people making positive changes in your company will pass you by. These folks are habitually happy and helpful to others. Their laughter and smiles attract similarly positive people. Each cheerful person increases the team's positive energy and ability to create innovative products. Members of this group will succeed, even when assigned the company's most difficult challenges, largely due to the collective positive mindset. Listen to the topics discussed within this group of achievers. Their conversations will be of new products and ventures to improve company performance. Senior managers see these people as the lifeblood of the company and quickly promote from this pool.

If you don't believe me, take my challenge. Find two people. They don't have to be at your work, but you should choose folks that you see regularly. Watch how they react to unexpected news and events. Find one person who reacts negatively, often with emotions of anger or disloyalty. Find another person who reacts calmly, seeking to understand why their wants, desires, and expectations were not met. Observe how each of these people goes through their day and the types of events and circumstances that enter their lives.

As you become aware of this phenomenon, you can expand your scope of observation. Watch people in restaurants, grocery stores, gas stations, or *any* government service agency. Observe the interaction between customer and customer service representative.

How do you become one of these positive people? Simple—act the part. Compliment folks you encounter throughout the day. Maybe their shirt, their smile, their cheerful attitude, or the fabulous work they did on a recent project. Give a hearty handshake, a warm hug, and thanks for their contribution to the company. I have found that giving praise throughout the day makes *me* feel better. I am happier, I eat healthier, and unexpected good things come my way. It starts and sustains a series of events that ultimately make me more successful. For example, I recently attended a training course where I met an old acquaintance, rekindled a friendship, and he became interested in my new business.

Closing

Success is really a mindset. I wake up each morning and give thanks for the tremendous day that lies ahead. I am grateful for my health, my loving family, my rewarding job, and my appreciative boss.

Focus on BIG ideas (and idea people), not on inconsequential details (or petty complainers). Embrace the opportunity for success—flaunt it! Don't dwell on possibilities of failure, all the ways it *might* not work.

Ultimate success is living in a state of happiness. If your daily activities result in happiness, then by definition, you are successful. This is the hidden secret to life. If you are unhappy, you may achieve a little success, but you will not achieve *big*, lifelong success, because what you are doing is not fun. If it is monetary success that you desire, then follow your heart and focus all thought on those activities that make you happiest. Enjoyable activities trigger your mind to think of creative ways to produce the money you need to continue the activity, or a better one.

Biography

Mike Pawlowski

MIKE PAWLOWSKI was the valedictorian of Northport High School and is a graduate of Oregon State University with a bachelor's degree in nuclear engineering and a master's degree in chemistry. He is a retired naval officer skilled in driving ships and operating nuclear propulsion plants. As project  manager, Mike adeptly integrated all facets of a $30 million project to paint the exterior of an aircraft carrier, nearly 600,000 square feet. He is currently launching a new business devoted to health and financial freedom. Mike's caring wife Joelle is the pillar of their family, which includes three lively boys and two cats.

Contact Information

www.FreedomCowboy.com
Pawlowski.gin@gmail.com
3056 Opdal Road E.
Port Orchard, WA 98366
206-317-3851

Chapter 34

The Breakthrough Mantra

by Joe Rodrigues

On the brink of a momentous decision, I paused. Did it make sense to quit a secure job to start out on my own—with no financial backing? I knew it did not. I also knew I was shying away from what I really wanted. For a full week I had been carrying my letter of resignation around with me. I signed and submitted it.

Only then did the mental debate, which had been raging for months, subside. After a brief lull, I was caught up in another round of thinking: What should I name my company? Waking and sleeping, sleeping and waking, thoughts crowded my copywriter brain, each clamoring for attention. One morning I willed them all to be quiet and put two questions to myself: (1) What had I achieved in the positions I had held? (2) What should my new company offer to attract and sustain clients?

Soon I had two sheets of hastily scribbled answers. Forcing myself to remain focused, I went through a process of sifting, eliminating, combining, filtering, and condensing, till it all crystallized into one word. And as I scrawled that one word, "BREAKTHROUGHS" across a fresh sheet of paper, I knew it was right! It triggered the same body response I got whenever I came up with a winning headline or slogan.

During my colorful career as publicity manager in Roussel Pharmaceuticals and then in Cipla Limited, I had scored outstanding successes with several innovative "first time in India" approaches in the restricted area of pharmaceutical sales promotion. Across the industry, they had been acknowledged (and soon imitated) as breakthroughs. That was what I would offer to clients: Breakthroughs—a *Promise* backed by *Proof!* And in 1981, Breakthrough Communication Services was born.

Our Breakthrough team was engaged in developing customized marketing strategies and a range of creative material for pharmaceutical products. One of our clients heard that while at Lyka Labs, in addition to my creative portfolio, I had trained medical representatives in selling skills. At his request, I conducted a few sessions for his company's field force. The positive feedback led to more such trainings being requested, also by other clients. This serendipitous "diversion" from my company's main business activity fanned the flame of my first love: Teaching.

Being a post-grad in philosophy and pedagogy, I had started out as a teacher in Don Bosco High School, Lonavala, and I often recalled those years as being a most fulfilling period of my life. Now, from schooling medical reps in selling skills, it was but a step to developing different seminar modules, and the range kept expanding in response to clients' requirements—Assertiveness Training, Communication Skills, Stress Management, Creativity, Teambuilding, Leadership, and more. My core program is "Making Life Work for You." It involves getting in touch with *self*, reprogramming, breaking out of mental blocks, overcoming fear, and gaining exposure to a whole new "technology of living." This taps the source of greater physical vitality and expanded mental powers, taking participants to a level where they wake to the realization: *Ad majora natus sum* (I am born for greater things). This happens to be the motto of my alma mater, St. Stanislaus High School, Bandra, Mumbai. Doubtless, it acted as a subtle subliminal stimulant in my own life. In fact, embedded in all the soft skills seminars we conduct, there are repeated exhortations to super-achieve, reflecting the thrust of our core program.

In time I landed assignments that took me all over India; my list of clients included the country's leading corporates, like Hindustan Lever, the Aditya Birla Group, The Times of India Group, Hoechst, Lupin Laboratories, Maersk Shipping, the Bank of India, Hindustan Petro- leum, Bharat Petroleum, Bombay Stock Exchange, ILFS . . . however, it had been far from easy to earn such recognition and command a price. What leveraged me up the ladder were word-of-mouth referrals, as each assignment well executed attracted fresh bookings. At the outset, I was considered a total outsider to the profession, and the doors of big-name companies were shut against me. I had to break through, first my own mental blocks and then the real-world obstacles.

As more and more participants began describing their experience of my seminars as personal breakthroughs, I was forcefully struck by the prophetic inspiration in my choice of that word for my company name. It had foreshadowed a mission more profound than cranking out creative ideas to help sell medical products; it had ushered me into the dimension of true breakthroughs—in peoples' lives! Still more marvelous, even before I named it by its name, Breakthrough had been an active force in successive phases of my life. Which brings me to the power of the mantra "Breakthrough." The more you meditate on, and the more you repeat your mantra, the more power you infuse into it, and the more power the mantra channels back to you—amplified X times.

Breakthroughs are about creating space. "Space" is the simplest and the most profound topic we take participants through, starting with the evidence of physical space and moving up through the levels of psychological, emotional, and operational space, to the imperative of opening up metaphysical space for creation to occur. "Every act of creation is first of all an act of destruction" (Picasso). Stop and say "breakthrough" aloud. The very sound is disruptive, with more than a hint of the tearing pain that might accompany it. Now picture a butterfly laboriously struggling out from the confines of its chrysalis. Then see it in the full glory of its new avatar, taking wing to claim its heritage of space. That vignette captures the essence of Swami Vivekananda's "All Expansion is Life; All Contraction is Death."

It was in March 1967 that I found myself taking serious stock of my personal space. I had completed almost seven years of religious discipline and study for the priesthood, and was poised to ascend the final steps of theological studies. As I contemplated life as a priestly religious, instead of feeling the joy and anticipation of fulfillment, I was gripped by a growing disquiet. I knew from deep within that I would not be truly happy; I would not be Me; and consequently I would never be able to do justice to that noblest of all callings.

However I knew that if I did leave the seminary, I would need to make a living for myself, starting from scratch; I would need to contend with background whispers of "failure" and "he-must-have-done-some-thing-wrong" circulating within the parish and far beyond. The *sane* course of action would be to allow myself to drift into priesthood by default. The turbulence in my mind and heart gave me no peace—till I *insanely* decided to leave.

Even so, the wrenching pain of that breakthrough took months to subside. It was a time when, like a butterfly just emerged from its chrysalis, I was most vulnerable, with no means and my self-esteem almost in tatters. That was when the most numbing blow came, from the most unexpected quarter. I was visiting a particular institute when the superior caught sight me. Telling me I should be ashamed of myself as an ex-seminarian, he conducted me to the entrance and asked me to leave and never return. This personage was a high-ranking member of the same religious community to which I had belonged and given my services for seven years . . . It took months to arrest the process of "contracting" with bitterness and hurt.

"Expanding," I had my reverse revenge when, 15 years later, I was requested to conduct seminars for members of the same religious order, and one priest-participant confided that I was doing more good to them all than I would have ever done if I had remained in the congregation. "All Love Is Expansion; All Selfishness Is Contraction" (Swami Vivekananda, continued).

Skipping over the eventful years that saw me move from the ad world to pharmaceutical marketing and then to corporate training, I come to one mFAQ (m = most): "What is your secret of success?" The answer I give in my seminars is, "Do *what works for you,* in your circumstances." Still, numberless people keep salivating for a precooked "formula for success." The truth is, I did not follow any formula. My strategy has been to go with the Zen flow, responding to situations as I thought best, and continuously monitoring what worked and what did not work.

I am greatly influenced by my reading and by the inspiration I find in quotations, to which I am addicted. I also grab every opportunity to attend talks and seminars to listen to and learn from others, especially spiritual seekers. The complex chemistry of all these elements, often barely at the level of consciousness, directs my moves. This is aligned with Kierkegaard's axiom: "Life must be lived forward, but can only be understood backwards." How often, looking back at some life-jarring upset, we thank God because were it not for that occurrence, we would never have broken through to a new plane of a better life.

In 1972 I married Brenda, a high achiever, an author, and a key player in our seminars. The learnings we distill from reviewing our life experiences become the "rules of success" that we then strive to consciously apply. This is what we have identified as the Ultimate Energizer: *Ubi amatur non laboratur; etsi laboratur, labor ipse amatur.* (Where there is Love, there never is "work"; and even if there is work, that very work is loved.) This is what carried us through a grueling six-year period from 1989 to 1995, when our ancestral property, in which family (my mother, brother, sister, and we ourselves) occupied three apartments and one shop, was targeted by the land mafia. We were enmeshed in over 100 legal and quasi-legal procedures requiring personal court appearances and reams of paperwork. We were battling a corrupt officialdom, there was a contract on my life, Brenda and my office staff were assaulted, and we had to hide our two young daughters in Dalhousie, 1,200 miles away. Through it all, Brenda held on to her 9-to-5 job, while I was running three companies and conducting seminars all over India; often I had scarcely three hours' sleep at night (and did land in the hospital with a bleeding stomach ulcer). Yet because we were fighting for family, we never felt it was work, and no law of physics could ever explain how we had such an inexhaustible store of energy to draw on. (It happens too in our seminars, because each is a labor of love.)

The struggle concluded with a settlement—we relocated to apartments valued at one-third the price of what we surrendered. Many considered this a foolish loss of money, but we were just following another tried and proven golden rule. If the environment is negative/hostile and cannot be changed, get out! You may lose money, but you will benefit immensely in more significant ways.

Small minds discuss people; mediocre minds discuss events; great minds discuss ideas. The level of success one is likely to achieve is largely determined by those with whom one discusses and interacts: friends, workmates, social contacts, and above all, one's life partner. Your life partner can lever you up to hero or drag you down to zero. In India, where arranged marriages are common, it is customary to give the go-ahead to a marriage proposal only if the horoscopes of both intending parties "match." My exhortation to Gen X has been, while bowing to tradition by checking horoscopes, get with it by matching personal *values*. This will ensure congruency in thoughts, decisions, and actions, especially in the pursuit of what each wants in terms of "success."

A rule I have not found in any book so far, and which I pass on when teaching presentation skills, is based on the process I myself use in creating ads, sales literature, articles, and talks. After outlining the main content, I tell myself that the target audience has not the slightest interest in my message—so what do I need to incorporate in order to grab their attention and sustain it?

That was the how I composed this very chapter. If you read it through to the end, you have proof that the rule works. Pass it on to others.

You may be gifting them a breakthrough.

Biography

Joe Rodrigues

JOE RODRIGUES is founder and former director of Breakthrough Communication Services Pvt. Ltd. He has a rich and varied experience conducting seminars on soft skills for some of India's best-known corporations for more than 30 years and has also lectured abroad. He is a post-grad in philosophy and pedagogy,  having completed his graduation at 18 and being awarded the Pianazzi Medal in Economics. Joe has merited biographical mention in Men of Achievement, U.K., and Dictionary of International Biography, U.K.

Contact Information

jbrodrigues@gmail.com (joe_rodrigues@vsnl.com)
Netto Apartments 3, St. Francis Road, Bandra (W) Mumbai
400050 INDIA
+91-22-26429138

"Osprey," Chorao Island Resort, Belbhat, Chorao, Tiswadi, Goa
403102 INDIA
+91-832-2239898;
+91-9324609797 (cell)
Skype: joeandbrendarodrigues
Linked-in: Joe Rodrigues

Chapter 35

What You Do

by Margie Stacey

People may doubt what you say,
but they will believe what you do.
—Lewis Cass

hroughout my life I have taken up many challenges and had many successes. Although my parents were postwar immigrants who didn't speak English, I still gained entry into university as a student of pharmacy and lived on the campus, truly a privileged opportunity. Since obtaining my degree, I have never stopped educating myself in areas as diverse as financial planning, law, life coaching, and Neuro-Linguistic Programming, to name a few. Throughout my career, I have also run several successful businesses, one of which started from just a concept that no one else had pioneered.

Success begins with "To thine own self be true" Know yourself and do only what you love. Follow your passion and the rest will follow.

In business I try to serve others as I would like to be served. I treat everyone with respect, as every link in the chain is vital.

If you can live your life and know that you have somehow improved people's lives, whether through service, words, actions, or support; if you laugh often and keep everything in its proper perspective; if you are generous with your spirit, your time, and your emotions; if you look for the good in people; if you don't worry about what you don't have, but focus and are grateful for all the gifts you *do* have, you are indeed a success!

One of the greatest successes I have had in my life to date was to run the New York Marathon in 2010. Although many people run marathons, on a personal level, it was an enormous mental and physical challenge, and as a result, my life has been profoundly changed forever.

In 2007 I accompanied a friend as a supporter when she competed in the NYC Marathon (any excuse to travel to the Big Apple). She confidently announced that after I witnessed the event live, I too would have a burning desire to run a marathon. Nothing could have been further from the truth. After watching the runners stagger over the line looking absolutely exhausted, I was horrified at what would drive people to do this to themselves.

Although I have always been athletic, my physique was more suited to sprinting and sports that required short bursts of energy. I had avoided long-distance running my entire life, and the farthest I had ever run without stopping was one kilometer. Hence I convinced myself that there was *no way* I could ever be involved in any sport that required endurance, as I had no stamina, or so I believed.

Things started to change when that same friend signed me up for a walk to raise money for OXFAM, the international charity. Although I had had knee reconstruction due to a torn anterior cruciate ligament in May 2007, my friend assured me that I could participate in the Oxfam Walk in August 2008.

The word "walk" lulled me into a false sense of security, thinking it would be like a stroll for charity. I subsequently discovered two more vital things:

1. It was a bushwalk with some very steep terrain.
2. It was 100 kilometers!

The first practice, we walked 20 kilometers of the course through the bush. We were certain the organizers had gotten it wrong: such steep terrain and 100 kilometers? There had to have been a mistake! Unfortunately, it was right, and only sheer hard work, determination, and preparation would get us through.

There were five women in our group. We all had different strengths and weaknesses, but each of us played a key role in our success. We trained hard! We gave up weekends with our families; we trained in the dark of night, in the rain, in the cold, and in leech-infested waterways, always with the goal that we would all complete this journey together. The camaraderie, laughter, support, and common goal helped us sail through it on the day, finishing strong and with the support of family and friends gathered to greet us at the end. We also managed to raise a substantial amount of money, finishing among the top group of noncorporate fund-raisers, which of course made our success that much sweeter.

Subsequently, a significant shift occurred for me. My mindset completely changed. I thought, if I can walk 100 kilometers, maybe I can do something I absolutely loathe: run long distance, maybe a half marathon? I was curious to see how much my mind controlled my actions.

In February 2009, I commenced training for a half marathon with a small group of women.

There were two problems I was facing:

1. All the other women had a history of running at least 10 kilometers regularly or had a more recent solid foundation of muscle memory. I had never run long distances before.

2. The half marathon was only three months away.

Once again, I adopted the same strategy.

1. Set a goal.
2. Make a plan to achieve that goal.
3. Chunk it down into achievable goals.
4. Begin.

On the day of the half marathon, I woke up with flulike symptoms. Everything in my being told me I should not be running this distance under these circumstances; however, I am stubborn, and I felt like I had put in the work and was familiar with the circuit. I was going to do it!

I managed to complete the run, but because I was battling the onset of the flu, it didn't deliver the high I was expecting.

I didn't run another step until February 2010, the following year, when I threw down the gauntlet. This time the run would be a full marathon for me and six other women, and it would be in New York City!

We would have nine months to prepare.

It's so easy to be overwhelmed when you are tackling something for the first time or outside your comfort zone, so much so that one can become so paralyzed by fear that nothing happens. As Albert Einstein wisely said, "Nothing happens until something moves."

My mantra became "How hard can it be?" No challenge is insurmountable provided there is a *will* coupled with *unfailing persistence*, and I was armed with plenty of both.

I learned this lesson when I was growing up. My father stubbornly refused to live in predominantly ethnic areas; hence my olive skin and dark eyes did not blend with the Australian surf culture of the '70s and '80s that I grew up in. Also the food we ate and our family life was vastly different from that of my friends. I spent most of my youth being embarrassed about my origins and having low self-esteem and self-confidence—definitely feeling like a square peg in a round hole. Of course, everything Italian is very trendy now, but back then, I was always being asked where I was from. It felt like I was from nowhere. The culture gap meant I didn't belong in either country, as I was neither one nor the other.

To be accepted, I excelled in sports and school. If you are sporty in Australia, it doesn't matter what you look like, and if you are good at sports it's okay to get good grades in the classroom; hence I managed to grow up relatively unscathed because my success protected me from ridicule. However, I still held feelings of being a second-class citizen. Going to university and obtaining a degree and then entering a profession that involved counseling and caring finally created a belief in myself that I had something worthwhile to contribute.

The challenges that I faced growing up have created a steadfast confidence in myself—I know that if I want something badly, I can achieve it. The only limiting factors we have are our own self-limiting beliefs, and with every success that we have in our lives, the confidence to set the benchmark higher and higher grows.

There is nothing like a fire in your belly to make you want to excel. My wanting to fit in created a drive, competitiveness, and focus that are now my greatest ally.

My pharmaceutical background and my propensity to research and be well informed before embarking on such an enormous undertaking as a marathon meant I suddenly felt myself feeling responsible for the well-being of the group and to ensure that our training and diet would be managed correctly so that we would be well prepared and *injury free* right up to and including the big day.

My aim was to motivate the group, to inspire and direct their actions and to carefully navigate them through the next nine months of mental and physical training, as well as educating them on correct hydration and energy requirements to support them through such a physical and mental challenge, but all the while maintaining a sense of humor. The journey had to be fun because it had to be just as important and memorable as the actual event.

When people questioned why I was putting myself through this training, my response was "why not?" Surely the more difficult the challenge, the greater the reward once it is conquered?

One of my favorite quotes is by Stephen Covey: "The best way to predict your future is to create it." I think this quote succinctly says it all. We were in the process of creating our future as marathoners!

Despite my lack of experience, it never occurred to me that I or anyone on my team wouldn't complete the race. I kept visualizing myself and the others crossing the line with big smiles on our faces and a feeling of elation, not exhaustion.

On the big day, the weather was perfect. Despite the chilly conditions, the citizens of New York came out in droves to support the event. It was all quite surreal and over far too quickly. The race was executed exactly as we had planned, and when I crossed the finish line, holding the hand of one of my friends, we were both smiling, and we just looked at each other and laughed. This scene was exactly as I had visualized nine months prior but 1,000 times better. I felt like an Olympian!

The journey that ended in running a marathon has had a profound impact on my mindset and belief systems. I now truly understand that the only reason I couldn't run long distances before is because I never truly believed I could.

Now I *know* if you have the *desire* coupled with the *belief* and the *tenacity* to see it through, anything is possible!

The other wonderful and unexpected benefit was the overwhelming support that we received postrace. So many people celebrated our success: friends, family, and strangers. Somehow the word had spread through the whole community, and there was an incredible amount of joy and positive energy that flowed through to all and sundry. Many said they were so in awe and inspired that they too would take up challenges in their respective lives as they had seen what was possible just by daring to try. What can be more rewarding than motivating others to be the best they can be?

We truly are responsible for our own success in every aspect of our lives, in sports, business, relationships, and so on. We just have to take action, and the time to do that is *now*.

Biography

Margie Stacey

For the past 25 years, MARGIE STACEY has worked for and owned businesses across many facets of pharmacy, including toxicology, drug rehabilitation, and clinical and community pharmacy. In the past 15 years, she has researched and developed an interest and knowledge base in preventive healthcare, which is based on natural techniques such as healthy diet, light effective exercise, vitamins, and a positive mindset. She is currently writing several books on disease management and prevention, anti-aging, weight loss, general well-being, and more. Small changes can make profound differences in good health.

Contact Information

www.ageyoungcentral.com
ageyoungcentral@gmail.com
P.O. Box 3946, Military Rd., Mosman, NSW 2088 Australia

Chapter 36

Letting Your Spirit Guide

by Christine Kasik

Success [suh k-ses]: noun

What is success? Is it having food to eat? Having water to drink? Never smoking a cigarette in your life? Taking care of your family? Making an insane amount of money? Never getting a divorce? Knowing a lot of people? Having a lot of people know you? Dying before your children? Is it finding faith? Having a really attractive husband or wife? Being loved? In your own words, what does it mean to be successful?

Believe me when I say, God never played a leading role in my life when I was younger. To me, church was adult talk and obligation that I didn't care to understand. I figure my ignorance toward Christianity as a child was the original sin we are all born with. I know now that I could not have rectified my faith until God intervened in my life with His grace. Believe me again when I say, God's grace is overwhelming and mysterious.

I am a sinner, and I'm very willing to admit it. I cheated off the hard-working students in class, I took what wasn't mine, I liked the boys my friends liked, I lied, I was jealous of what I couldn't have, I kissed girls the way I would kiss a boy, I tested the Lord's love, and sex was a game to me. When I think about my past decisions, I can see that I was extremely selfish. The only redeeming factor to the choices I made is that I put a lot of thought into everything I did before I engaged myself. I acknowledged the fact I was ready for whatever consequences may come of my actions. My whole heart may have had good intentions, but I've learned the road to hell is paved with good intentions.

I did not start exploring my faith until after my g-ma couldn't recover from a routine colonoscopy. Josephine was a religious woman with a strong heart and a stubborn soul. She was my idol, my big sister, my grandmother, my favorite human being. Seven months later, October 11, 2007, she passed away while I was enrolled in my freshman year at Miami University. I felt alone in Oxford, and I really didn't want to be counseled by my new friends about how to handle death; they didn't know me or anything about the relationship I had with my grandmother. They didn't understand how unbearable it was for me to see her in a hospital bed. You could see it in her eyes when she looked at you; Josephine wanted to die. My dad was the only person who could make me feel somewhat at peace with the whole situation, and he was 250 miles away. Instead of asking for help, I ended up finding my own ways of coping with her upcoming death and my lingering depression. Attending church was not one of those ways either.

After I told her "I love you," and said my last goodbye, I asked my grandmother to wait for me when I leaned in for a hug and kiss. I didn't know how to deal with having her gone for the rest of my life. It hurt, badly. In my eyes she was the glue to our family. Josephine kept us all together with her simple traditions. Spending time with her was the definition of joy to me. By saying those last three words, I avidly to believed my grandmother would be forever alive in my soul.

After she died, I spent most of my time looking for her presence, that she was actually waiting for me like I had asked her to. She became my new imaginary friend. I talked to her constantly and apologized frequently for the mistakes I made. I walked aimlessly whenever I could, playing music into my headphones and smoking cigarettes, listening to the atmosphere and soaking in my surroundings. The thing is, I'm certain my grandmother was with me on those hikes across Oxford; at least, someone was with me. They listened and continuously guided me to where I needed to be. I refused their help in the beginning out of fear. I was lost in a world of insecurities and was bound to find my way through the chaos I had created. Life is an outcome of all the input submitted, and I had a lot of input to organize and file away before I kept repeating the same cycle continuously. I was going nowhere and was becoming increasingly alone. Scared, battered, and bruised, I was determined to fight my battle till the end because I had faith in myself. Trust was always a challenge for me, but I trusted my grandmother to be there for me spiritually, and I knew she would help guide me in my endeavor.

A year after my grandmother's death, my spiritual guardian told me I would find solace in my father if I was willing to be honest. I quit hiding my true self from my dad, in hopes that if he could accept me, then maybe I could accept myself too. I cannot be a true "me" unless I start telling people who "me" really is. I told him exactly how I was feeling; I was miserable and couldn't shake it off no matter what I did. My sister was one of my angels who was there for me through thick and thin. I knew Michaela loved me for me. I kept a lot of feelings bottled up, and my sister was there to let me say anything without holding it against me. I was always in a lot of pain emotionally, and

I tried desperately to ignore it by acting like I was happy. I created an alter ego to distract myself from my real feelings. Unfortunately, my fake happiness only made my life more complicated. I was in a very dark, empty place for what seemed like most of my life. I prayed to my grandmother, to God, to whoever would hear my prayers that I would do anything to be okay again, and here I am better than okay, confronting and comprehending my emotions for what they are.

The most significant sign I was given from the spirit world was my daughter's name. I originally wanted to name her Josephine for obvious reasons, but instead my grandmother gave me another name in her honor. Ever since that double line showed up on my first pregnancy test, I was inspired to name my child meaningfully. A name that reminds me every day how lucky I am to be a healthy mother with a healthy daughter. I had no previous knowledge of the name Lillian (other than from the television cartoon *Rugrats*), but for some reason when I was lying awake at five in the morning on my cousin's apartment floor in Berlin, Germany, I knew Lillian would be my baby's name. There I was, six months' pregnant in Germany, reciting name after name in my head without any clue as to where I was coming up with them—Harper, Ella, Anastasia, Liberty, Elizabeth, and then Lillian. The moment the name Lillian crossed my mind, nothing sounded more fitting for my daughter. I couldn't escape the integrity, and I instantly sent a text message to my boyfriend proclaiming that I had chosen my baby's name and he could not persuade me otherwise. To make my daughter's name even more perfect to me, Anthony actually approved and loved her name just as much as I did, and this was after rejecting every other single name I had suggested prior to that day. I later found out that Lillian was my great-grandmother's name, Josephine's mother. The joy I felt knowing Josephine was still a part of me and now a part of my daughter is indescribable. I felt truly loved and blessed knowing my grandmother didn't forget about me. Josephine is not only waiting for me, but I'm waiting to be reunited with her again.

I had a spiritual experience, and I found God in the end, but finding God is not my success story. My success came through the emotional journey I survived with the guidance of God and Josephine. For the longest time I couldn't forgive myself for the person I was and the lies I told. Life was a wreck when it was controlled by all the falsehoods I lived by. Once I stopped being afraid of the truth about who I am, I was able to like myself—the sinner, the liar, the lover. I was able to forgive my family for all the lies and mistakes they made because I was able to forgive myself first. I'm okay with not knowing what will happen tomorrow after all that I've done yesterday or three years ago as long as I have my family by my side. My grandmother taught me how family is a team, not a burden on your social life.

My success story won't lead you to fame or fortune, but I hope my story can bring light into your life wherever it's needed. It's a true story about overcoming misery, no antidepressants necessary. The devil truly had five of his hands wrapped tightly around me. One hand was over my eyes, to blind me from spiritual things. Another hand was over my hands, to keep me from doing good deeds. A third hand was over my feet, to keep me from walking to that which is good. A fourth hand lay over my reason and understanding, so I would not be ashamed to sin. The fifth hand rested over my heart, where I would be held from ever returning to the right way of the Lord through remorse and penance. The hands of Satan feel powerful when they're embracing your body, but your soul is genuinely lost when it's not in the hands of God. I was brought back into the light of God by Josephine. I am forever grateful and eternally loyal to Him for allowing me to join His family. Without family, we're nobody.

As I said, finding God is not my success story. God brought His presence and grace into my life, but the greatest success I've achieved is knowing I don't have to be contrite about who I've been. The people who truly love me, as God loves me, will be able to see through my younger years and see me as who I am now. The past and the present make me the person I will be tomorrow. I have learned that the choices I made growing up never led me in the right direction, and now I'm traveling down a different road, one I have yet to leave my footprints on—a road that I think will take me where I've been trying to go. This is me, living everything I've learned and still wanting to learn more. I'm not afraid of who I am. I love who I am.

A big thanks goes out to all the people I love, and all the people I will never love. We make each other's world go round. A bigger thanks goes out to my family for loving me. You know who you are. Xoxo.

Biography

Christine Kasik

CHRISTINE KASIK is an everyday twenty-two-year-old trying to graduate college on time and work to pay off her expenses. Her life is not what she expected, but you cannot plan for life; it just happens. Her daughter, Lillian, was born September 20, 2010, and she is an honest blessing by being one of those  unanticipated additions in life. Christine loves being a single mom, especially with an amazing baby like her, and she's anxious to see what else the universe has in store.

Contact Information

christinekasik@gmail.com

Chapter 37

What Everybody Ought to Know for Success in the 21st Century

by Evelyn Cole

1. The Art

Art is intuitive, imaginative, and powerful. Success is a state of mind—your mind—and you define it.

For example:

- Sometimes I enjoy wonderful success, sometimes abject failure that keeps me awake at night. Old phrases haunt me: "You have to be practical. You're so naive! You trust everyone. You gotta do the research."

- Other times I glow. After three bad marriages, I have a heavenly one. Big success!

- People like my poetry, even pay for it. So what that my novels get no money yet get great reviews.

- Friends love my cooking.

- My two sons-in-law love me. Now that's an unusual success.

I am developing the practice of daily success. When I help someone, clean something, make something new for dinner (even if it's only Normandy meatloaf), win a doubles ping-pong game, or give a loving hug at the right moment, I feel successful.

I need to count my successes every day in order to count my blessings, and vice versa.

Love is my greatest success. I am not religious, but I agree with Rob Bell, a Christian pastor who wrote *Love Wins*, a book that "stuck a pitchfork in how Christians talk about damnation" (review by Cathy Grossman in *USA Today*). Bell says, "God is love. . . . Love demands freedom. Making definitive judgments about other people's destiny is not interesting to me."

In other words, "Who am I to insist on someone else's punishment in hell?"

I add, "Does any kind of punishment work?"

Everyone, I suppose, has experienced some form of punishment. Each of us angered our parents who, being human, lashed out to stop us from doing whatever angered them. "Stop crying or I'll give you something to cry about!"

But when punishment is administered rationally through legalized paddling in schools and the death penalty in a civilized society, does punishment really work, or is it simply justified revenge?

Most schools have stopped paddling children who "misbehave," but few states have recognized that it costs three to five times as much to execute a prisoner than to feed and shelter him for life. Lawyers on both sides of the issue take advantage of our collective confusion, as they should, and litigation takes decades. That's what adds to the costs of executions.

A loving approach to influence behavior, whether Christian, Muslim, or Atheist, is far more effective than punishment. We need to recognize that we are simply acting out of our anger collectively when we vote to imprison and ignore torture—any kind of torture.

A loving approach includes simple physical removal from the scene, whether it be removing a screaming toddler in a grocery store or deterring or rerouting criminal action in a community. Adding punishment or torture to incarceration or spanking after removing a toddler from a store does nothing to prevent future tantrums or future crimes. In fact, punishment does no more than create another punisher. Many of us grew up with misguided punishment, and we continue to ply it onto the next generation.

When you smile at a baby, he smiles back. Is he—or she—just imitating you, or does he feel the pleasure? Instinctual pleasure begins at birth, despite moments of pain. Those who succeed in life maintain the baby's smile, feel the pleasure of interaction with others who love them, and develop delightful laughs that stay for life.

Those who are punished regularly may succeed in business but in nothing else—except punishing others.

If you suffer from the results of childhood punishment in your adult life, you can learn the art of total success in several proven ways: audio discs that help you let go of negative self-concepts and past traumas, audio for hypnosis to help you change your perceptions, visual instruction on painting your pains onto canvas. All art takes imagination. My chosen art is writing. It changed my self-concept and my ability to love so much that I created an e-course called *Brainsweep*.

May you define seven successes a day. May you imagine seven successes a day.

If you're overweight, imagine yourself thinner.

If you're overworked, imagine yourself strolling through spring wildflowers or along a beach.

If you're undersexed, imagine . . . .

It's fun to create success; just let it flow.

2. The Science

The Mathematics of Success

The following concepts come from an interview with Martin Nowak, Ph.D., professor of mathematics and biology at Harvard University (*New Scientist*, March 24, 2011).

Introduction: "Using mathematics to tackle some of biology's biggest questions, Martin Nowak has concluded that an ability to cooperate is the secret of humanity's success. He talks about the perils of punishment and devising the mathematical equivalent of the rules of religion."

On punishment:

> Many people feel that punishment is a good thing, that it leads to human cooperation. So their idea is that unless you cooperate with me, I punish you. It might even cost me something to punish you, but I do it because I want to teach you a lesson. One cannot deny that punishment is an important component of human behavior, but I am skeptical about the idea that it's a positive component.
>
> I have analyzed the role of punishment using mathematics and experiments. I think that most uses of punishment are very much for selfish interests, such as defending your position in the group. Punishment leads to retaliation and vendettas. It's very rare that punishment is used nobly.

(I don't understand how mathematics describes the effects of punishment on cooperation, but I want to.)

Nowak says, "Without a mathematical description, we can get a rough handle on a phenomenon, but we can't fully understand it. In physics, that's completely clear. You don't just talk about gravity, you quantify your description of it. The beautiful thing about mathematics is that it can decide an argument. Some things are fiercely debated for years, but with mathematics the issues become clear."

(Measurements do tell a true story. Whether you like it or not, they tell you what size clothes to buy.)

On religion: "When you look at mathematical models for the evolution of cooperation you also find that winning strategies must be generous, hopeful, and forgiving. In a sense, the world's religions hit on these ideas first, thousands of years ago. Now, for the first time, we can see these ideas in terms of mathematics. Who would have thought that you prove mathematically that, in a world where everybody is out for himself, the winning strategy is to be forgiving, and that those who cannot forgive can never win."

This is a powerful statement. I can attest to it on a personal level. Long after my mother's death, I began writing to her, asking questions. In the process, I understood and forgave her, finally. As a result I met and fell in love with a man who is now my husband. I know now that I would not have loved him before I forgave her. He is nothing like my former husbands, who criticized me daily as she did.

More on the Science of Success

How do we win a war? When we win a war, are we successful?

In a beautiful interview with Captain Paul Chappell by Leslie Goodman in *Sun Magazine*, April 2011, we learn how to wage peace. Paul is a graduate of West Point, veteran of the Iraq War, and advocate of success through cooperation. He shows us how to relate to people with opposing views.

He says, "One thing I learned at West Point is that in order to think strategically, you must be able to see the world from your opponent's point of view. And from the point of view of the average Afghan, the U.S. military is there to keep a corrupt government in power."

More and more leaders are beginning to consider this fact, but have yet to act on it.

"Human beings," Paul says, "aren't naturally violent. . . . Military history shows how nonviolent we are. . . . Look at war propaganda. In every culture the warmongers tell us that we have to protect our families, our freedom, and our way of life from evil people in some foreign land. War propaganda manipulates our most powerful instincts: love of family, love of freedom, and the desire to help others. . . . If we were naturally violent, our leaders could just say, 'I'm going to give you a chance to kill people. I'll even pay you!' I've never seen a military-recruiting commercial that even *mentions* killing people."

But that is exactly what military training does. Our veterans suffer to the point of suicide. A young Navy junior officer in the Pacific during World War II became suddenly in charge of a landing boat when his superior officers were killed. For two years he had to take boatloads of U.S. Marines to their death on Pacific Islands. Seven years after the war, he committed suicide.

Warfare now can have a growing disconnect. Consider the following:

Young boys fight hand-to-hand, kick, scream, swear, spit, push, bite, back away crying, and then go play together.

Gloved men fight, left uppercut, right to the jaw, knockouts by the rules, and then go drink together.

A soldier in battle sees the enemy's eyes looking into his as he kills him. Those eyes stay with him always. A bombardier shoots from the sky. Curled tight, he studies the map, looks down on his target, aims, drops, flies away, and then drinks to collateral damage.

The command programmer guides a missile from a Predator into a car in a desert two hundred miles away and then pats his own back.

A four-star general dictates the code that destroys a whole city on the other side of the world and then watches results on six o'clock news. After driving his Hummer to pick up his daughter, he returns home and clutches the steering wheel. The woman in the doorway should be his wife, but he cannot recognize her face.

The brains in babies light up in one place for faces, another for things. Not so in autistic babies. Things and faces look the same.

This why it's so important to heed Paul's strategy to influence cooperation successfully. He calls for understanding other people's worldviews. He says, "If you attack someone's worldview, they are likely to react as if you are attacking them physically. It's part of who they are. When Martin Luther King Jr. challenged segregation, he was challenging everything that white Southerners believed. . . . So King took an innovative approach: he tied his ideas to his opponents' existing worldview by likening black Americans' fight for civil rights to the Hebrews' struggle for freedom from oppression in Egypt. This made the challenge less threatening."

The science of success includes recognizing the faces of those opposing you and leads me to one final quote:

"Are you aware that a shift in human consciousness is occurring even as you read [about] celestial triggers such as supernovas and Earth's alignment with Galactic Center in the year leading up to 2012 to trigger the evolution of our species?"
—Sol Luckman

May we evolve successfully!

Biography

Evelyn Cole

EVELYN COLE taught English for 23 years. To get high school freshman interested in Greek mythology, she persuaded them to teach it to sixth graders across town by email. To get college freshman to understand why they were required to analyze literature, she showed them how semantic analysis relates all subjects.

She has three published novels, short stories, poems, one textbook, two self-help e-books, called *Brainsweep* and *Your Inalienable Right*, and a related series of articles called "Mind Nudges."

Contact Information

evymae@hughes.net
1748 Deer Canyon Road
Arroyo Grande, CA 93420
805-473-0230

Chapter 38

Possibility

by Joanne Haslam

Any fact facing us is not as important as our attitude toward it,
for that determines our success or failure. Believe in yourself!
Have faith in your abilities! Without a humble but reasonable
confidence in your own powers, you cannot be successful or happy.
— Norman Vincent Peale

I had huge reservations about sharing my simple story. It is not grand, but it is real. I hope that in sharing the truth of where I am and who I am, I can help you in some small way.

I want to talk to you directly, as though we were sitting together. This book is about success, and I don't know if I am successful. There is certainly nothing I need or want for. I have taken care of my children and provided them with a good education. I have a good job, work with great people, and travel all over the world. Help me as I share this inquiry with you. What got this girl to where she is today?

I am South African. Yes, born in South Africa. Many people are surprised to hear this, thinking this should make me black. Growing up in such a racist society, as a child I was simply not aware of it, and later I felt it had nothing to do with me, as I felt neither guilty nor responsible. I now believe if you are not part of the solution, you must be part of the problem.

My parents are divorced. I have a brother and an extended family. My father remarried so I also have a stepbrother and sister and a half brother. My mother also remarried much later to a lovely, kind, intelligent man, but this tragically did not last as he died from liver cancer. I left school in a hurry to be independent and earn a living fast so I would no longer have to choose between my parents or have to ask them for anything. This sounds like a good enough excuse for getting married young and not getting a degree, but if I dig deeper, the truth is that I probably did not know what I wanted to do. I feel I have to mention my marriage, which can't possibly be described as a success. I got divorced after 16 years. I do not want to go into the reasons it did not work, as they are too personal and sad to share here. Much of it was related to me, but a good portion of our problems were related to his issues as well. I don't expect anyone to believe I am capable of telling an unbiased version of the story. I have read that all issues are relationship issues. I challenge you to have your own personal inquiry on this one. I am not comfortable, however, leaving this part of my life classified as unsuccessful. I have no regrets and have two beautiful children, so let's put this piece down to experience and learning.

I am an IT professional with 20 years' experience, including roles as project manager, regional lead, and CIO. My job focus is to maximize business value through the effective and relevant use of technology, to achieve the most efficient operations, providing highest business value through effective management of IT resources (people, financial resources, services). I developed an environment that fosters high performance and innovation in the organization. I have lived in several countries, and I moved halfway across the world with two children to take the role as a project manager for a huge global IT application rollout. I saw this through to completion, but the success was not just mine—I was a small part of a big team.

Maybe to have this conversation, we should be clear on the definition of success. I think it is very personal. A dictionary can give you a definition of success, but real success is determined only by you. My success must encompass all my roles, at work and as a family member. It is extremely important to have balance in all roles to be truly happy.

Success

So how do you get success in life and business? You must make sure people can trust you. If you don't let people down, and they know they can trust you implicitly, then opportunity will come to you. Be authentic and genuine without any hidden agenda. Success is as much internal character as it is anything else. If I were pushed to choose one key attribute in achieving success, it would be integrity. Not from the base of right or wrong, good or bad, but wholeness and completeness. Of course, there is more to success than this. I will try to give you what I have found to be the most important steps in creating success in life.

1. *Believe in yourself.* If you don't have confidence that you will achieve, then no one else will either.

2. *Develop others.* Leading includes challenging others to do more than they have before and empowering them to make efforts that will achieve your vision.

3. *Be goal oriented.* Success is generally decided long term, and it can only come from achieving the smaller steps and milestones. You must be able to set clear targets with deadlines and meet

them! This is the same as being action oriented. You actually have to get off your butt and do something.

4. *Be tenacious.* Stick-at-it ability. Don't let failures stop you. Pause only long enough to see what you can learn from the experience and move on. That which does not kill you makes you stronger. Persistence and courage are most often needed.

5. *Think positively, with great imagination.* Albert Einstein said, "Imagination is more important than knowledge." Doing things with enthusiasm makes such a difference. Have a passion for life!

6. *Release your belief in one absolute truth and attachment to being right.* Achieving the end goal is more important than being right.

7. *Practice daily gratitude.* There is always so much to be grateful for, and concentrating on that will help you complain less and be at peace with yourself. This will draw people to you who will want to follow your lead.

8. Accept personal responsibility. Be fully responsible for your life. Your thoughts are creating your reality in every moment. Blaming others never helps and only slows you down.

Obstacles

No road in the real world is a smooth one; there are always challenges. You have to face them and learn from them, in the hope that you can turn them into strengths. I grew up as a happy child but never feeling good enough. Whatever I did, my parents thought I could do better. This taught me a great work ethic, however. I had to work hard to constantly prove myself. I never took anything for granted.

After my parents' divorce, I had a huge fear of being dependent on anyone. I have learned, however, that you might succeed, but you will be lonely. Vulnerability is not bad, and many people get pleasure helping you. You can't become yourself by yourself. Others offer a unique refection that can help you grow and develop quicker. Finding a good mentor is invaluable.

Stress and lack of time were major issues for me. The more you do, the more you are expected to do, but there are no medals for overwork. You have to learn to say no.

My biggest roadblock to date has been illness. Do you know what it feels like to be sick and tired? It hit me like a ton of bricks. I simply had no energy and could not get through a normal day. After an initial diagnosis of chronic fatigue syndrome and a doctor who advised me to simply take antidepressants and a year sabbatical, I finally discovered that I had a tropical intercellular infection called Rickettsia. Depression might keep you from wanting to get out of bed, but with this disease, you want to but simply lack oxygen to give you the energy to move.

I felt completely out of control. Everything else in my life could be fixed with self-discipline and hard work. I did find help and am living on pulse antibiotic therapy. More recently I discovered the power of energy healing. But the more important discovery is this: *You alone* are responsible for creating your state of health and for making health-related decisions. Not even your doctor has this responsibility! He's certainly a consultant and an adviser, but ultimately, the final decisions about your health are yours and yours alone. You cannot allow doctors to push you into treatments that may not be the best option for you. Ask questions. Get second and even third opinions. Any doctor that objects to you getting another opinion should no longer be your doctor.

Illness is a great teacher, however. I was forced to slow down, take stock, and reprioritize my life. I could not run, so I could not run away. Keeping continually busy ensures you have no time to reflect. It is so important to find solitude and space to think. It is not only what you do but how you are being in any situation that counts. My strength and learning from this is radical self-care. You have to be your own best friend. Look after your body because you hopefully have a long road to travel together. If you don't have your health, what you are able to do is severely restricted. Never give up. Keep an open mind and get all the help and advice you can.

Through this experience I feel a bigger calling to help others realize their fullest potential; maximize their health; and navigate the mass of information that is available to get optimal results. Integral is my new passion. Integral health and integral life, a strong belief that a 360-degree view is needed to truly find powerful solutions to the very real challenges we face together today (see http://integrallife.com/learn-more).

Leadership

Chris McCusker, chairman and CEO of Motorola, said, "Leadership is going first in a direction—and being followed." Leading begins with realizing and clearly envisioning the overall mission. "Starting with the end in mind," as Steven Covey wrote in the *7 Habits of Highly Successful People*, is how you point the way to others who can't yet see it. A leader must be able to envision an outcome and be able to communicate that vision in a way that engages and inspires others; have tenacity and courage to take action and let others know they are on track; and stay confident even in the face of disappointments.

Mentors

We all need people to inspire us. My role models and mentors are too many to list here, but two stand out:

Les Brown—He said, "You have the power to change and you are never too old to set another goal or dream a new dream." He started with nothing and had the courage to find his voice. He has spoken to millions of people and has had a profound effect on people's lives.

Sean Stephenson—This incredible three-foot giant is living proof that anything is possible, and if for a second you have doubts or feel sorry for yourself, just look at this man to shame you back into action and fill you with gratitude.

Choose Success

Be clear about what you choose to have or achieve. Think about what you think about! What you put your attention on grows stronger. Don't stress. Stress will only make you ill and will not help you reach your goal. Try to relax and do what you do with enthusiasm and a passion for life.

My success so far has only been focused on *me*, the need to survive and care for my children. Now it is time to move on to the *we* focus, the deep desire to make a difference by adding value. My success can at best be described as ordinary. Extraordinary success I believe is an option for all of us.

Biography

Joanne Haslam

JOANNE HASLAM is a 46-year-old South African living in London. She has worked in the life science sector as an IT professional for 15 years, and is currently head of the IT Project Management Office for Asia, the Middle East, and Africa. This region has 32 countries and spans 11 time zones and more  than 40 languages— an exciting region with huge economic growth but also huge political uncertainty. Nearly 2.5 billion people live in these countries—almost one-third of the world's population. Joanne is the mother of two beautiful girls ages 19 and 23.

Contact Information

www.bestwaystomarketonline.com
www.bestwaystohealth.com
joanne.haslam@gmail.com
44 148 3420164
44 777 8040706 (cell)

Chapter 39

A Success Bigger than Self

by Sabrina Williams

As a young vulnerable child, I was molested and physically abused by people whom I thought loved me. I cried for many years, ran away from home, and eventually dropped out of school. Sometime later, I married and had four children. I thank God for my children, but my marriage became a living hell. I was falsely accused on a daily basis of cheating with another man. The accusations became so bad that I dreaded him coming home because I knew that I would have no peace. He would keep me up until the early morning hours questioning me about cheating, and when he wasn't home, he would constantly call to check up on me to see if I was doing something with another man. And that was just one of the many problems in my marriage.

I had many sleepless nights not knowing whether my kids and would have a place to live because we were constantly faced with being evicted from our home. A lot of the evictions came as a result of my husband's misuse of money and gambling problems, and him not being able to keep a job because of inappropriate actions on the job and being late for work. Having a place to live was not my only worry. I had to worry about the utilities being disconnected. There was a time when I had to live in government housing, and we had next to no food in the house, so I fed my children and husband what was there, and I made myself flour bread (flour and water mixed together) to eat.

I can remember locking myself in the bathroom and just crying my eyes out because one school year, my husband was not going to be able buy our children clothes for school because of misuse of money. So I ended up turning to a friend for help, and one day I decided that enough was enough, so I got a job and moved myself and the kids out.

I later went back to school, earning my high school diploma. I also become a licensed insurance agent for one of the largest insurance agencies in the country. After being in the business of selling insurance, I decided I needed something more challenging, so one of my fellow church members and I decided to partner with a company and go into business together. Our new business partner made a lot of promises about day-to-day business dealings and other aspects of the company. We would sometimes work 12–16 hour shifts each with the belief that the company would make good on its promises. After a period of time had passed, we realized that the company was just using us for its own gain.

Now I could have run with my tail between my legs and cried over it, but that's not what I'm made of. I am always reminded that if I can survive being molested (which was far more tragic), then I can survive whatever obstacle is thrown my way.

After this unfortunate event, I later became the president of a company whose main focus was purchasing and renovating houses for low-income families. We were very successful until the city placed a lien on the company's houses, a lien that was later determined to have been placed without merit. But by this time the company had suffered great loss and was forced to shut its doors.

Now I know that there are a lot of businessmen and women who would have given up on ever owning and operating their own business, but we must always remember: "What doesn't kill you makes you stronger." After some time had passed, I earned my mortgage broker's license and began to process mortgages. During this period, my partner and I were inspired to develop a unique, innovative, anticipated Nobel Prize-winning concept that would reverse the obesity epidemic, drastically reduce poverty by 25%–75%, reduce the need for government subsidies, restore the American dream of homeownership, provide employment, prevent foreclosures, eliminate our government debt, decrease the crime rate, assist with resolving our Social Security problems, and much more. (The prelaunch is set for 2011. For additional information, please visit www.thevillagemovement.com.)

A tip for success in life is to commit to a belief system that is greater than you and commit to a system that teaches against selfishness. The idea of being successful in your personal life or in your business endeavors without removing selfishness is an illusion.

Can you imagine a man refusing to go into a burning building to save his son, his daughter, his wife, or maybe all three because he is unwilling to sacrifice his own life for the benefit of others? Can you imagine a mother keeping a man in her life who rapes or molests her daughter or son? I am reminded of the movie *Precious,* starring Mo'Nique, who played the role of Mary (Precious's mother), who was so selfish that she allowed her husband to rape their daughter at a very young age up until her teenage years. She then allowed her daughter to bear two children from her biological father. She thought only of what she wanted or what she thought was best for her to the point of destroying any hope or chance for her daughter to ever live a normal life.

What about a person who works for a company or the EPA and uncovers a situation that causes people to develop cancer or babies to be born deformed? These people believe that making this information known will cost them their job or any chance of starting their own independent business. What about investment companies who set forth policies that the companies' in-house stock must be sold first before other companies' stock, even if the other stock is more profitable and has less risk? Let me take a moment and remind you of Bernard Madoff, who swindled billions of dollars from an investment account where people trusted him with their life savings, thinking that he was loyal and honoring his fiduciary responsibilities. However, we all know that he was selfish, greedy, and self-centered. He sought only to satisfy himself and caused many people to be hurt both mentally and financially. Selfishness is a destructive trait that will destroy you and cause you to justify harming others, being dishonest to them and to yourself.

In my humble opinion, I believe that true success is composed of many elements that are entwined to achieve higher levels of success. Much like the human body has a heart, brain, lungs, kidneys, liver, eyes, nose, ears, and so on, each element of success has a separate and distinctive function. Under normal circumstances, they join together to achieve life in its perfect form (the human body). If you remove a lung or kidney, the body will still function but not at the level it's meant to perform. For example, we have two eyes designed by nature to give us peripheral vision, but if you lost the vision in your right eye, then you would have lost the full use of peripheral vision on your right side.

For a moment look straight ahead, then take your right hand and raise it about 12 inches away from your right ear directly from the side. You should be able to see this without turning your head. Now close your right eye as you continue to look ahead. You won't be able to see your right hand because you have lost the use of one of your eyes. The more elements of success you combine and use in conjunction with each other, the greater level of success you will achieve—the more complete will be your vision.

Success is having achieved or accomplished certain things in your personal or business life without compromising your moral values or breaking the law. It's about overcoming problems no matter how big or small without giving up. There are steps to consider and follow in an effort to become truly successful:

Self-evaluation: Self-evaluation is important because it forces you to analyze your strengths and weaknesses. It is mandatory to be completely honest when conducting this phase because lying to yourself will only hurt you in the long run. Believe it or not, you can be your own worst enemy. During my marriage, after so many other heartbreaking events, I decided that enough was enough and I could do badly all by myself. So the first thing I did was performed a self-evaluation to determine my weaknesses and strengths. This process allowed me to recognize what I had to offer my employer if I chose to get a job or what I had to offer my customers if I chose to own and operate my own business. You cannot plot a path of success without first evaluating where you are. Since that time, I have not looked back.

Planning: Failure to plan is a plan for failure. Planning is mandatory for personal and business success. Can you imagine a ship captain setting sail without a plan or map? He will no doubt get lost and wander the sea trying to get his bearings. Planning requires deciding where, when, and how you will get where you're going. It requires you to take inventory of yourself and of the vehicle you will be using to get there.

Forgiveness: Someone once said, forgiveness is the key to action and freedom. When the mind is preoccupied with thoughts of who did you wrong, when they did you wrong, why they did you wrong, and so on, it has become imprisoned with thoughts of resentment, hatred, revenge, and anger toward those who have wronged you. These feeling and thoughts are so strong that they can lead to hypertension, stomach ulcers, forms of depressions, and the prevention of success. The key to unlocking the prison doors and freeing yourself to focus on achieving the greatest inside of you is forgiveness. Lewis B. Smedes said, "To forgive is to set a prisoner free and discover that the prisoner was you." Through forgiveness, I was able to take back control of my life from my abuser.

Remember that true success is not measured by whether you have a big home, an expensive car, a lot of money in the bank, or your level of social status; it is measured by overcoming life's obstacles. So I would like to encourage you to set goals, take it one day at a time, and stay on the path regardless of challenges. Consider each step you take to be an accomplishment, and remember that the more steps you take, the more accomplished you will become.

Biography
Sabrina Williams

MS. WILLIAMS is the president and CEO of Legacy Rent 2 Own, the former president of WWDF, Inc., a licensed mortgage broker, and a licensed insurance agent. For the past seven years, she has been developing an antici- pated Nobel Prize-winning concept that will  reverse the obesity epidemic and drastically reduce poverty through home ownership.

Contact Information

sabrinawms.com
Sabrina@sabrinawms.com
265 SW Port St. Lucie Blvd., #238, Port St. Lucie, FL 34984
772-236-9552

Chapter 40

The Power of Thought

by Melanie Greenough

*A problem cannot be solved
on the same level of thinking it was created on.*

*L*ife is amazing with all its mystery and evolution, how some figure life out while others waste away in poverty, misery, and misfortune. How can we be assured we are not the latter? There is a serious danger for people who don't realize they are the masters of their own destiny as this master wordsmith describes:

Invictus

by William Ernest Henley

*Out of the night that covers me
black as the pit from pole to pole,
I thank whatever gods may be
For my unconquerable soul.*

In the fell clutch of circumstance
I have not winced nor cried aloud.
Under the bludgeonings of chance
My head is bloody, but unbowed.

Beyond this place of wrath and tears
Looms but the Horror of the shade,
And yet the menace of the year
finds and shall find me unafraid.

It matters not how strait the gate,
How charged with punishments the scroll,
I am the master of my fate:
I am the captain of my soul

The question has to be asked of life: Who or what decides our fate or destiny? The true answer is we do. No matter where we come from or what has happened to us, we have the final say in what will become of our lives. I know that for some this will be hard to understand, but the truth is that every person has free will, and we can use it be a success or not.

As a slim shaving of an example, here is my story:

I grew up with an alcoholic father, was abused by many people, on alcohol and drugs by 13, a dropout by 16, pregnant by 19, lost my son at birth, and worked in a very harsh industry by the time I was 21. This was the start of my journey. I then met and married the father of my daughter, and things got very difficult—I ended up in a woman's shelter completely homeless, no car, no job, no bank account, and not a cent to my name. I found myself at the bottom of bottom at 25, hopeless and scared. I woke up one day at the shelter faced with an uncertain future, stripped of every belonging and all dignity, and I was left alone with a one-year-old baby counting on me. That's when I realized I had a decision to make.

What would it be? More of the last 25 years, or was I going to change, do things differently, learn a different way to live? The answer came quickly. I would do everything in my power to give my daughter a different life than I had lived. My desire to see her safe and living a good life outweighed my desire to blame others, to cower and hide in being a victim.

In my responsibility to her, I found the inner conviction to move forward, to never surrender. But to have different results, I had to become different. So I set out on a journey, very unsure of the path that lay before me but certain that if I did not change, my daughter's life would look like mine or worse.

*There is no question but that he who is "wise enough to understand" will readily recognize that the **creative power of thought** places an invisible weapon in his hands and makes him a **master of destiny.***
—Charles F. Hanaal

Now I would like to say that because of this life-changing aware- ness, everything fell into place and success overtook me, but I would be doing success a great disservice to talk of her so flippantly.

Success is something that is earned by hard work, persistence, good character, and commitment. So the decision I made to change my life was the *start* of the process, not the end. It was the first step on a long ladder of choices that I had to make to get from where I was to where I am today. Working on myself, changing the way I thought, was and still is the hardest work I have ever done, but I promise it is worth it.

The first step was taking responsibility for where I found myself. It was not what had happened to me that was the problem; it was the way I chose to respond to what happened that got me in trouble. Unfortunately, society is highly victim friendly. We blame everyone for everything that happens. We even blame people for the way we feel.

He made me feel this way or that. He did this, so I did that. Reacting to our circumstances does not bear the mark of a master. Quite the contrary, victims blame others and circumstances for their woes. Masters take ownership and decide how to respond to attain the highest good.

This is what I had to do. First, forgive the people who had deeply hurt me—release them and bless them and then take full responsibility for how I reacted to their actions. As soon as I started taking responsibility, I was able to apply my will to each situation and become committed to walking toward my highest good.

My commitment to success removed the chance of failure, because now no matter how long I had to work, I was working toward what I wanted instead of being batted around by life, ending up a victim of what happens to me.

My level of awareness began to grow, and I was faced with the fact that my thinking had gotten me to where I was, and for my results to change, my thinking had to change. I had to become a different person. Successful people think a certain way, dress a certain way, talk a certain way, and do things a certain way. This is where your path could begin if you chose—to learn a different way, to change your thinking, to figure out who you would like to become. What do the people who have what you want do? How do they think?

As I went through the process of personal development, positive creation through thought, and consistent action, my life began to change and now is drastically different from the one I had created before. Now my past annual income has become my monthly income; I travel and speak to crowds of thousands across North America and coach and mentor hundreds if not thousands of people on how to create the life of their dreams. Can I say I have arrived? No. I may not be where I want to be, but thank God I am not where I used to be either.

Here is what I do know for certain: Whatever problems or circumstances you face in your life, they cannot be solved on the same level of thinking that you created them on; therefore, you must change your thinking to change your life.

The good news is that you are the master of your destiny; the bad news is that you are the only one who can or will change your life for the better, which means the work is up to you. Most people will argue that they are not responsible for their circumstances or are victims of the actions of others, but we all must take 100% responsibility for where we are before we can move forward.

So let's assume that you are willing to take responsibility and move forward toward the life of your dreams, toward success beyond your wildest imagination. The next step is to become aware of the power you have to create through your thoughts. Every time you create a scenario in your head, whether it be in the right direction or not, you are creating a pattern for your life to follow. If your scenarios are based on your past level of thinking, you will get that level of result again, but if you elevate your thinking, you can get a higher, more desirable result.

How do you do this? Through the books you read, the people who mentor you, and the personal development material that you learn and apply. This is the way to change your level of thinking by allowing others who are more successful, who have gone before you and gotten the kind of results that you want, to coach and mentor you to higher heights.

One of the first things I learned along this path is that we need to have a crystal clear picture of what we want our life to look like. What would your life look like *exactly?* What house would you live in, what car would you drive, how would you dress, where would you shop, who would you hang out with, where would you travel?

Find pictures of the things you want, find out how much they cost, and make a plan to create a stream of income that will give you the lifestyle that you want. Be as exact as you can because you get what you think about and you become a product of the thoughts you are currently generating. By focusing on where you are going and keeping the life of your dreams before you, you naturally create a map of success.

Of course, wanting things you can never have is not the point of this exercise. Really take the time to feel how it feels to have that thing or that relationship. Be there—feel the feelings of it already being accomplished. Feel your pride swell, your happiness expand, your joy explode, and stay in the mindset of it being yours already. When you feel that thing as if it were already done, you are creating feelings of gratitude, and when you are grateful, you are setting yourself up for more great things to come your way. Then act as though your success is certain. It is in picturing what you want that you figure out what kind of person you need to be to have the level of success you are seeking. To have more, you must be more.

Shut out all negative input that goes against what you are creating. Remember, your life can look anyway you choose. What someone else says you can have, be, or do is immaterial. As you remember to feel the feelings of already having, being, or doing it now, your creative thinking is engaged and the "how to" will appear. Once it appears, *act immediately!* You must act as though your success is certain, and it will be.

So why is it so important to feel the feelings? Your feelings super-charge your thoughts. For example, if you have ever been in love, you know that you could not stop thinking of that person all day long, and you would do anything for them. If you've ever wanted something really badly, all you could think about was how to get it. Your positive emotions toward that person or thing is what created the thoughts that moved you to be the person you needed to be to have a relationship with the person or get the object of your desire.

Therefore, the power of your thoughts is the key to your success. All success starts with a decision to have, be, or do something. Then once you've decided where you want to go, it is a matter of feeling good about the fact that you are exactly the type of person you need to be to obtain the object of your success and acting as though your success is certain.

So you see, everything you want is already there, just waiting for you to organize your thoughts in a way that will enable you to have, be, or do what you want. To unlock the unlimited power of your mind, you must become aware of what you are creating with your thinking, choose to build the world of your dreams, and allow yourself to feel successful now. It is up to you. Make no mistake: You can will for yourself whatever you please, so what are you waiting for? Go get whatever life you desire and start creating now.

Biography

Melanie Greenough

MELANIE GREENOUGH is a business developer, coach, mentor, public speaker, and author. She has ranked as a top performer in the network marketing industry for several years, being in the top 10 world-wide in her company as well as first in her country. She travels and speaks to thousands internationally,  has been featured in *Success at Home* as well as many other publications, and is one of the best coaches and trainers in the industry.

As a mother and a wife, her greatest success is her family. Having created a six-figure income from home, she has the time to spend with them and to devote to her passion, which is setting girls free who are enslaved across the world. Melanie has been involved in creating a school and home for rescued girls and educating the public on what they can do to stop slavery. For more information or to contact Melanie, see her information below or find her on Facebook and Twitter.

Contact Information

www.melaniegreenough.com
melaniegreenough@gmail.com
778-808-2228

Chapter 41

From a Poor Farm Boy to a College Professor and an Entrepreneur

by Robert Boyd

I was born on a small, 40-acre farm in the city of Rayville, Louisiana, in a house built by my father. This house was in a very remote area. It had no indoor plumbing or utilities. My father owned this farm, and he taught me at an early age basic business principles. He taught me the value of having my own business, of getting a good education, and of not prejudging people. He educated me about the importance of gaining the respect of people, even if they disliked me. As a rule, my father used to carry his gun everywhere he went, and the people he interacted with left him alone, because they said he was crazy.

Mother Moved Out

When I was nine, my mother left my father. When she left, I felt like my world had fallen apart. Because my father and I had a close relationship, I looked up to him as my hero. My mother's departure subjected me to an agonizing experience that was one of the worst periods of my life. Consequently, I accepted Jesus Christ as my Lord and Savior. This gave me the faith, spiritual courage, and assurance to carry on.

Later, my mother and I moved five miles away to another local community, and I attended a one-room schoolhouse for two years. The school I attended was about five miles away, so I rode my bike every day until it broke down. As a result, I started walking to school. On one occasion, it was raining, and my bike was broken, so I began to walk. On my way, some of my classmates drove by me in their cars, splashing water all over me. I cried out to God because I was in pain. Then, I said to myself I did not care what happened. I was determined to go as far as my classmates went through school. Today, to my knowledge, none of those classmates has earned an advanced college degree. That afternoon when I saw my father, I told him what happened to me on my way to the school. As a result, he bought a new motor bike for me.

Working for 15 Cents Per Hour

I can vividly remember how poor I really was during those years. I remembered I was working for one person in a yard for 15 cents per hour. Although this was not a lot of money, to me it was sufficient money for me buy tickets to see movies.

Newspaper Business

When I was 12 years old, my mother and I moved to the city of Monroe, Louisiana, where I worked for a newspaper. I was a delivery boy, and I had one route. Because I provided good service to my customers, they referred me to other people. Eventually, I developed one of the largest routes in the city. The highest percentage of my customers were professional people. They did not like to go out in the rain or cold weather to get the paper, so they told me to leave the paper behind their front or back doors. From time to time, I used to inform them that I needed to slow down and get off my bike to deliver their papers appropriately. For this extra service, my customers provided me with additional rewards.

Good Samaritan

One day my bike broke down, and I took it to the shop. I told the mechanic that I needed the bike the same day to go to work. He asked me how old I was, and I told him. He said he had a son about my age, and he invited me to his house to meet his son. During our conversation, he told me his son owned a motorcycle and knew how to repair bikes.

His son and I became good friends, and he taught me how to repair my own bike, so I did not need to take it to a mechanic. After these experiences, I found another way to expand my business. I bought used motorcycles and fixed them. After fixing them, I allowed other boys to ride the bikes, if they agreed to work for me.

U.S. Navy

When I was 17 years old, I joined the U.S. Navy because I knew I could repair motorcycles. They thought I enjoyed working with diesel and other engines. Following boot camp, I went aboard a ship to see what they did. The heat was unbearable, so I told them about this problem, and they agreed to change my rank from a fireman to a seaman. After a short stay there, I was transferred to a naval air station. I went to work for GS 18, who was in charge of civil defense. I managed all the audiovisual equipment and took care of all the administrative matters in his office within one month. He asked me about my plans. Under his guidance, I studied and passed my first test for promotion in the Navy. Then I passed the third class petty officer examination, and I was transferred to my first ship.

Duty on Board the USS Grapple (ARS-7)

I was assigned to the *USS Grapple* (ARS-7), which had only three African American males, and I was the only one who was ranked petty officer third class. The captain had problems with people of color, and he told me it would be only a matter of time before I lost my rank. After listening to him, I realized he wasn't too smart because if he knew how to read the computer codes, he would have known beforehand that I was African American. My father told me whenever I meet dumb people, I should just out-think them. Later, I reported to the executive officer, and I asked him about the pass problems with our officer. I listened to his explanation; then I told him I would fix the problems with his permission.

When I started my survey, I found a young man who was typing some forms, and I asked him why he was doing it? One of the divers came over and told me, "Your officer never paid us on time." I told him I would be upset about that too; however, I had just arrived, and I would take care of this problem. If he reassigned this young man to our office, he would never have this problem again. He said he would do so, if the executive officer approved the transfer.

The executive officer was very pleased because the problem had existed for many years. At that point, he became my greatest supporter and suggested that I needed to find a way to work with the captain. When the captain called me, I sent this young man, who looked like him, to meet him. I told the young man, no matter what the captain asked him to do, I would show him how to do it. Within a year, the executive officer had recommended me for advancement to petty officer second class, and I passed the examination.

One of the advantages of being on a small ship is that we have to learn to do everything. The Navy operates on a simple system, and it had a manual that explained everything. I made all the updates to this manual myself, and I read everything; therefore, the job became easy.

Community College

After I was discharged from the Navy, I could not get into the Merchant Marines as a staff officer purser. Therefore, I decided to enroll in a community college to pursue a degree in accounting because that would be part of my job as a purser. I was very active in student affairs at the college. I established the accounting society at the institution. My goal was to make the dean's honor role and to graduate with honors. I accomplished both of these goals, but the best thing that happened to me there was meeting my future wife and mother of our three children. All our children are college graduates, and our two oldest children have earned advanced college degrees.

Educator's Life

After I graduated from the community college I attended, I started my own insurance business. One day, one of my professors called and asked me how things were going. I thought I knew him well enough to tell him the truth. I told him I was making money, but the cost of leads was too high. He said that if I liked the work, he would arrange for me to meet his friend, the president of Educator's Life, a company that had been founded by teachers for teachers.

Within two years, I was the second leading producer in the company, and a member of the President's Council. I was promoted to district manager and relocated to manage our Berkeley and San Francisco offices. After three months, my office surpassed five other offices in the state that had operations throughout the year.

Continued Education

While working for Educator's Life, I earned a bachelor's degree in management from Golden Gate University in 1974, which is located in the financial district in downtown San Francisco, California. In 1976, I earned a master's degree in a public administration from Pepperdine University in Los Angeles. This was the university where I taught business and business management to managers and business owners.

A few years later, Educator's Life merged with another company, and my offices were closed. Consequently, I opened my own office, and I began teaching part-time at a community college. After many years of exemplary performance at the college, I was promoted to professor of business and management, then to director of the small business training center. I was elected chairman of the business division at the college.

People tend to look at success in different ways. I believe doing something that fulfills or uplifts others is just as important as anything else. I'm very appreciative and thankful that God used me to help others with the skills that I learned throughout the hardship years of my life. I was very successful helping students whom many in our society had abandoned.

I believe that success is a journey and not a destination. When we achieve a goal, we need to set a new one. Today, I'm a very successful entrepreneur and a problem solver in countless situations. I am the founder and president of Successful Marketing Solutions, LLC. In everything we do, we must first decide what we want. We must have clearly defined goals and take the necessary actions with the help of God to get there.

Biggest Challenge

I suffered a stroke in 1997, and it left me completely paralyzed on my right side. In three different hospitals, the doctors told me that they had never seen a person who suffered a stroke in the area that I did survive. My main insurance provider, Kaiser, told me that they knew I would retire. I told them that they were only in charge of the insurance, but God was in charge of my life. Despite these dire statements, I recuperated and returned to my employment one year after the incident. Today, I am able to move around successfully without using a mechanical aid, but not only that, God has restored my mind.

Biography

Bob Boyd

BOB BOYD is a successful entrepreneur and problem solver and the founder and CEO of Successful Marketing Solutions, LLC. He is a professor of business and management and has a lifetime community college instructor's creden-  tial. Bob is also a captain in the Naval Volunteer Reserve/USV-JSC and a staff officer in the U.S. Merchant Marines.

Bob has an urgent desire to help others in need, particularly inner city students and veterans. Thus, his immediate goal is to start a foundation to provide scholarships to students in the inner cities. He also plans to provide a support ministry for veterans and other causes that he cares about.

Contact Information

www.SuccessInLA.com
www.bestcashblueprint.com
(800) 778-1492

Chapter 42

Success Turned Upside Down

by Wayne Sharer

They were the best years of my life. I had started from a tiny duplex in Wheaton, Maryland, and now I was the commanding officer of a US Navy E-2C Hawkeye Squadron.

This was what life was all about. My career was a complete success by all measurements in the Navy. My first commanding officer, Ray Bunton, had told me early on that I would be a commanding officer—and I had listened.

Ratchet things back to my beginnings: I grew up in a house not even close to being the bedrock of success. There were my two parents and seven of us kids in a duplex with three tiny bedrooms, one closet-sized bathroom, a living room, a small dining room, and a miniature kitchen all split between two floors.

There was never enough money, and there were no excesses in our home. We barely had enough food to have a bowl of cereal for breakfast, a sandwich and cookies for lunch, and some sort of meal for dinner. More times than I care to remember, dinner was a pancake, or a bowl of cereal. However, this all seemed normal to us. We knew no other way of life.

My dad grew to be an alcoholic, and my mother did, too. They ultimately became very cold and distant. When my parents "interacted" when I was in high school, it wasn't for pleasure.

My mother slept on the sofa, and my dad slept upstairs in the bed. For some number of years, they both went to bed drunk. Yet my dad instilled a drive in me to succeed no matter what.

He did it through fear. If I failed, I would meet the wrath of his heavy hand. He was 6 foot, 1 inch tall, and 210 pounds. That was really big to me as a kid.

He made me literally fear failure through punishment, threats, and spankings that could make my butt burn for days. Good or bad, as you may judge this, it resulted in me getting mostly A's, earning my own money from the time I was 13 years old, getting a NROTC scholarship to Tulane University, and moving steadily and unimpeded up the responsibility chain in the Navy.

In the Navy, I succeeded with a drive for success that was still fueled by fear of failure. I was awkward in socializing and timid in my personal life. Nevertheless, my life in the Navy flourished. I knew I was a poor networker, so I learned to create success by helping others realize their true worth.

Then I made myself an expert in everything I did. I advanced on my record alone as matter of necessity, which I created.

As more and more people worked under me, I saw how many of them came from backgrounds similar to mine. I also developed my skill at making them feel they could succeed, too. I truly believe that the single thing I did to make this possible was being a very good listener. The strange thing is, I did this quite subconsciously.

I didn't interact at all on a personal level, yet I knew all their names, what their strengths were, and most important, what they wanted for themselves. I got the "what's in it for me" information by always working among them and rarely working in a separate office. I heard everything they did. So I learned what they wanted by listening, and then acted on as much as I could through the chain of command.

I worked 10- to 12-hour days when stationed ashore, and 16- to 18-hour days at sea. I wanted to know what was happening on the day and night shifts, so I stayed and listened. I was all about mission success.

But this life nearly killed me. Midway through my career, as a lieutenant commander, my first wife decided drugs were more important than I was. She did amazing things, including selling almost everything I owned while I was deployed, opening credit cards in my name and maxing them out, buying a handgun and threatening to kill me, and creating a story to tell the Navy how I was beating her at home. She was deliberately trying to destroy me for drugs.

Those years threw me into a deep depression. The real problem was, I never knew I was depressed, and I compensated by working even harder. I was a lonely character, now letting success be the only thing worth living for.

My commanding officer at the time was the first person who openly went out of his way to save me (though I don't believe he really understood how depressed I was—frankly, neither did I). Skipper Patrick stood by me as the Navy indirectly put me on trial for wife abuse from the my ex's trumped-up charges.

Because she had emptied my bank account and sold everything I had, I was left with literally nothing but my uniforms, a few clothes, my car, a foreclosed house, and $80,000 worth of debts.

Now, don't think I'm writing this because I enjoy it. This is the first time I've ever told this story publicly. It brings tears to my eyes when I think about it. So you can believe I didn't want to share this, but it is an important part of my success, and why you can find your success, too—no matter what!

So my life became my career. Skipper Bunton's words were all I lived by. Many of my peers openly and covertly tried to take me down. I never retaliated. My successes spoke for themselves. My success was all that I had.

Though I remarried just before my command tour, I had never recovered from the depression of my first marriage. You see, my life was about success, and my marriage had been a failure. So this proved bad for my second wife. Though she was a wonderful lady, and marvelous to be with, I, on the other hand, was not.

I tried hard, but I had sunk so deeply into isolating myself in my Navy success and the success of those under me, I had little real time for her.

As my command was ending, my depression was growing. Senior officers told me how great everything I did had been while they stabbed me in the back when I wasn't looking. It was my fault, because I had gotten to a level requiring a network to advance. I had none, and I made no effort to develop it. They tossed me to the wolves, regardless of my performance.

This crashed my whole well-being. I was now moving into another deep depression and never really knowing it. This time it would be worse.

I had one more sea tour to go before I could retire. I wanted out but didn't know how to get out. I went to sea, and my last tour concluded with the most unique aircraft carrier operation ever executed, in response to the 9/11 terror attacks. I was a big part of that plan. I should have been so proud and uplifted.

Well, I was too far gone. I was now going to the Pentagon for a short tour and was quickly told by my seniors that the Navy was likely to send me on another sea tour as a ship commanding officer. This nearly flattened me. I should have been ecstatic, but I was horrified. I had been selected to be a Navy captain, and now I was looking at more endless, thankless time at sea.

Once again, I have never told this part of my life publicly because of my utter and deep embarrassment of this label, depression, and of my actions. I caused embarrassment to many I don't know, and possibly even harmed people I never met. I actually have to pause now to do this. . . .

I lost control of my life, and I didn't know what to do. I didn't even share it with my wife. I was shameful. I got lost in the darkest corners of the Internet as my solution. I created a character and started chatting with every creep on the web. It ultimately ended up in chat rooms with minors and carrying on in the most egregious manner I could or can ever imagine, short of being an actual rapist or murderer.

I scheduled a meeting with a minor under my fake name. I never wanted to do this, though I played it out as if I did. And as I was trying to undo my connection to prevent my wife from finding out it ever happened . . .

. . . it all ended. I was arrested. My life was over in an instant. Success was lost. No one in the Navy would stand up for me. Nine months later, I was in prison as a sex offender (yes, even without having sex). The judge told me my career as a Navy officer didn't matter and was meaningless.

I was so depressed. Yes, even more than before. I weighed 205 pounds when I entered prison. Six months later, I weighed 162. I'm 6 foot, 2 inches tall, by the way. There was nothing left of me. My family pretended I didn't exist, and my wife divorced me.

I had only one extremely valuable possession. My mind. My mind is the root of success. It is gold.

No one could take my will unless I let them. After six months in prison, I started self-talk about the power of my mind and my road to success. I started to take control of myself.

I had to figure out my way to success. I knew no one was going to help me. So I began a business plan. I developed handwritten spreadsheets and calculations. I analyzed everything I had ever done to succeed. I created a plan for success.

My family never visited me, and when I was free, they never offered me a thing. Not a bed for one night, not a pillow or a blanket. Not even a cold can of soup. I had known this would happen, but I had spent the last 26 months preparing my willpower to succeed no matter what.

When I got out, the economy was booming. Despite the amazing resume I had, I was turned down for nearly 80 jobs of every kind. I expected this too.

So I found a place to live. I had my suitcase, a box, and a plan— and most important, I had a will to live and a real reason to succeed. I started a new road toward creating value for others like I never had before. The formula is something like this:

1. Never let other people tell you how far you can go and what you can achieve. You determine this.

2. Always remember that what happens to you is because of your actions. Even accidents involve your actions. When you can accept full responsibility for yourself, then you will have no limits.

3. Develop strong personal and professional relationships. This is very important, something I was missing that has made my rebuilding even more difficult. These relationships must be built on trust and your value to others.

4. You own your will. Your mind is a high-value vault that only you can access. Many people will try to control it and even

destroy it. But in reality, only you control it, and you can stop anyone from tearing you down.

5. Always analyze yourself and be your harshest critic. You will rarely find anyone willing to tell you the truth about you. When you find someone who does, cherish that person.

6. If there is one skill you must develop to accelerate past your competition, it's your listening skill. Master it and you can achieve things others never imagined you could.

7. Always see yourself taking the next two big steps. There will be no limit to where you go.

8. Never put yourself ahead of creating value for others. In that way, you are highly valuable in and of yourself. If you cherish the value you can create for others, you will never find yourself alone, or looking to cheat others for your short-term success.

9. Work toward the end, and know what the end is—that way you can always build a bigger future.

In my last years in the Navy, before I came crashing down, I started to study rare success and found Abraham Lincoln. He is where I discovered most of these realities and tied them all together. He was truly born out of obscurity, ridiculed to no end, but he succeeded in his listening skills, creating value for others, building a powerful network, and having unbelievable control over his will.

No amount of education gives you these things. They are already in you—you just have to find them, nurture them, and grow.

Biography

Wayne Sharer

Born in Washington, DC, and raised in Wheaton, Maryland, WAYNE SHARER earned a ROTC scholarship to Tulane University, culminating in a highly successful career as a U.S. Navy officer. He served from 1981 to 2002 from aircraft carriers on 12 major deployments, including as a squadron commanding officer. He's now helping entrepreneurs succeed with online training and coaching.

Contact Information

www.WayneSharer.com
wayne@thinkbigandgrow.com
4500 Connecticut Ave., NW B1, Washington, DC 20008
202-243-3128
Skype: webtrafficman

To receive over $2,000 in free bonus gifts
for purchasing this book, visit

www.SuccessYouPublishing.com/gifts

CPSIA information can be obtained at www.ICGtesting.com
Printed in the USA
LVOW011007170911

246612LV00005B/104/P

9 780983 077015